# History of
# LATIN AMERICA

BY

HUTTON WEBSTER, Ph.D
*Lecturer in Stanford University*

THIRD EDITION REVISED AND AUGMENTED BY

ROLAND DENNIS HUSSEY, Ph.D.
*University of California at Los Angeles*

DC H
& CO

1885

## D. C. HEATH & COMPANY

Boston

27671

980

# Preface to the First Edition

The twenty republics of Latin America are little known in the United States. Their history — a very interesting and significant part of American history — has usually no place in our historical textbooks. Their contributions to New-World culture are seldom understood or appreciated by us. We remain too unfamiliar with their problems, aspirations, and achievements.

This neglect of our southern neighbors, though deplorable, may be excused. The Latin American countries long preserved an almost Oriental aloofness and self-sufficiency, not only during the colonial era, but also for many years following the separation from Spain and Portugal. Now, however, the same currents of modern industrialism and science that begin to penetrate the Orient sweep even more rapidly over Latin America. Railways, steamships, oceanic cables, and all the other great inventions of the nineteenth and twentieth centuries, by fostering travel, stimulating commerce, promoting immigration, and facilitating the investment of foreign capital, break down the barriers between the Latin American countries themselves and between them and the outside world. The isolation of Mexico, Cuba, Chile, Argentina, Uruguay, and Brazil is already ended; it is ending for the other countries as well.

The time seems propitious, therefore, for an elementary book that shall introduce pupils in school and college and the general reader to Latin American history and civilization. The narrative, though brief, is comprehensive; it may be expanded either by lectures on the part of the instructor or by additional reading on the part of the student. Some of the more important works on Latin America are mentioned in the Bibliographical Note. The Index gives the Castilian pronunciation of the more important names, by means of a phonetic respelling. However, many of them have now become Anglicized, and these it would be pedantic not to pronounce as English words. The modern Spanish practice as respects the spelling and accentuation of proper names has been followed both in the text and on the maps, with a few exceptions.

I wish to express my indebtedness to Dr. José Padin, of New York City, for reading the proofs and for his helpful comments thereon. My colleague, Dr. Jacob Warshaw, Professor of Modern Languages, has also been good enough to put his wide knowledge of contemporary Latin America at my disposal in revising the later chapters of the book.

Thanks are further due to the officials of the Pan American Union and to Dr. E. L. Hewitt, Director of the School of American Research, Santa Fe, New Mexico, for several photographs included among the plates. The map of the Expansion of Brazil is based upon one in Professor W. S. Robertson's *History of the Latin-American Nations* (D. Appleton and Co.), by kind permission of the author and the publishers of that work. The three maps of modern Spain, South America, and Mexico and Central America are taken, also by permission, from the *First Spanish Course* by Professors E. C. Hills and J. D. Ford.

HUTTON WEBSTER

# Preface to the Third Edition

In my preface to the second edition (1936), I remarked, "In view of the success met with by the original text, and considering that the generalized treatment adopted by Professor Webster avoids the difficulties likely to result from changes in our knowledge of details, I have altered the old text as little as possible. No two men entirely agree on interpretations, on minor facts, or on judgments of what should be included. But with rare exceptions, the only changes that I have permitted myself in the text as printed in 1924 involve facts of too recent occurrence in

1923 for accurate knowledge, or facts which were omitted by Professor Webster but are necessary for an understanding of events discussed in the new chapter. As a result, no changes will be found in the first five chapters. Chapter six is much altered, and chapter nine is entirely new except for one paragraph borrowed from the former chapter seven. Chapters seven, eight, ten, and eleven, though very different in places, generally follow the original version fairly closely. The bibliography is greatly augmented, but is still largely confined to general histories, all of them in the English language."

The present revision is somewhat more general. There has been no occasion for creating a new chapter division, but changes have been made within every chapter, and they become increasingly important from chapter three. Some were caused by narration of events since 1935, or by a desire to incorporate the results of recent research. But most of them reflect a desire to equalize the emphasis upon the various countries, or recognition of the arrival of a new era in Pan-American relations. In 1935 one could only hope that he was seeing that new era. Five more years have justified a belief in its permanence, and as a result a considerable portion of chapter eleven, and its whole viewpoint, is new.

A new printing of this third edition permits a number of additions and alterations to bring the domestic and the international story to August, 1942, and to make several other desirable changes.

ROLAND DENNIS HUSSEY

Los Angeles, California
*August, 1942*

## Publisher's Note

The study and project material at the ends of the several chapters has been provided by Professor Kenneth A. Bernard of Boston University.

# Contents

# Maps and Illustrations

# HISTORY OF LATIN AMERICA

These states lying to the south of us, which have
always been our neighbors, will now be drawn closer
to us by innumerable ties, and, I hope, chief of all, by
the ties of a common understanding of each other.
— WOODROW WILSON

AMÉRICA DEL SUR

# CHAPTER I

# Geographic Environment and Native Peoples

**The Atlantic Abyss.** There existed during the period of geological time called the Tertiary, a land-bridge across the Atlantic Ocean between Greenland and Norway. Iceland and the Faroe Islands are today its remnants. The collapse of that land-bridge, perhaps during the early Quaternary period, left an Atlantic abyss dividing America on the one side from Europe and Africa on the other side. The islands of the Atlantic, few and scattered, provided no avenue of intercourse between the Old World and the New. Excepting the Canaries, all of these islands, from Greenland in the far north to Tristan da Cunha in the far south, were uninhabited when first visited by Europeans. The Atlantic thus effectually separated the two hemispheres until late historic times.

**America.** An historical accident led to the use of a common name, America, for the two continents included in the Western Hemisphere. Scientific justification also exists for this one name. North America and South America, from the point of view of the geologist, are really "twin continents," which developed as a result of more or less similar strains in the earth's crust. They resemble each other in general plan of construction.

**Physical Resemblances between North America and South America.** The two great land masses present the same triangular shape, with base running from northwest to southeast and with sides tapering southward to the apex. In area, there is not a great difference between them, for the northern triangle scarcely exceeds the southern by one eighth. Each continent is traversed from north to south by a huge mountain chain, geologically speaking, of recent age; in each this chain approaches much nearer to the Pacific than to the Atlantic side; and each has a far older mountain mass on the eastern side, comprising the Appalachian system in North America and the Guiana and Brazilian highlands in South

America.   Both continents have enormous central plains —
prairies, llanos, savannas, pampas — which are inclosed by mountain ranges and are penetrated by extensive rivers.   Excepting the
Mackenzie, Yukon, Columbia, and Colorado rivers, in North
America, all the important streams empty into the Atlantic.
Other physical resemblances between North and South America
include active and extinct volcanoes throughout the Cordilleras;
a desert, which in North America stretches from the Rockies
to the Sierras and in South America from the Andes to the Pacific;
and in that desert an inland river basin with elevated lakes.

**Physical Contrasts between North America and South America.**
These result, in the first place, from their differing position in
respect to the poles.   Frigid waters bathe the northern shores of
North America;   great glaciers are found in its northwestern
mountains;   and Greenland, its prolongation toward the northeast,
is shrouded in perpetual ice.   South America, on the other hand,
has frigid waters and extensive glaciers only at its remote southern
extremity.   In the second place, there is their differing position
in respect to the equator.   Whereas in North America the bulging,
and consequent greatest average breadth, of the continent occurs
north of the Tropic of Cancer, in South America the bulging takes
place about the equator, and beyond the Tropic of Capricorn
the land tapers so rapidly southward that only a relatively small
area lies outside of the torrid zone.   The one continent is essentially
a temperate region;   the other, essentially a tropical region.

**Area of America.**   The combined land and water area of North
America, excluding Greenland (estimated area, 827,000 square
miles), is about 8,575,000 square miles.   For the different divisions
of North America the figures are:   Canada, Newfoundland, and
Labrador, 3,885,000;   the continental United States and Alaska,
3,614,000;   Mexico, 767,000;   Central America (including British
Honduras), 219,000;   and the West Indies, 90,000.   The area of
South America is estimated at 7,325,000 square miles.   The greater
superficial extent of North America becomes less significant, however, when one recalls that northern Canada consists so largely of
archipelagos with extensive intervening water surfaces.   Furthermore, much of Canada and Alaska lies within or near the Arctic
Circle, where harsh climatic conditions oppose so stern a resistance
to man.   From this point of view the southern continent actually

surpasses its northern neighbor in extent of land available for human habitation.

**Areas of Anglo-America and Latin America.** Still more striking are the results of a comparison between Anglo-America and Latin America. The former contains about 7,500,000 square miles; the latter, about 8,400,000 square miles. Even after deductions have been made for the Guianas and for European colonies in the West Indies, we find that Latin America is considerably larger than Anglo-America, that, in fact, it occupies more than half the area of the New World. Brazil (3,275,510 square miles), though surpassed in size by Canada, has an area greater than that of the United States exclusive of Alaska. Argentina (1,153,119 square miles) is about as large as all the United States east of the Mississippi, together with the three Pacific states. Perú (722,461 square miles) is larger than Alaska. Colombia (440,846 square miles) somewhat exceeds in size the combined area of Arkansas, Louisiana, Oklahoma, and Texas. Even Uruguay (72,153 square miles), the smallest of the South American countries, is larger than the six New England states. As for the rest of Latin America, it is perhaps sufficient to point out that Mexico and Central America together more than equal the combined area of Montana, Idaho, Wyoming, Colorado, New Mexico, Nevada, and Oregon.

**Mountain Systems of Latin America.** The mountains of Mexico are a southern prolongation of the Cordillera of Canada and the United States. They consist, essentially, of two ranges, the Sierra Madre Occidental on the west and the Sierra Madre Oriental on the east. Both ranges run nearly parallel with the shore line. On the south, below the City of Mexico, a lofty, snow-clad chain, containing both active and extinct volcanoes,[1] runs transversely between the two oceans. The ranges of the Mexican Sierra Madre converge in Central America. Here, however, the mountains form a system distinct from that of North America and South America. Geologically speaking, Central America, which connects the northern and southern continents, is really not a continuation of either. The Cordillera of South America, commonly known as the Andes, extends without a break for 4400 miles along the Pacific from Panamá to Cape Horn and attains a greater elevation than any

---

[1] The highest are Orizaba (18,209 feet), Popocatepetl (17,888 feet), and Iztaccihuatl (17,343 feet). All three volcanoes are extinct.

other range except the Himalayas. The Andes consist of a single chain in the southern part of the continent. They begin to diverge into two chains from about 25° below the equator, and in the extreme north they divide into three chains. The western slope of the mountains is steep; the eastern slope is more gentle. The Andes contain some of the highest peaks in the world, the most elevated being Aconcagua in Argentina (23,080 feet). Volcanoes, such as Cotopaxi and Chimborazo in Ecuador, continue to be still active, especially near the equator. The Atlantic side of South America has lower groups of mountain ranges, known under the general name of Serra do Mar. North of latitude 20° the mountains swing inland and fall away in gently sloping tablelands.

**Plateaus and Plains.** Mexico is mainly an immense elevated plateau, extending from the boundaries of Texas and New Mexico on the north to the Isthmus of Tehuantepec on the south. This plateau, called by the Aztecs Anáhuac,[1] ranks next to those of Tibet and Bolivia among the largest and loftiest on the globe. It covers 69,000 square miles and rises from 6000 to 8500 feet above sea level in the middle part. The lowland region, which lies between the Sierras and the Mexican coasts, widens on the eastern side into the peninsula of Yucatán. Central America has low and narrow coastal plains along the Atlantic, but along the Pacific side the mountains generally come down to the ocean. The plateaus and plains of South America include the Pacific coastal plain, with an average breadth of only 40 miles; the Bolivian and Peruvian plateaus, between divergent ranges of the Andes; the Brazilian highlands; the Guiana highlands; and lastly, the llanos of the Orinoco, the selvas or forested lowlands of the Amazon, and the grasslands called savannas and pampas, which in the far south merge into the bleak Patagonian steppes. Altogether, South America has the most extensive plains in the world.

**River Systems.** Apart from the Rio Grande, whose northern bank is now held by the United States, and the Colorado, which penetrates for a short distance into Mexico at the head of the Gulf of California, that country does not possess a single stream much over 600 miles in length or accessible to seagoing vessels for 50 miles above its mouth. The rivers of Central America, on the Pacific side, are mere mountain torrents, while those of the Atlantic

---

[1] Meaning, "Amid the waters," a reference to the lakes in the Valley of Mexico.

## CHIMBORAZO, ECUADOR

Chimborazo, a volcano in Ecuador, which soars 20,700 feet above sea level.

littoral, though longer and less impetuous, are seldom available for anything but canoes and barges. A similar deficiency of navigable streams characterizes the dryer portions of the Pacific coastal plain of South America, though central and southern Chile is well watered. The eastern side of the continent contains the magnificent river systems of the Orinoco, the Amazon, and the Plata, which jointly drain nearly 3,700,000 square miles. The Orinoco, the smallest of the three systems, is about 1500 miles in length. The Amazon is not only the largest of South American rivers, it is also the largest in the world. For 250 miles from its mouth the river has a width of 50 miles, and during the rainy season it spreads over a vast flood plain. The total length of the Amazon is 3000 miles, a figure that must be multiplied nine or ten times to include all its navigable affluents. The Rio de la Plata is the long and shallow estuary formed by the junction of the Uruguay and the Paraná. It discharges more water into the ocean than any other river in the New World, except the Amazon. The Paraná is navigable for deep-sea vessels for 1200 miles or more above Buenos Aires, and with its numerous tributaries reaches to the Andes and to the Brazilian highlands. Other important fluvial systems include the São Francisco, the largest river lying wholly in Brazil, and the Magdalena in Colombia.

**Lakes.** The lakes of Mexico are mostly small and few in number. Those of Central America are more numerous, in proportion to the total area. Lake Managua reaches 50 miles in length, and Lake Nicaragua, with which it communicates during the rainy season, is 90 miles long. Most of the South American lakes are found in the Andes or along their base. Lake Titicaca, between Perú and Bolivia, is surpassed in size only by the great inland waters of North America. It covers about 2000 square miles (exclusive of islands and peninsulas) and lies at an altitude of over 12,000 feet. Titicaca is so deep that it never freezes over. Maracaibo on the coast of Venezuela may be included among the other South American lakes, but it is a large indentation of the sea, rather than a true lake.

**Coast Line.** Mexico has about 6300 miles of coast, more than two thirds being on the western side. The coast facing the Gulf of Mexico contains no bays of importance. Of the principal Gulf ports, Vera Cruz is an open roadstead and Tampico and Matamoros are on rivers. The east coast of Yucatán, however, affords several good anchorages. The Pacific side of Mexico has a number of deep, well-sheltered bays, including Salina Cruz, Acapulco, Manzanillo, and Mazatlán; unfortunately for commerce they are separated from the interior by difficult mountain ranges. There are also excellent ports in Lower California. The indented coast line of Central America provides commodious natural harbors. The same cannot be said of South America, for the coasts of the continent, always excepting Chile and southern Argentina (Tierra del Fuego and Patagonia), have few windings or inlets. Among these are the gulfs of Darién and Venezuela in the north, Guayaquil on the west, and the still smaller bays of Rio de Janeiro and Bahía on the east. The other indentations are not marine inlets, but great pluvial estuaries, such as those of the Plata and the Amazon. In general, South America is much more accessible on the Atlantic side than on the Pacific side, where the harbors are not deep enough for large, ocean-going vessels to land at piers. Freight and passengers must therefore be landed in small boats. The Caribbean seaboard, also, lacks good harbors. '

**Peninsulas and Islands.** While Mexico has no large islands, it possesses the two extensive peninsulas of Yucatán and Lower California. Yucatán, lying between the bays of Campeche and Honduras, is a low tableland, diversified by hills and lakes, without running streams, but provided with a great store of underground water. The soil is generally productive. Lower California, on the other hand, is so arid that little of it can be brought under cultivation or even made available for herding. South America is poorly endowed with peninsulas and islands, except for those fringing the Chilean seaboard. Marajó is a large island between the mouths of the Amazon and Pará rivers. The islands at a considerable distance from the mainland include the Galapagos group, belonging to Ecuador, Juan Fernández,[1] a dependency of Chile, and the Falklands, a British possession.

**The West Indies.** The islands of the West Indies, or Antilles,[2] stretch in a vast curve from the peninsulas of Florida and Yucatán in North America to Venezuela in South America. They are the

---

[1] Associated with Defoe's immortal hero, "Robinson Crusoe."

[2] So called because Columbus, on his arrival in the archipelago, was supposed to have reached the fabled land of Antilia.

summits of a submerged mountain range — all that now remains of the land which in remote geological times occupied the basins of the Caribbean and the Gulf of Mexico and joined the northern and southern continents. Including rocks, keys, and raised banks, the West Indies must be reckoned by the thousand. Their size varies from islets, scarcely five miles in area, to Cuba (over 44,000 square miles).

**The Greater Antilles and the Bahamas.** The four large islands of Cuba, Jamaica, Haiti, and Puerto Rico, forming the Greater Antilles, comprise nine tenths of the total area of the West Indies. They are highly mountainous throughout their entire length. The mountains culminate in Haiti, with peaks nearly 12,000 feet high. North of the Greater Antilles lies the Bahama Archipelago, which consists exclusively of low coralline reefs and islands. In this respect it resembles the neighboring peninsula of Florida, which is largely a consolidated coralline archipelago.

**The Lesser Antilles.** The graceful curve of the Lesser Antilles forms the eastern boundary of the Caribbean Sea. The inner islands of this group are of igneous origin; they contain still active volcanoes such as Mont Pelée in Martinique. The outer islands are of marine origin, the work of the coral polyps. The inclusion of Barbados in the Lesser Antilles is only for the sake of convenience. Geologically, this island, together with Tobago and Trinidad, forms a continuation of the Venezuelan coast.

**Rainfall.** The Atlantic slopes of Latin America, being open to the moisture-laden winds, receive a much heavier rainfall than the Pacific slopes. The precipitation is naturally greatest in the equatorial belt of South America, east of the Andes. It is least on the western coast of the continent, where for a distance of over 2000 miles, from Guayaquil in Ecuador to Coquimbo in Chile, stretches the arid, barren, and saline region known as the Atacama Desert. Here the cooling influence of the Andes combines with the so-called "Humboldt Current" from the Antarctic to draw moisture out of the winds. Southern Chile, however, enjoys so heavy a rainfall that the inhabitants are playfully said to have webbed feet.

**Climate.** Climatic conditions throughout the tropical and subtropical parts of Latin America are determined rather by altitude than by latitude. The climate is, so to speak, vertical and not

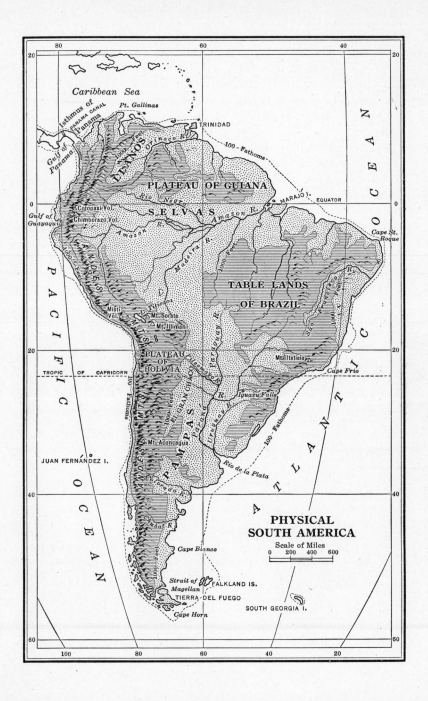

Caribbean Sea

Isthmus of Panama
PANAMA CANAL
Pt. Gallinas
Gulf of Panama
Gulf of Guayaquil

TRINIDAD
100 - Fathoms

LLANOS

Orinoco R.
Rio Near

PLATEAU OF GUIANA

SELVAS

Cotopaxi Vol.
Chimborazo Vol.

Amazon R.
Napo R.
Amazon R.

MARAJO I.
EQUATOR

Cape St. Roque

Amazon R.

Madeira R.

100 Feet

TABLE LANDS

OF BRAZIL

Misti Vol.
Mt. Sorata
Mt. Illimani

Titicaca L.

San Francisco R.

100 Feet

PLATEAU
OF
BOLIVIA

TROPIC OF CAPRICORN

Mt. Itatiaia

Cape Frio

100 - Fathoms

EL GRAN CHACO

Pilcomayo R.

Paraguay R.

Iguazu Falls

Paraná R.

Uruguay R.

100 - Fathoms

PAMPAS

Mt. Aconcagua

JUAN FERNÁNDEZ I.

Colorado R.

Rio de la Plata

P A C I F I C

O C E A N

A T L A N T I C

O C E A N

100 Feet

Negro R.

Cape Blanco

Chubat R.

100 Feet

Strait of Magellan
TIERRA-DEL FUEGO

FALKLAND IS.

Cape Horn

SOUTH GEORGIA I.

## PHYSICAL
## SOUTH AMERICA

Scale of Miles
0   200   400   600

horizontal. There are three zones: a tropical (*tierra caliente*), from sea level to about 1500 feet; a temperate (*tierra templada*), from 1500 to 5000 feet; and a cold zone (*tierra fria*), above 5000 feet. It thus results that in Mexico the elevation and vast area of the central plateau produce temperate conditions over the greater part of the country. Only the lowlands on each side of the plateau are hot, humid, and consequently unhealthy. Central America, likewise, exhibits wide diversities of climate, due partly to variations of altitude and partly to the proximity of the two oceans. The temperature of such low-lying territories as British Honduras and northern Guatemala differs widely from that of the alpine districts of Nicaragua, Salvador, and Costa Rica. For this reason a majority of the important Central American towns have been located on the lofty tablelands of the interior. The higher parts of the West Indies enjoy a marked degree of coolness, and even during the summer months the extreme heat of the islands is moderated by sea breezes. Two thirds of South America lies within the torrid zone, but the climate is not uniformly torrid. Colombia, Ecuador, Perú, and Bolivia contain extensive elevated areas with a cool, invigorating climate. Beginning with the southern half of Brazil, one passes into the south temperate zone, in which lie most of Paraguay, Argentina, and Chile, and all of Uruguay. This part of South America is indeed a "white man's land."

**Mineral Resources.** The wealth of the Latin American countries in minerals is almost limitless. The precious metals of Mexico and Perú first attracted European notice to this part of America, and mining formed the principal occupation of the Spanish conquerors for three centuries. Practically all the countries are rich in minerals, the chief mining centers being Mexico, Colombia, Perú, Bolivia, Chile, and southern Brazil. Mexico still leads in the production of silver; Chile is next to the United States in the production of copper. A recent government report estimates the iron deposits of Brazil at 4,000,000,000 tons. Chile has long supplied the world with nitrate of soda, her most valuable export. Venezuela and the neighboring island of Trinidad are the world's principal source of asphalt. Mexico, Venezuela, Colombia, the Amazon slopes of the Andes, and Patagonia contain valuable oil fields. These mineral resources have not been fully utilized because of difficult transportation.

**Forest Products.** Latin America, as might be expected from the variety of climates there, is unsurpassed for the beauty, luxuriance, and variety of its forests. Such cabinet woods as mahogany, rosewood, cedar, and ebony, together with palms, bamboos, and giant hardwood trees, abound in the tropical areas. Oaks, pines, magnolias, and similar trees characterize the more temperate regions. As yet this forest wealth has scarcely been tapped; indeed, the exuberant jungle of the hot lands of Mexico, Central America, and the Amazonian plains is almost impenetrable by man.

**Economic Plants.** More food, medicinal, and other economic plants have been derived from Latin America than from any other part of the world. Maize, or Indian corn, is believed to have been first domesticated in Mexico. The potato, both white and yellow, and the tomato formerly grew wild in the Andes. The cassava or manioc plant, yielding tapioca, and the cacao tree, whose seeds yield cocoa, are indigenous to Latin America. Another food plant is *yerba maté*, a South American holly, which yields "Paraguay tea." Among native medicinal plants may be mentioned ipecacuanha, sarsaparilla, cascara, the coca shrub, from which cocaine is prepared, and the cinchona tree, the bark of which furnishes quinine. Tobacco, "Sea Island" cotton, the most valuable of all cottons, and *henequén*, or sisal hemp, are other economic plants originating in Latin America. To these may be added red peppers, vanilla beans, peanuts, pineapples, and various resins and gums, the latter including chicle (the chief ingredient in chewing gum) and caoutchouc, or India rubber. Many plants, such as sugar cane in Cuba, coffee trees in Brazil, and the grapevine in Argentina and Chile, were imported by Europeans and have become the basis of important industries.

**Domesticated Animals.** Though remarkable for an extraordinary variety of animal life, the New World had few species capable of domestication. The dog was generally domesticated throughout Latin America, together with the turkey in Mexico and the guinea pig in Perú. The aborigines of the Andean regions also succeeded in taming the llama and the alpaca. These animals are related to the African camel, though smaller and without a hump. The llama still forms the beast of burden in Perú and Bolivia; its flesh serves as meat; and its coarse wool provides garments for the natives. The alpaca is highly prized for its fine fleece. Of domestic animals introduced by Europeans, one need only mention cattle, sheep, and horses, which find ample pasturage on the llanos and pampas. South America, especially Argentina, is now an important contributor to the world's production of meat and hides.

**Geographical Advantages of America.** As a home for man, America has much to offer. It contains a smaller proportion of stony steppes and arid deserts than Asia, Africa, or Australia. It possesses the longest rivers on the globe. The St. Lawrence, with its five great lakes, forming the largest connected surface of fresh water in any continent, the Mississippi-Missouri, the Orinoco, the Amazon and the Plata, with all their tributaries, provide a natural system of inland navigation. In length of coast line as compared with total area, North America ranks next to Europe and South America next to North America. The climate is likewise favorable to man, being mainly temperate in North America, while in South America the tropical heats are moderated by the great elevation of the Pacific and Atlantic highlands and by the ocean breezes. As a food-producing region the two continents are unrivaled, though many of the most useful cultivable plants and domestic animals were introduced by Europeans. Similarly, it was reserved for Europeans to uncover the wealth of America in metals, fisheries, and forests. The American aborigines, at the time of their discovery, occupied an environment which they had scarcely begun to exploit and of whose possibilities they had little conception.

**Antiquity of Man in America.** The discovery, in western Europe during the nineteenth century, of rude stone implements and human bones associated with the remains of extinct animals, such as the mammoth, woolly rhinoceros, and cave bear, placed beyond doubt the high antiquity of man in the Old World. He has lived there for tens of thousands of years, certainly since the latter part of the Ice Age and quite probably still earlier. On the other hand, archæologists have not found in either America any implements or human bones more than a few thousand years old. No satisfactory evidence exists that man lived here during preglacial or glacial times. Until this evidence is forthcoming, if ever, we are obliged to believe that man migrated to the New World long after he had inhabited the Old World, that is, long after he had reached substantially his present physical and mental development. The

migration probably began at an epoch contemporary with the last
phase of the Old Stone (Palæolithic) period in Europe or with the
opening there of the New Stone (Neolithic) period.

**Origin of Man in America.**  It has been suggested that the first
immigrants to America came from the Old World by way of the
Atlantic bridge between the two hemispheres.  This land-connec-
tion disappeared, however, in the late Tertiary or early Quaternary,
long before America must be presumed to have received its first
inhabitants.  Furthermore, evidence is lacking of any Caucasian or
Negroid blood in the Indians until recent historic times.  The only
possible route to America was from Asia.  Bering Strait, at its
narrowest point between Siberia and Alaska, is but 56 miles wide,
while the Aleutian Islands and Commander Islands form an almost
complete series of steppingstones across Bering Sea.  Here there
is, in effect, a North Pacific bridge from the Old World to the New.

**The American Race.**  The natives of America, whom Columbus
called Indians, still present many resemblances to Asiatics.  Such
physical traits as the skin color, ranging from yellowish white to
dark brown, the hair of the head, uniformly coarse, black, and
straight, the scanty beard and hairless body, the brown and often
more or less slanting eye, the high cheekbones, the shovel-shaped
upper incisor teeth, and the short stature of some tribes are Mon-
goloid characteristics.  On the other hand, the large, straight or
aquiline nose, bold features, and tall stature of many tribes are
non-Mongoloid characteristics.  The American race, in fact, does
not distinctly duplicate any Oriental type of man.  It is a new race.
It gradually developed as the Asiatic peoples, representing different stocks and coming in several migratory waves, spread
throughout the Americas, multiplied, and blended with one another
during centuries of isolation.

**Unity of the American Race.**  This conclusion, which is that of
the majority of contemporary anthropologists, means that the
American race is substantially one in both continents.  Even the
Eskimo of the Arctic regions are ranked as Indian, though in
physical traits and material culture they resemble northern Asiatics more closely than do other red men.  They seem to be comparatively recent arrivals in America.  It is possible that in pre-
Columbian times the western coast of America was on more than
one occasion reached by small parties of Polynesians, as we know

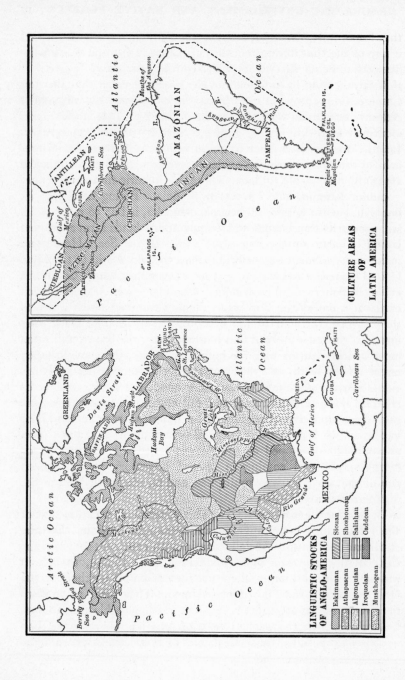

CULTURE AREAS OF LATIN AMERICA

LINGUISTIC STOCKS OF ANGLO-AMERICA

Eskimauan
Athapascan
Algonquian
Iroquoian
Muskhogean
Siouan
Shoshonean
Salishan
Caddoan

that Europeans (the Northmen) reached the eastern coast. Nor is it impossible that during the early centuries of our era, when Buddhism was being carried so widely throughout Asia, devotees of that faith should have landed on the shores of America. But the Chinese account of journeys by Buddhists during the later fifth century A.D. to a kingdom called "Fusang," which has been identified with America, is agreed by present scholars to refer to Japan. In any case, such visitors, whether Polynesians, Northmen, or Buddhist missionaries, must have been too few in number to affect the mass of the Indians, who remained one in race as before.

**Indian Languages.** The racial unity of the Indians did not imply linguistic unity. Aboriginal America was a babel of stock languages, as irreducible to a single mother tongue as are the Indo-European and Semitic groups in the Old World. Fifty-six such stock languages have been distinguished in Canada and the United States,[1] 29 in Mexico and Central America, and at least 84 in South America. The total for the New World thus approximates 200, embracing over 1000 idioms and dialects. Not one of them can be traced outside of America. They all differ from other linguistic systems in vocabulary, grammar, and structure. Their most striking feature is "polysynthesis," that is, the tendency to merge all the words of a sentence in a single term, often of prodigious length. An example, by no means the longest, is Eskimo *takusariartorumagaluarnerpa?* ("do you think he really intends to go to look after it?"). By means of such portmanteau words the native can say a number of things in, as it were, one breath. This unique mode of expression, which prevails from Alaska to Tierra del Fuego, testifies to the long isolation of the Indians from the rest of the world's peoples.

**Indian Culture.** Because of their isolation the Indians had to work out for themselves many arts, inventions, and discoveries. Their tools and weapons consisted of polished stone, occasionally of unsmelted copper, and among certain peoples of Mexico, Central America, and South America, of bronze. The use of iron was unknown to them. They cultivated maize, but lacked the other great cereals. They domesticated only the dog, and in Perú the llama and the alpaca. They lived in clans and tribes. Sometimes these were grouped in confederacies, like those of the Iro-

---

[1] Of these, six are now extinct, and twelve are on the verge of extinction.

quois and Mayas; and the Aztecs, Chibchas, and Incas established real empires. Government was solely by public opinion among the lower cultures, but was strong among the others. The religion of the lesser cultures probably did not involve a belief in a "Great Spirit," as is so often said, but rather recognized in all nature the abode of spiritual powers, mysterious and wonderful, whom man ought to conciliate by prayers and offerings. Among the higher cultures, however, a real hierarchy of gods, with temples, altars, ceremonies and a priesthood, was well developed. Although human sacrifice existed, it was extensive only among the Aztecs. Most of the Indians had a rigid code of morals. Much of the code differed from that of Europeans, but it was well observed, and many of the European ethical ideas were also found among the Americans. In short, the majority of the Indians were not savages, but barbarians fairly well advanced in culture.

**Cultural Areas of Latin America.** Seven or more cultural areas may be distinguished among the aborigines, corresponding to basically different geographic conditions. The most civilized groups were the Mayas, Nahuas or Aztecs, Chibchas, and Incas. They and related groups inhabited the smaller part of Latin America, being confined to Middle America and Andean South America, but made probably nine tenths of the aboriginal population.

**The Mayas.** Guatemala, adjoining parts of Salvador, Honduras, British Honduras, the Mexican states of Chiapas and Tabasco, and the peninsula of Yucatán were inhabited in pre-Columbian times, as today, by the Mayas. There are at present upwards of twenty tribes speaking various dialects of the Maya language, and numbering about half a million in all. But their civilization is a thing of the past. Such knowledge as we possess of it rests upon the incomplete descriptions by Spanish writers and upon the examination of its surviving monuments.[1]

**History of the Mayas.** The Mayas are believed to have emerged from barbarism as early as the first or second century of the Christian era. The period to about 600 saw the rise of Palenque, Quiriguá, Copán, and other great cities in the southern part of the

---

[1] There is also some historical material in the so-called *Books of Chilan Balam*, which were copied or compiled by natives in Yucatán subsequent to the Spanish conquest. These records are written in the Maya language, but in Latin characters.

Maya territory.  Sculpture reached its highest development at this time.  The southern cities subsequently sank into decay, if not into oblivion, and Maya settlements began to be made in Yucatán.

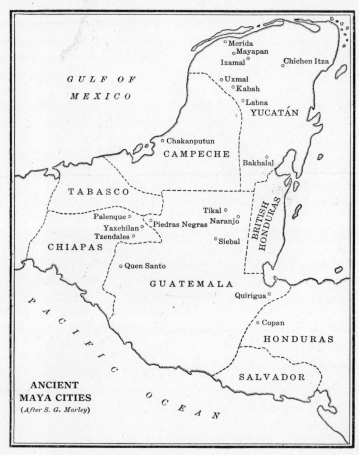

GULF OF MEXICO

o Merida
o Mayapan
Izamal o       o Chichen Itza

o Uxmal
o Kabah

o Labna
YUCATÁN

o Chakanputun
CAMPECHE

Bakhalal o

TABASCO

Tikal o
Palenque o      Naranjo o
Yaxchilan o  o Piedras Negras
Tzendales o          o Siebal
CHIAPAS

BRITISH HONDURAS

o Quen Santo

GUATEMALA
Quirigua o

o Copan
HONDURAS

PACIFIC

SALVADOR

OCEAN

ANCIENT
MAYA CITIES
(After S. G. Morley)

Here about 1000 the cities of Chichen Itza, Uxmal, and Mayapan formed a confederacy, each having an equal share in the government of the country.  Maya culture during this age was revealed particularly in architecture.  Extensive ruins, scattered throughout the length and breadth of the peninsula, testify to the numerous, industrious, and peaceful people who once inhabited it.  Later, however, Yucatán split into warring sections under petty chief-

PYRAMID TEMPLE OF CHICHEN ITZA, YUCATÁN

An imposing monument of Chichen Itza is the so-called Castillo, or Castle. It is a stepped pyramid, about eighty feet high, with a block-like superstructure forming the temple proper. A broad stairway of hewn stone ascends each face of the pyramid.

tains; population and culture declined, and when the Spaniards arrived they found the country in chaos and ripe for conquest.

**Maya Architecture.** Remains of the Maya cities — the Ninevehs and Babylons of the New World — now lie buried in the tropical jungle. Some of the cities in Yucatán were still inhabited at the time of European discovery, though soon abandoned thereafter. The surviving ruins are chiefly those of temples and shrines, which were placed on terraces or pyramids. Staircases led up to the top from one or more sides. Most pyramids were built in steps. The material of these structures is a soft limestone, which could be cut with flint chisels; the filling is a cement made of mortar and small stones. Cornices and lintels consist of hardwood. Some buildings rise to as many as three stories and contain a number of rooms with vaulted ceilings. The principle of the true arch was unknown; hence the builders overlapped the slabs of the side walls in succession until the narrow space at the top could be spanned with a single flat stone. It is an interesting fact that many structures have a definite orientation to particular points of the compass.

**Maya Sculpture.** The Mayas lavished decorations on the walls of

A MAYA FIGURINE

Found in 1903 in the Mexican state of Vera Cruz and now in the U. S. National Museum at Washington. It is about 6½ inches in height and 3¾ inches in diameter at the base. The upper part represents a human head. Part of the face is covered by a mask-like device, which extends down over the chest like a beard. The lower part of the stubby figure bears a general resemblance to a bird, and the bird-form is further emphasized by wings at the sides. This little idol doubtless represents a bird-man deity. It is covered with Maya glyphs. These embody the earliest date yet determined in America, a date which corresponds to 100 B.C.

temples, on pillars and roofs, and even on the faces of the pyramids which supported the temples. Their stone reliefs, and especially their stucco designs, were often executed in a masterly manner.

Animal, human, and divine figures are represented. No statues completely in the round have been found. All this work in sculpture, as in architecture, was accomplished with stone and wooden tools, for the Mayas were unacquainted with the useful metals.

STUCCO RELIEF FROM PALENQUE, YUCATÁN

An altarpiece from the "Temple of the Beau Relief" at Palenque. It shows a single figure, nearly life-size, seated on a cushioned throne, which rests on two tigers. The grace, vigor, and refinement of this work make it a masterpiece of aboriginal American art; unfortunately most of it has now been obliterated.

**Maya Science.**  Still more remarkable were the scientific achievements of the Mayas.  Their priests — the leaders and teachers of the people — knew enough astronomy to calculate the duration of the revolution of Venus and perhaps of other planets as well. They coördinated the lunar month with the solar year and devised a calendar consisting of eighteen periods of twenty days each, with five supplementary days at the end.  In arithmetic they understood the principle of local value, used a zero symbol, and were able to write down and handle numbers exceeding a million.  Their writing was at least occasionally phonetic. Pictures which stood for objects or ideas were being displaced by symbols for the sounds of words and syllables.  Maya glyphs were usually carved in stone or painted on fiber-paper books (codices). Modern scholars have been able to decipher those glyphs which indicate numbers and refer to the calendar system, thus gaining an insight into the age of Maya culture, but as yet little progress has been made in reading the script as a whole. But it is now clear that the Mayas were a literary people, who had begun to give permanent form to their history, philosophy, and poetry.

**The Aztecs.**  The group of Indian tribes calling themselves Mexicas, or Aztecs, belonged to the Nahua linguistic stock,[1]

MAYA BAR AND DOT
NUMERALS

The Maya arithmetical system was vigesimal, being based on the number 20.  Maya numerals were of two kinds, which have been compared to our Roman and Arabic systems.  It is the latter that is shown here.  A picture of the moon stands for twenty.  The commonest sign for zero was a shell.

[1] Represented today by the Pimas of southern Arizona and northern Mexico, the Seri of Lower California, and the Yaqui, Cora, and Huichol Indians.

which is related to the Shoshonean stock in the Rocky Mountain region of the United States. Nahua-speaking peoples entered Mexico from the northwest in successive waves and spread over the country as far as the Isthmus of Tehuantepec. The Aztecs, the last Nahua wave, presumably arrived in the eleventh or twelfth century. About 1325, under a chief named Tenoch, they founded their lake settlement Tenochtitlan, on the site of the present City of Mexico.

**The Aztec Empire.** The Aztecs before long began to expand over the plateau of Anáhuac, where they united with two other tribes or pueblos on Lake Tezcuco. The triple alliance, thus formed, subjugated many neighboring peoples. The Aztec war chief (emperor, as the Spaniards described him) ruled over an imperial domain, extending between the Gulf of Mexico and the Pacific Ocean, and at Tenochtitlan the Aztec war god towered supreme above the idols of the conquered tribes. The empire of the Aztecs had lasted less than a century, when in 1520 Cortés and his Spaniards brought it crashing to the ground.

**Sources of Aztec History.** Our knowledge of the Aztecs, as of the Mayas, is derived partly from the examination of the scanty monumental remains and partly from the accounts — often fantastic — by early Spanish historians and Spanish-educated natives. Fortunately, additional information of high value can be gleaned from Aztec picture writing, which was executed in bright colors on skins of animals or on maguey paper. The picture writing is often full of detail, indicating festivals, sacrifices, and other features in the life of the people, together with the dates of important events and the names of prominent persons. The majority of these priceless records disappeared after the Conquest, but some have survived, either in the original state or as copies, among them the so-called codices in Rome, Paris, and Oxford. Students of Aztec history are thus able to consult the actual documents on which that history is based.

**Culture.** When the Nahua peoples first entered Mexico they were migratory hunters and fishers, with no arts save those pertaining to a barbarous state of existence. Their new environment, with a genial climate and a soil adapted to the production of maize, favored agriculture and a sedentary mode of life. Accordingly, the Nahua in time settled down and developed the culture best known to us among the Aztecs. This Aztec (Nahua) culture seems to have been much indebted to the Mayas, who once occupied the plateau of Anáhuac at least as far north as the Valley of Mexico.

**Social Classes.** Aztec society was based on the clan (*gens*), each tribe being divided into a number of clans, each clan owning in common a section of the tribal territory, and each family holding and tilling a share of the communal lands. Above the freemen of a clan stood a so-called nobility, whose members monopolized all the higher positions in the state. The relation of the nobles to their retainers recalls some features of the European feudal system. Below the freemen were the slaves, recruited from prisoners of war, persons enslaved for punishment, or children sold by their parents.

**Government.** Compared with the American Indians generally, the Aztecs had a highly organized government. Two chiefs held sway, a civil chief ("snake woman") and a war chief ("chief of men"). As befitted so militant a people, it was the war chief who cut much the greater figure. The despotic power and luxurious- ness of Aztec rulers may be inferred from the picture writing, which enumerates by hundreds and thousands mantles, skins, bags of gold dust, bronze hatchets, and other objects, regularly furnished by the towns as taxes or tribute.

**Occupations.** Aztec farmers raised maize, the principal food crop, together with the tomato (*tomatl*), the *chili* pepper, and the beans now called by the Spanish name *frijoles*. From them the Spaniards learned to prepare the beverage chocolate (*chocollatl*) and the intoxicating drink *pulque*, which was produced from the juices of the maguey plant. Though unacquainted with iron, artisans worked in both copper and tin and also in the alloy of these two metals known as bronze. Metallic implements had not superseded, however, those of obsidian and other hard stones. The Spaniards, on their first entry into Mexico, saw barbers' shops in which men were being shaved with obsidian razors. Merchants formed an important and honorable class. Regular markets were held in each important town every fifth day, and a currency consisting of quills of gold dust, with cocoa beans for small change, was used for trading purposes. It remains to add that the Aztecs made fair pottery, spun and wove cotton cloth almost as fine as silk, excelled in featherwork, using for this purpose the

gorgeous plumage of tropical birds, built skillfully in stone, and
carved in both wood and stone.

**Intellectual Life.** The Aztecs, as well as the Mayas, had a solar
calendar, without any correction for the six hours by which the

AZTEC CALENDAR STONE

The stone is basaltic porphyry, 12 feet in diameter and 3 feet in thick-
ness. It was found buried in the soil of the cathedral square of Mexico
City, about the middle of the sixteenth century. The central figure of
the carving represents the sun. The hieroglyphs and other signs form a
record of the cosmogonic myth of the Aztecs and the creations and de-
structions of the world. It is believed that the stone served as a sort of
altar upon which human victims were sacrificed.

year exceeds 365 days. The division of the year into eighteen
periods of twenty days each, with five remaining days, was the
same as that of the Mayas. Both peoples considered the extra
days added at the end of the year to be unlucky, and nothing of any
importance was ever done at this time. Aztec numerals were
based on the vigesimal system, being reckoned by scores. Thus a

flag stood for the figure 20, a feather for 400 (a score of scores), and a purse for 8000 (a score of scores of scores). For convenience such symbols might be halved and quartered. Aztec picture writing, above referred to, resembled the Maya glyphic system. It was on the road to becoming phonetic, through the use of the rebus. This method of expressing words by pictures of objects, whose names resemble those words or syllables in them, was employed by the Aztecs for names of persons and places. After the Spanish conquest, the natives adapted the rebus for the Latin words of their new Christian religion, expressing *amen*, for instance, by the picture of water (*a*) and an aloe (*me*). Writing, arithmetic, and other branches of knowledge were regularly taught, at least to the children of the upper classes, in schools attached to the temples.

STONE IDOL OF THE
AZTECS

A large stone figure, more than 8 feet high and 5 feet across. Probably represents Coatlicue, mother of the war god Huitzilopochtli. Coatlicue was an earth goddess and, as her name (Serpent-Robe) implies, wore a skirt woven of snakes.

**Religion.** Aztec religious beliefs centered in the worship of natural objects and phenomena — the sun, the moon, the morning star, fire, and vegetation — which were regarded as divine beings and were represented by idols. Huitzilopochtli, the war god, stood at the head of the Aztec pantheon. Tezcatlipoca personified the breath of life, and as such both gave and took away men's lives. Centeotl, the maize deity, presided over agriculture, and Tlaloc, over rainfall. Quetzalcoatl, god of the winds and the heavens, came to stand for law, order, and enlightenment. The worship of these and other deities, save the gentle Quetzalcoatl, was marked by human sacrifice on a more extensive scale than has been known anywhere else in the world. War captives and children were led to the summit of a pyramidal temple, there were stretched upon a stone, their breasts slashed with an obsidian knife, and their still palpitating hearts torn out as an offering to the bloodthirsty god.  Spanish chroniclers tell of thousands of prisoners annually slaughtered at the various festivals.  Back of these ugly rites lay the belief that the gods needed to be sustained by food and drink; hence the Aztecs engaged in ceaseless hostilities with other tribes in order to provide human material for sacrifices.  This feature of Aztec religion was naturally very repulsive to the Spaniards, who seem to have exaggerated its prevalence.  At any rate, it existed side by side with such rites as baptism and confession, indicating consciousness of sin.  Many Aztec prayers, marked by spiritual feeling and expressed in refined language, have been preserved, together with hymns in honor of divinities.

AZTEC SACRIFICIAL KNIFE

British Museum, London

Length, twelve inches.  The blade is of yellow, opalescent chalcedony, beautifully chipped and polished.  The handle is of light-colored wood carved in the form of a man masked with a bird skin.  Brilliant mosaic settings of turquoise, malachite, and shell embellish the figure.

**Tenochtitlan.**  Few architectural works of the Aztecs survived the Conquest.  Their capital, Tenochtitlan, we know only by the descriptions of the Spaniards.  The city lay on two islands in Lake Tezcuco.  Three long causeways, built of cement, maintained connection with the mainland.  The center of the city was marked by a great square, which formed the place of trade and public gathering.  Twenty or more temples stood in this square.  Surrounding it were quarters for the priests, educational buildings, official residences, and huge communal houses in which the people lived.  These structures were built of stone, in one or two stories.

**The Chibchas.**  Another Indian people who had made considerable progress in civilization were the Chibchas.  They occupied the plateau of Bogotá, east of the Magdalena River, but their influence seems to have penetrated from Colombia into Central America and Venezuela on the north, while on the south it reached into Ecuador.  The culture of the Chibchas resembled that of their Inca neighbors.  It was less advanced, however, for they lacked domestic animals and did not work in copper.  Nor do we find among them any evidence of writing and calendar systems comparable to those of the Mayas and Aztecs.

**The Incas.** The ancestors of the Incas, according to the most plausible theory, were the ancient people who left behind, as evidence of their civilization, the ruins of Tiahuanacu at the southern end of Lake Titicaca. Here, on a plateau nearly 13,000 feet above sea level, are the remains of a great city, or, if not of a city, of sanctuaries, fortresses, and palaces. The ruins, which once covered the plateau for a distance of ten miles, consist of enormous and perfectly chiseled stone blocks. No such imposing architecture is found elsewhere in America. This Megalithic civilization seems to have arisen at least as early as the beginning of the Christian era. Though subsequently overthrown by barbarian invaders, it survived among Indians belonging to the Quechua linguistic stock.[1] About four hundred years before the Spanish conquest some of these Quechua-speaking peoples settled in the fertile valley of Cuzco. They were called Incas — "children of the sun" — a name which originally applied only to their ruling family.

**The Inca Empire.** Legend makes Manco Capac the founder of the Inca dynasty and the builder or rebuilder of the city of Cuzco. His successors, by prowess in war and judicious marriages, brought many Andean tribes under one government. The Inca Empire, when the Spaniards came early in the sixteenth century, stretched for approximately 2700 miles from the River Ancasmayu north of Quito in Ecuador to the River Maule below the present Santiago in Chile. Its area about equaled that of the United States east of the Mississippi River; its population numbered perhaps ten millions.

**Organization of the Inca Empire.** Whereas the Aztecs only exacted tribute and soldiers from the subject peoples of Anáhuac, the Incas took pains to consolidate their vast dominions. They built fortresses at strategic points in the conquered territory, established colonies of Quechua-speaking peasants, and maintained military roads, or rather trails, running from Cuzco to every part of the empire. These administrative measures, which present a curious resemblance to the Roman organization of Italy, seem to

---

[1] Machu Picchu, a stone city recently uncovered by the Yale University expedition led by Professor Hiram Bingham, is believed to be the Andean fortress where the remnant of these Megalithic folk took refuge. The ruins of the city are situated about two days' journey from Cuzco, in an almost inaccessible canyon in the valley of the Urubamba River.

Courtesy Pan American Union

MONOLITHIC GATE, TIAHUANACU, BOLIVIA

The monument stands about ten feet high. The material is hard trachyte, decorated with bas-reliefs. The central figure represents a god, probably the creator-god Huiracocha; on either side are figures, human or bird-headed, kneeling in adoration. The style of the sculptures is pre-Inca.

Courtesy Grace Line

SACSAHUAMAN FORTRESS, CUZCO, PERÚ

Part of the mighty fortress that stood watch over the ancient capital of the Inca Empire. It consists of 3 parallel walls, each over 300 yards long. Some of the stones measure 17 × 12 × 7 feet. In the masonry work no mortar was used, the blocks being cut accurately to fit into one another.

have been effective. One of the Spanish Conquistadors testifies that "the Incas were feared, obeyed, and respected by their subjects as men capable and versed in the arts of government."[1]

**Inca Society.** The Inca Empire might be described as a religious despotism. All authority centered in the ruler, who, as the Child of the Sun, bore divine attributes and enjoyed reverence akin to worship. He was politically an emperor and religiously a god. His officials regulated the distribution of the arable land, which, with its produce, belonged partly to the royal family, partly to the priesthoods of the Sun, and partly to the clan or local community. There was no individual ownership of land; consequently a peasant could not sell or bequeath his holding. The Inca officials had also to see that everybody lived in a fixed district, followed a fixed occupation, and did a proper share of the work. Persons who refused to perform their allotted tasks were severely punished. An all-powerful State, in association with a State Church, constantly supervised and regulated the activities of the people. Personal freedom did not exist in ancient Perú.

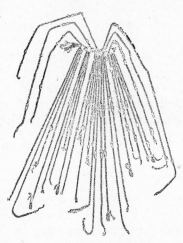

A PERUVIAN QUIPU
American Museum of Natural
History, New York

The result was a habit of passive obedience and a lack of initiative which prevented any determined resistance on the part of the natives to the handful of Spaniards who overthrew the Inca Empire.

**Inca Culture.** The Peruvian Indians were skillful farmers, raising maize, manioc, potatoes, and cotton. They understood the use of fertilizers, built aqueducts and irrigation ditches, and carried terraces for cultivation high up the mountain sides. As has been noted, they domesticated the llama and the alpaca. The Peruvians also excelled in the practical arts — stone working, spinning and weaving, the manufacture of pottery, and the metallurgy of gold, silver, and bronze. In some of these respects they

[1] Will of Leguisamo, Cuzco, 1589.

perhaps surpassed the Mexican Indians.  On the other hand, the
Peruvians had no solar calendar and no writing system, by either
pictures or glyphs.  The *quipu* (colored strings with knots) was
used very ingeniously for enumeration according to the decimal
system.  Inca religion, centering in the adoration of the Sun, a
deity who but seldom required human sacrifice, marked an improvement over the bloody Aztec rites.  Elaborate ceremonies,
festivals, and pilgrimages characterized the solar worship.  Early
Spanish authorities assert that the people were very peaceful and
orderly and that theft and crimes of violence were almost unknown
among them.  On the whole, their culture bears witness to the
high intellectual and moral capacity of the Indian race.

**Cuzco.**  The once sacred City of the Sun lies about one hundred
and fifty miles northwest of Lake Titicaca, in a mountain valley
more than 11,000 feet above sea level.  When Cuzco was captured by Pizarro in 1533, the size and magnificence of its palaces
and temples filled the Spaniards with astonishment.  These structures were all swept away by the conquerors or were incorporated
in their own buildings.  But one still finds long stretches of Inca
walls, the masonry of which exhibits much expertness in cutting
stones and fitting them together without cement.  Above Cuzco is
the hill of Sacsahuaman, crowned by the ramparts of a fortress
that may well be older than the Inca Empire.  The extent of the
fortress, its solid construction, and the enormous size of many of
the individual stones combine to produce here the most impressive
prehistoric monument in the New World.

**General Indian Cultural Status.**  The Mayas, Aztecs, Chibchas,
and Incas present many aspects in common.  They all developed a
sedentary maize culture on fertile uplands, in or near the tropics,
where the heat was moderated by the great altitude.  All of them
lacked iron, and the Mayas and Chibchas even lacked copper.
Except for the feeble assistance of the llama and alpaca in Perú,
they did not have the coöperation of domesticated animals.  They
possessed no wheeled vehicles.  None of them invented an alpha-
bet or syllabary, while the Chibchas and Incas knew nothing of
picture writing.  In arithmetic, astronomy, and the calendar only
the Mayas and Aztecs seem to have made conspicuous advance.
Such scientific knowledge as existed was not widely diffused; on
the contrary, it was confined to an aristocratic and priestly class,

sharply separated from the mass of the plebeians.  The Spanish conquest led to the destruction of this class, and in consequence the natives soon lost their intellectual culture.  When we consider, however, the material obstacles in the way of progress and the further fact of isolation, preventing the mixture and contact of peoples who otherwise might have learned from one another, we may well wonder that the Indians of Mexico, Central America, and South America accomplished so much.  It is one of the tragedies of history that their incipient civilization should have perished so completely at the hands of Europeans.

## Words and Phrases You Should Know

| | | |
|---|---|---|
| aborigines | Humboldt Current | religious despotism |
| Anglo-American | Incas | savannas |
| Antilles | Latin America | selvas |
| archæologist | linguistic stock | Sierra Madre Occidental |
| archipelago | llanos | Sierra Madre Oriental |
| Aztecs | lunar month | solar calendar |
| Cordillera | Mayas | steppes |
| dialect | pampas | twin continents |
| glyph | polysynthesis | |

## Questions You Should Be Able to Answer

1. Why may North and South America be called twin continents?
2. How are these two continents unlike one another?
3. How do you account for the fact that South America, although smaller than North America, contains more land suitable to human habitation than North America?
4. How would you compare the mountain ranges and river systems of the two continents?
5. Why are the large trading centers of South America located on the eastern side of the continent?
6. What is meant by the statement that the climate of Latin America is vertical rather than horizontal?
7. What are some of the chief mineral resources of Latin America?
8. What lumber products are found in Latin America that we do not have in North America?
9. What foods of common use do we obtain from Latin America?
10. What evidence is there that the earliest inhabitants of America came from Asia?  How did they probably come?

11. In what part of Latin America did the Mayas live? the Aztecs?
12. What were the classes of people in Aztec society?
13. How do we know that the rulers of the Aztecs were dictatorial?
14. Why was human sacrifice so important in Aztec religion?
15. In what way did the Incas show greater governmental ability than the Aztecs?
16. Would you rather have lived in the Inca empire or in the land of the Aztecs? Why?
17. In what ways were the Incas more advanced than the Aztecs? the Aztecs than the Incas?
18. How would you compare the civilizations of the Aztecs and Incas with that of the Indians in New England at the time of the Pilgrim Fathers?

## PROJECTS AND ACTIVITIES

1. Let a committee plan a day with the map of Latin America. Each member of the committee might draw or trace a map of Latin America, and by pictorial drawings or printed descriptions make his map tell the story of one of the topics below. The committee's report to the class might consist of discussions of the maps by the committee members. The maps could then be posted on the class bulletin board for future reference. Topics for map stories: the countries of Latin America as it is today; comparisons between Latin America and Anglo-America; mountains, plateaus, plains, rivers, and lakes of Latin America; the Antilles; mineral, lumber, and food resources of Latin America; the land of the Mayas, Aztecs, and Incas.

2. Prepare a brief oral report on the importance of plateaus in South America.

3. Using a bar of soap, carve the Maya figurine on page 21 or the Aztec stone idol on page 27.

4. Give a short talk on the tools and weapons of the Latin Americans.

5. Make a chart in which you compare and contrast the Mayas, Aztecs, and Incas. Use these headings: government; classes of people; architecture and sculpture; occupations; religion; writing; calendar.

6. Work out a comparison of Indian civilization and accomplishments with the civilization and accomplishments of some other primitive people whose history you have studied.

7. Prepare a short talk on monuments and remains of Indian civilizations. Use the pictures in this chapter.

8. Make a chart showing the privileges and duties of each class of Aztecs.

# CHAPTER II

# European Background: Spain and Portugal

**The Old World Elements.** Spaniards, Portuguese, and African Negroes appeared in America from the late fifteenth century. Since the white man was dominant, his ways of life receive the most attention, but the Negro deserves more thought than he usually gets. Slaves brought to America nearly all originated on the coasts between the Niger and the Congo rivers. Their cultural status there was at least equal to that of the higher Indian groups, in politics, religion, economic activities, and social organization. They were inferior to the Mayas and Aztecs in intellectual life, but superior to all Indians as herdsmen and ironsmiths. Much of their skills survived transplanting to America, and the influence of their music and religion [1] is still visible.

**Hispanic-American Nations.** Eighteen independent nations in the New World developed from Spanish colonies. Brazil sprang from Portuguese settlement. Haiti had a mixed Spanish and French origin. All of them inherited Romance languages (Spanish, Portuguese, French), the Roman Catholic faith, and Latin culture. They constitute the Latin America of today. Omitting Haiti, as partly French, they may be called still more definitely the Hispanic [2]-American nations.

**The Iberian Peninsula.** The geography of the Iberian Peninsula in some ways visibly molded its history. The Pyrenees, lofty, forbidding, and provided with few passes, isolated Spain and Portugal from the rest of Europe far more effectively than the Alps isolated Italy. The mountains (*sierras*) of the interior, though nowhere an insuperable barrier, cut up the country into several distinct regions, unlike in climate and natural productions, and consequently in the characteristics of the inhabitants. At

---

[1] Ophiolatry, or serpent worship, often confused with a minor outgrowth called voodoo.

[2] Hispanic from *Hispania*, the Roman name of the Iberian Peninsula.

the same time, the nearness of the peninsula to Africa brought it
into intimate relations with the northern coast of that continent.
Much as Russia has formed a link between Asia and Europe, so
Spain and Portugal have been a highway from Africa to Europe.

**Settlement of the Iberian Peninsula.**  Men of the Old Stone
(Palæolithic) period once lived in the Iberian Peninsula, as we know
from the discovery of human relics and remains in Spanish and
Portuguese caves.  What became of these first settlers we do not
know.  Several thousand years ago Neolithic men, generally called
Iberians, reached the peninsula from North Africa.  They belonged
to that short, brunette, longheaded Mediterranean type of the
White Race which is also found in central and southern Italy,
Greece, and the adjacent islands.  After them Celtic-speaking
tribes entered from central Europe.  It seems probable that Celts
and Iberians became more or less fused in the course of centuries,
thus forming the mixed people known as Celtiberians.  Romans,
Germans, Moors, and Jews, who settled in the Iberian Peninsula
during ancient and medieval times, have also contributed considerable elements to its population.

**Phœnician Trade with Spain.**  The Iberian Peninsula (more
briefly, Spain) first became known in antiquity through the trading
expeditions of those redoubtable mariners, the Phœnicians, who
reached the southern coast, called by them Tartessus,[1] perhaps as
early as 1000 B.C.  Here they planted their most distant colony,
the city of Gades, which survives to this day as Cadiz.  It is perhaps the oldest town in Europe that has kept a continuity of life
and name since its foundation.  The Phœnicians exchanged their
purple cloths, tools and weapons, and other finished products for
the tin, lead, and silver yielded by the Spanish mines.

**Carthaginian Possessions in Spain.**  After the rise of Carthage,
the great Phœnician colony in North Africa, Spain comes definitely
within the purview of history.  Numerous Carthaginian settlements were established in the peninsula, the most important being
Nova Carthago (New Carthage), from which the modern city of
Cartagena takes its origin.  The authority of Carthage finally extended along the fertile eastern coast as far north as the Ebro
River.  This expansion took place chiefly during the latter part
of the third century B.C.  It was the work of the Carthaginian

---

[1] The Biblical "Tarshish."  See *Ezekiel*, xxvii, 12.

general and statesman Hamilcar Barca (father of the still more famous Hannibal), who, seeing his country deprived by Rome of Sicily and Sardinia as the result of the first Punic War, determined to build up a new colonial dominion in Spain. The produce of the Spanish silver would fill the depleted Carthaginian treasury, and the hardy Spaniards would provide a soldiery equal even to the legions of Rome. But that city had already fixed her eyes on the Spanish mines and men, and in the second Punic War (218–201 B.c.) she drove Carthage finally and completely out of the peninsula.

**Roman Conquest of Spain.** The expulsion of the Carthaginians did not imply the subjection of the Spaniards. The Spanish tribes loved freedom and in their mountain fastnesses long kept up a desperate struggle against the Roman power. In Viriathus, a chief of Lusitania, they found a leader who for years baffled the best commanders Rome sent out to the peninsula. Not long after his death, the last embers of Spanish liberty blazed up in the heroic defense of Numantia, an unwalled city in the northern part of the country. The capture of the city (133 B.c.) put an end to organized resistance on the part of the natives. Henceforth all Spain, except the inaccessible mountain district in the northwest, became Roman territory.

**Romanization of Spain.** Rome continued in Spain the process of Romanization which she had begun in Italy and Sicily, and which she was to repeat in Gaul and Britain. Many farmers and traders went to Spain; even Roman soldiers, quartered there for long periods, married Spanish wives, and, on retiring from active service, settled in the peninsula. The uncivilized Spaniards, on their side, accepted Roman ways gladly. By the close of the republican era southern Spain had become practically Roman in speech, in customs, and in religion. The process of Romanization went on even more rapidly under the empire. The country at this time was studded with Roman cities, including Cæsaraugusta (Saragossa), Toletum (Toledo), Corduba (Cordova), Hispalis (Seville), Olispo (Lisbon), and Brigantium (Coruña). These were all connected by magnificent highways. Spain under the empire consisted of three provinces: Terraconensis, in the north and northwest; Lusitania, roughly equivalent to the modern Portugal; and Bætica, in the south. These divisions closely coincide with the natural geographical features of the peninsula.

**The Germans in Spain.** The long period of peace, prosperity, and settled government ended for Spain, as for the other parts of the Roman world, with the inruption of the Germans. In 406 Suevi, Alans, and Vandals, taking advantage of the defenseless state of the frontiers, crossed the Rhine and swept almost without resistance over Gaul. Three years later they marched through the unguarded passes of the Pyrenees and entered Spain. The invaders then proceeded to divide the country between them in some rough fashion. The Suevi took Galicia in the northwestern corner of the peninsula. The Alans settled in Lusitania. The Vandals for a time occupied the former Roman province of Bætica, but subsequently established themselves in Africa. These barbarian peoples were too few in number really to subdue Spain and too lacking in political capacity really to govern it. What they did was to rove about in hordes, plundering, levying blackmail, and fighting both with the provincials and with one another.

**The Visigothic Kingdom (415–711).** Not very different, at first, were the Visigoths, or West Goths. Under their famous chieftain, Alaric, they had harried Greece and Italy and had even sacked Rome. The Visigoths came to Spain, however, as allies of the Empire and duly commissioned defenders of the provincials. After destroying the Alans and pushing the Suevi farther back into the mountains of the northwest, they settled down on both sides of the Pyrenees. Their possessions in southern Gaul were seized by the Franks after less than a century, but the Visigothic kingdom in Spain lasted for nearly three hundred years. Its barbarian rulers sought to preserve the institutions of Rome and to respect the rights of their Roman subjects. Near the close of the sixth century one of the Visigothic kings made Roman Catholicism the religion of the state, in place of Arian Christianity. This change, by breaking down the religious barrier which had formerly existed between the orthodox (Catholic) provincials and the unorthodox (Arian) Germans, helped greatly to blend them into one people.

**The Moors in Spain.** But the Visigothic kingdom was nearing its end. Islam, the new religion of Mohammed, had now appeared in the East. It was an aggressive religion, which its Arab adherents prepared to spread by the sword. They quickly annexed Egypt, and by the opening of the eighth century had subdued the Berber tribes of North Africa as far as the Atlantic. Next came the turn of Spain. In 711 a small force of Arabs and Berbers, under Tarik, crossed the strait that still bears his name,[1] entered the peninsula, and in a single battle overthrew the army gathered by Roderic, the "Last of the Goths," to meet the invaders. The Visigothic kingdom, already much enfeebled, could not withstand the shock. The Moors, as the Arabs and Berbers in Spain may henceforth be called, soon extended their sway to the foot of the Pyrenees.

**Moorish Spain.** The Moors introduced into Spain the Arab language and the culture and faith of Islam. After the establishment there of an independent Arab emirate, which in 929 became a caliphate, Cordova,[2] the capital, took its place as a center of art, learning, and refinement by the side of Damascus, Bagdad, and Cairo. According to the statements of Moorish writers it had a population of half a million. Other cities in Spain were noted for commerce or manufactures — Almeria for silks, Chincilla for carpets, Seville for cotton goods, Tortosa for shipbuilding. In short, Moorish Spain seems to have enjoyed great material prosperity. The Moors treated the Christians with liberality. No massacres and no persecutions occurred. The conquered Spaniards were allowed to retain their own laws and their own religion, on condition of paying taxes. In course of time, however, many Spanish Christians adopted Islam, in order to acquire the rights and privileges of Moslem citizens. Various features of Moorish art were also taken over by the Spaniards, who afterwards reproduced them in the cathedrals and missions of Latin America.

**Christian States of Spain.** The Moors never wholly conquered the fringe of mountain territory in the extreme north of Spain. Here a number of small Christian states, including León, Castile, Navarre, and Aragón, came into existence. In the west there also arose the Christian state of Portugal. Acting sometimes alone and sometimes in concert, these states fought steadily to widen their boundaries at the expense of their Moslem neighbors. The contest was blessed by the pope and supported by the chivalry of Europe. Periods of victory alternated with periods of defeat, but by the middle of the eleventh century the Spaniards and Portuguese had recovered half of the peninsula. The decisive battle of Las Navas de Tolosa, won in 1212 by the united forces of León, Castile,

---

[1] Gibraltar = *Gebal al Tarik*, "the mountain of Tarik."   [2] Sp. Córdoba.

INTERIOR OF THE GREAT MOSQUE OF CORDOVA

The great mosque of Cordova, begun in the eighth century, was gradually enlarged during the following centuries to its present dimensions, 570 by 425 feet. The building, one of the largest in the world, has now been turned into a cathedral. The most striking feature of the interior is the forest of porphyry, jasper, and marble pillars supporting open Moorish arches.

THE ESCORIAL, MADRID

This remarkable edifice, at once a convent, a church, a palace, and a royal mausoleum, is situated in a wilderness about twenty-seven miles from Madrid. It was begun by Philip II in 1563 and was completed in 1584. The Escorial is dedicated to St. Lawrence, that saint's day (August 10, 1557) being the day when the Spanish king won a great victory over the French at the battle of St. Quentin. The huge dimensions of the Escorial may be inferred from the fact that it includes eighty-six staircases, eighty-nine fountains, fifteen cloisters, and miles of corridors. The Escorial contains a library of rare books and manuscripts and a collection of valuable paintings. In the royal mausoleum under the altar of the church lie the remains of Charles I, Philip II, and many of their successors.

Aragón, Navarre, and Portugal, laid Moorish Spain at the feet of the Christians. Cordova and Seville, the two chief cities of Andalusia, were captured by them not many years after. The Moors now retired to the kingdom of Granada, which they kept for more than two centuries.

**The Cid.** The long struggle with the Moors made the Spaniards a patriotic people, keenly conscious of their national unity. The

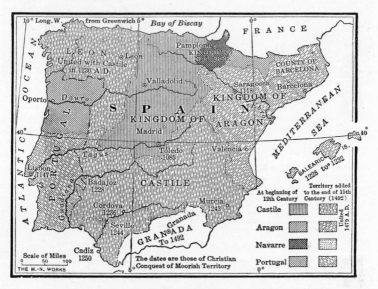

UNIFICATION OF SPAIN DURING THE MIDDLE AGES

achievements of Christian warriors were recited in countless ballads, especially in the fine *Poema del Cid*. It deals with the exploits of Rodrigo Díaz, better known by the title of the Cid (lord) given to him by the Moors. The Cid of romance was the embodiment of every knightly virtue; the real Cid was a bandit, who fought sometimes for the Christians and sometimes against them, but always in his own interest. The Cid's evil deeds were forgotten after his death, and he became the national hero of Spain.

**Union of Castile and Aragón (1479).** Meanwhile, the separate Spanish kingdoms were coming together to form a nation. León and Castile in 1230 combined into the one kingdom of Castile, so named because its frontiers bristled with castles against the Moors.

THE ALHAMBRA, GRANADA

A fortress and palace of the Moorish rulers of Granada. The outer walls are severely plain, but the interior, with its marble pillars and arches, walls paneled with painted tiles, fretted ceilings, and courts, is a miracle of beauty.

The next important step in the making of Spain was the marriage of Ferdinand of Aragón to Isabella of Castile, leading in 1479 to the union of these two kingdoms. About the same time the Castilian language began to crowd out the other Spanish dialects and to become the national speech.

**Conquest of Granada (1492).** The king and queen of Spain continued their unifying work by conquering the Moorish kingdom of Granada. No effort was made by the Ottoman Turks, who had recently captured Constantinople in eastern Europe, to defend the last stronghold of Islam in western Europe. The Moors, though thrown on their own resources, made a gallant resistance. At least once Ferdinand wearied of the struggle, but Isabella's determination never wavered. Granada surrendered in 1492, and the silver cross of the crusading army was raised on the towers of the Alhambra. Moorish rule in Spain, after an existence of almost eight centuries, now ended.

ISABELLA
Palacio Real, Madrid

**Annexation of Navarre (1515).** The little kingdom of Navarre, lying on both sides of the Pyrenees, had long been a bone of contention between Spanish and French monarchs. The southern part of the kingdom was finally incorporated with Castile in 1515. All the Iberian Peninsula, excepting Portugal,[1] henceforth came under one Crown.

**The Spanish Monarchy.** Ferdinand and Isabella accomplished more than territorial union. Like their contemporaries, Henry VII of England and Louis XI of France, they labored with success to create in Spain a powerful monarchy in place of feudalism. Spain had found, as England and France had found, that feudalism

---

[1] In 1581 Portugal was joined to Spain by a personal union under Philip II. Its dissolution in 1640 ended what Portuguese writers call the "Sixty Years' Captivity."

spelled disorder and that only a strong central government could keep the peace, repress crime, and foster industry and trade. Ferdinand and Isabella consequently struck hard at the feudal nobles. Private warfare was forbidden, castles could not be erected without the royal consent, and much land which the nobles had seized was reclaimed for the Crown. The centralizing policies of

the two monarchs were further revealed in their efforts to codify the mass of laws that had descended from earlier times, to build up an efficient national army in place of feudal levies, and to bring the Church under royal control. The development of the Spanish colonial empire still further increased the authority of the Crown, which ruled the dominions overseas directly and derived from them, not only an immense prestige, but also an enormous revenue. It is significant that the discovery of America was contemporaneous with the conquest of Granada.

**Royal Absolutism.** Aragón and Castile possessed representative assemblies in the Cortes or Courts, which, like

PHILIP II

the English Parliament and the French Estates-General, embraced the several estates of the realm. In Aragón at one time the Cortes insisted that grievances must be redressed before taxes would be granted and that no laws were valid which lacked the consent of all the estates. But nothing came from this hopeful beginning. Ferdinand and Isabella and their two successors during the sixteenth century, Charles I [1] and Philip II, had no love for parliamentary govern-

[1] As Holy Roman Emperor, Charles V.

ment. Henceforth the Cortes was rarely summoned and then only to vote supplies; for the work of legislation it was no longer needed. Royal absolutism in Spain, as elsewhere, repressed popular liberties.

**The Nobility.** The Spanish nobles, having been brought to a proper respect for the Crown, were left in possession of their social rank, landed property, and numerous privileges, including exemption from various taxes. As in France and other European countries, where feudal ideas still prevailed, the nobles despised all gainful occupations. A nobleman's son lost caste, were he to engage in farming, manufacturing, trade, or the professions. The Castilian proverb that a Spaniard who wished to make his fortune must seek the Church, the sea, or the Court, expressed the contempt of any sort of useful labor on the part of the upper classes.

**The Spanish Church.** (The State dominated the Church in Spain.) Ferdinand and Isabella successfully asserted the right of naming candidates for ecclesiastical offices, in order to exclude the foreigners so frequently appointed by the pope. Their successors on the throne also compelled the pope to agree that no bulls should be published in Spain without the royal consent. Such measures nationalized the Spanish Church, making it an effective instrument of government in the hands of the sovereign.

**The Clergy.** In no European country at this period were the clergy more numerous, more wealthy, and more powerful than in Spain. Over 400,000 ecclesiastics — archbishops, bishops, secular priests, monks, and nuns — administered to the religious needs of a population of not more than 10,000,000. The clergy were freed from the burden of taxation; they were also allowed to devote to ecclesiastical uses the huge gifts and bequests of property made by pious laymen. No wonder that the Church became exceedingly rich, so rich, indeed, that by the middle of the eighteenth century it owned one fifth of all the land and enjoyed a yearly income equal to the entire revenue of the Crown. As in Catholic countries generally, the Church had special courts and a system of "canon" law for the trial of persons charged with any offense against religion, including heresy, apostasy, and the practice of witchcraft. All cases involving Church officers likewise came before these ecclesiastical courts, for Spanish priests still possessed the right called "benefit of clergy," which exempted them from civil jurisdiction.

**Religious Orders.**  To the influence of the clergy must be added that of the religious orders.  At the accession of Ferdinand and Isabella the Franciscans and Dominicans had most prominence. The former preached especially in the slums of the cities; the latter addressed themselves rather to educated people and the upper classes.  The Dominicans took particular interest in the extirpation of heresy, and the religious persecution of the Inquisition was largely directed by these "Dogs of the Lord" (*Dominici*

ST. IGNATIUS LOYOLA

After the painting by Sanchez de Coello in the House of the Society of Jesus at Madrid.  No authentic portrait of Loyola has been preserved.  Coello's picture was made with the aid of a wax cast of the saint's features after death.

*canes*).  The Society of Jesus, which was founded by a Spanish nobleman, Ignatius Loyola, in 1540, subsequently became very influential, through the activities of its zealous members as preachers, confessors, teachers, and missionaries.  The Jesuits, as their Protestant opponents styled them, entered all the lands which the maritime discoveries of the age laid open to Europeans.  In India, China, the East Indies, Japan, the Philippines, Africa, and the two Americas their converts from heathenism were numbered by hundreds of thousands.

**The Inquisition in Spain.**  The crusade of centuries against the Moors engendered a spirit of intolerance which culminated in the Inquisition.  This institution had been established in Aragón and Navarre as early as the thirteenth century.  Ferdinand and Isabella revived it in 1480, extended it to Castile, and had its operations transferred from papal to royal control.  One of the great councils of the realm, called the Council of the Inquisition, was set up, with Tomás de Torquemada, the queen's favorite cleric, at its head.  The Inquisition had authority over all Christians, whether Spaniards, converted Jews (Marranos), or converted Moslems (Moriscos).  Jews and Moslems who had never aban-

doned their faith for Christianity were not subject to its jurisdiction.

**Work of the Inquisition.** This dread tribunal found much to do,
judging from the number of people fined, imprisoned, or con-
demned to death by it in the earlier years of its operation. According to the lowest estimate, Torquemada is said to have burnt
2000 persons while inquisitor-general. The ferreting-out of heretics and of apostate Jews and Moslems continued during the next
three centuries,[1] until at length religious dissent became a rare phenomenon in Spain. The Inquisition likewise exercised a censorship
of books and the press, with the purpose of preventing the spread of
new and dangerous ideas. All these activities met the general approval of the Spanish people, to whom the principle of religious
liberty was intolerable. They and their rulers felt that the greatness of Spain depended as much on uniformity of belief as on
political unity.

**The Jews.** It is from this point of view that the dealings of the
government with the Jews must be considered. Many Jews had
settled in Spain during the Visigothic and Moorish periods. They
received kind treatment, participated in the general life, and
often rose to high places in the service of the state. From the
Moors, in particular, the Jews caught the contagion of poetry,
philosophy, and science, and a brilliant Jewish culture arose in
medieval Spain. The crusading era brought a change for the worse
in their condition. Christian knights, who warred against the
infidel Moors, equally despised and hated the Jews as unbelievers.
Popular antagonism toward them developed rapidly in the fifteenth century, and the Inquisition, after its establishment, demanded that they should either be baptized or expelled from the
country. If the Jews were baptized, then the Inquisition could
deal with them. If they quitted Spain, it would be a good riddance.

**Expulsion of the Jews (1492).** The "Catholic Monarchs,"
Ferdinand and Isabella, at length yielded to the demands of the
Inquisition. Soon after the fall of Granada the sovereigns issued
a decree ordering all Jews either to embrace Christianity or to
leave the kingdoms of Castile and Aragón within three months.
The number of those exiled, according to a very conservative

---

[1] The first suppression of the Inquisition occurred in 1808, when Napoleon
Bonaparte annexed Spain, but it was not finally abolished until 1834.

estimate, was 200,000; and thousands more perished on the way to exile. Spain, to be sure, only treated the Jews as England and other European states had treated them during the Middle Ages, when Jew-baiting flourished. But Spain suffered most as a result of this harsh policy, for she could ill afford to lose the professional men, skilled artisans, traders, and farmers who formed the bulk of the Jewish population.

**The Moors.** Another racial and religious problem was presented by the Moors. They were more numerous than the Jews, though more concentrated, especially in Valencia and the southern provinces of Castile. The annexation of Granada made the entire Moorish population of that kingdom subjects of Spain. Efforts to convert the Moors to Christianity met little success, and they were now confronted with the alternative of baptism or exile. Ferdinand and Isabella adopted this policy in Granada and Castile. Charles I, their successor, enforced it in Aragón and Valencia. Many Moors fled to North Africa, while the rest became Christians, or Moriscos. The mosques were turned into churches, the Koran gave place to the Bible, and Islam as a recognized faith finally disappeared throughout Spain.

**Expulsion of the Moriscos.** The Moriscos — only nominal Christians — continued to be an alien and hated class. Religious intolerance alone did not dictate this attitude toward them; there was also fear of their coöperation with the Moslems in an attack from Africa. Various proposals were made for dealing with the Moriscos; that which finally found favor was for their complete expulsion. Philip III, urged on by the Inquisition, issued a decree to this effect in 1609. It forced some 200,000 hapless persons to sell or dispose of their property and embark for Morocco, which many of them reached only to die of starvation or to be kidnaped into slavery. The king's treatment of the Moriscos found favor with the nation, but economically it was a more crushing blow to Spain than had been the earlier expulsion of the Jews. Spain had now begun to decline, both in population and in wealth, and by expelling the Moriscos she lost her most skillful, thrifty, and industrious inhabitants.

**Economic Spain.** But we must not anticipate our narrative. In 1500, when Spain began to enter upon colonial activities, she was not a declining but a rapidly ascending power. She was

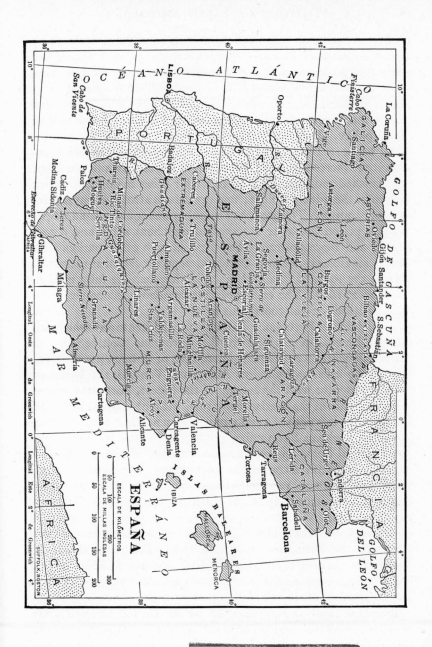

ESPAÑA

strong in economic organization, as well as in political unity and religious enthusiasm.  Christian Spain throughout the Middle Ages had produced only raw materials, exporting wool, iron, and wine and importing manufactured goods, chiefly in foreign ships. Ferdinand and Isabella, among their other activities, did much to foster manufacturing and commerce, and Charles I followed the same policy.  During his reign, it is said, the industries based on wool supported nearly a third of the population; the silk manufacture so increased that Spain began to import raw silk and export the finished product; large factories for other manufactures were set up in the principal cities; and great fairs attracted buyers from all over Europe.  The growth of shipping was equally rapid.  Spain at this period had over a thousand merchant ships and a navy larger and more powerful than that of any other nation.  The forces making for national decadence scarcely revealed themselves before the reign of Philip II, nor did they become fully manifest until after 1600.  The causes of that decadence, economic, social, and political, do not concern us here.

**Kingdom of Portugal.**  Throughout the centuries which witnessed Phœnician trade with the barbarous Celtiberians, the establishment, first of Carthaginian, then of Roman, power in Hispania, the invasion by Suevi, Alans, and Vandals, the settlement of the Visigoths, and the coming of the Moors, Portugal remained simply a part of the Iberian Peninsula, without a separate name or history.  It was not yet a state, much less a nation.  Its origin dates from 1095, when a Burgundian knight, one of those many crusaders who visited Spain to cross swords with the Moors, received the northern part of the country as a fief of León.  Two centuries later Portugal attained complete independence as a kingdom and reached its present boundaries.  Lisbon was henceforth recognized as the capital.

**Portuguese Nationality.**  The almost incessant border wars between the Portuguese and both their Christian and Moslem neighbors made them an intensely patriotic people.  Their national feeling was strengthened by the steady growth of the royal power at the expense of the feudal nobles, by the development of a comprehensive legal system, and, above all, by the formation of a common language and literature.  When the era of overseas expansion began in the fifteenth century, Portugal had already become a real nation. It stood ready to embark on that wonderful career which, for a time, made it the greatest colonial and commercial power among the nations of Europe. Germs of decay had entered by the sixteenth century, but were not at first apparent. Dynastic troubles led to the so-called "Sixty Years' Captivity," 1580–1640, when the kings of Castile became also the kings of Portugal. This improved Portuguese governmental mechanisms and did not seriously harm other aspects of life, but was displeasing to the national patriotism and was ended by revolt.

**Hispanic Culture.** As might be expected from their common origin, environment, and history, Spaniards and Portuguese presented many resemblances. They were the most Oriental of western Europeans, partly as the result of intermixture with Arabs, Berbers, and Jews, partly through contact for many centuries with Moorish civilization. "Africa," as has been aptly said, "begins at the Pyrenees." Upon both of them the struggle against the Moslem invader, lasting for nearly eight centuries, exerted a profound influence. It made them intensely religious. While the chivalry of France, Germany, and England fought for the Cross in the Holy Land, the knights of Spain and Portugal waged a private crusade in their own country. The natural outcome of the almost continuous fighting between 711 and 1492 was the exaltation of war and the development of an intolerant spirit which found expression in the Inquisition and in the wholesale expulsion of non-Christians. Politically and economically, Spaniards and Portuguese also resembled each other. Each had a strong centralized monarchy and a frame of government that mirrored the king's autocratic power. Each retained from the age of feudalism a system of land tenure that was based essentially upon the existence of large estates tilled by a dependent, semiservile peasantry. And each preserved, on the part of the upper classes, the feudal contempt for manual labor. Differences were those to be expected from the fact that Portugal was smaller than Spain and had poor land resources, but possessed excellent harbors on the Atlantic. Her religious, cultural, and political life was somewhat less developed than that of Spain, whereas her interest and skill in seafaring and trade were greater.

**Transplanting of Hispanic Culture.** These national characteristics, customs, and institutions of the Hispanic peoples were reproduced in the New World. The motives leading them to overseas expansion may be summed up in the three words "gospel, glory, and gold." As for the first motive, it was natural that the occupation of America should assume in their eyes the character of a crusade. The holy war against the Moorish infidel had just ended, but here in America Providence had bestowed upon them a vast region teeming with heathen peoples to be converted and given the blessings of a Christian civilization. Priests regularly accompanied the explorers and conquerors, and the propagation of the true faith formed an essential object of almost every expedition. As to the second motive, it was equally natural that to the knights of Spain and Portugal, who no longer had any occupation at home, the New World offered entrancing prospects for adventure and valorous feats of arms. But religious and martial enthusiasm was never allowed to interfere with the purely business aspect of conquest. Like the Dutch, the French, and most of the English, the Spaniards and Portuguese sought in America the means of making money. The Dutch did this by commerce; the French, by exploiting the fisheries and the fur trade; the English, as it turned out, chiefly by cultivation of the soil. The Spaniards and Portuguese, whose interest in agriculture and actual settlement was slight, wanted precious metals and precious stones. Their first object was to seize all the available wealth of this sort and next to locate mines and make the Indians work them. The development of Mexico and Perú may be traced directly to the silver mines in those countries, whereas Brazil, which showed no promise of mineral wealth, for a time was on the verge of official abandonment. When, subsequently, the more fertile parts of tropical and subtropical America were appropriated by the Spaniards and Portuguese, they introduced the plantation system, allotting to each adventurer his share of the natives as laborers along with his share of the lands. The great temperate regions of North and South America proved uninteresting and indeed repellant to the Hispanic colonists; such regions, yielding neither gold nor tropical products, they called "worthless territories," *tierras de ningun provecho*. Though Columbus first landed in the tropics by "chance," it was not by chance that later men explored and settled there. Arriving before other Europeans, the Spaniards and Portuguese picked what seemed most valuable, to the later envy of England, France, and the Netherlands. The tropical highlands combined wealth, labor supply, and climate, and only late arrivals or nontypical men cared to take up lands elsewhere.

## Words and Phrases You Should Know

Alhambra
apostasy
Aragón
"benefit of clergy"
canon law
Castile
Conquistadors
Cortes
feudalism
"gospel, glory, and gold"

Granada
heresy
Hispanic America
Iberian Peninsula
Inquisition
Islam
Jesuits
Moors
Moriscos
mosque

parliamentary government
Phœnicians
Punic Wars
religious orders
Romance languages
Romanization
royal absolutism
the Cid
Torquemada
Vandals
Visigoths

## Questions You Should Be Able to Answer

1. Why should we study the history of Spain and Portugal as an introduction to the study of Latin America?
2. How was European expansion into America different from European expansion into Asia and Africa?
3. Why were the Phœnicians and Carthaginians attracted to Spain?
4. What was the effect of Roman conquest on Spain?
5. Did the barbarian tribes contribute anything to the development of Spain?
6. In what ways did Spain benefit from the rule of the Moors?
7. In your estimation were the Moors in Spain more or less tolerant than the Christians?
8. Why is the Cid worshiped as a national hero in Spain?
9. For what reasons was the year 1492 important in Spanish history?
10. How did Ferdinand and Isabella become absolute monarchs?
11. What was the purpose of the Inquisition? How did it do its work?
12. What was the effect upon Spain of the expulsion of the Jews? the expulsion of the Moors and Moriscos?
13. How did Ferdinand and Isabella build up the economic life of their country?
14. How would you compare the Spanish attitude in the days of Ferdinand and Isabella toward racial and religious tolerance with our attitude today?

15. Why was it natural for explorers and adventurers of Spain and Portugal to look upon colonization as a sort of holy crusade?

16. Why did so many Spanish nobles seek glory and adventure in the New World?

17. Were the reasons why Spanish and Portuguese adventurers went to the New World any different from the reasons that caused English, Dutch, and French colonizers to go abroad?

## PROJECTS AND ACTIVITIES

1. Using the following dates, make a time line for early Spanish history: 1000 B.C., 201 B.C., 133 B.C., 415 A.D., 711 A.D., 929 A.D., 1212 A.D., 1479 A.D., 1492 A.D., 1515 A.D., 1609 A.D.   Under each date indicate its significance.

2. Write imaginary newspaper headlines for an important event that happened in each of the years given in Project 1.

3. Write an imaginary account of the effect of the Inquisition upon a Jew or a Morisco who has had to leave Spain.

4. Trace or draw a map of the Iberian peninsula.   By means of drawings or brief legends indicate thereon several important events in Spanish and Portuguese history.

5. On page 37 the statement is made that "Rome continued in Spain the process of Romanization which she had begun in Italy and Sicily . . ."   From your knowledge of Roman history or from a book on the subject enlarge upon the statement.

6. Imagine that you are a monk living in the times of Ferdinand and Isabella.   Write some passages in your diary that reveal some of the changes occurring in Spain during the reign of these monarchs.

7. Make a chart showing the accomplishments of Ferdinand and Isabella. Use these headings: Unification of Spain;   Control of the nobles; Control of the Cortes;   Control of the Church;   Strengthening economic life.

8. Write a short play in which you show how the Inquisition worked.

9. A priest, a nobleman, and a merchant are discussing an expedition to the New World.   Give an account of their conversation as you imagine it might have taken place.

10. Work out an explanation of the statement that "America . . . has become an annex of Europe."

11. Compose a dialogue between Ferdinand and Isabella as they discuss their policy toward the Moors, the nobles, the Cortes, heretics, and the Jews.

# CHAPTER III

# Discovery, Exploration, and Conquest of Latin America [1]

**The Indies.** The discovery of America and the circumnavigation of Africa came almost simultaneously at the end of the fifteenth century. These two events, which produced a geographical Renaissance, were intimately related. Back of both was the desire of Europeans to open up direct maritime intercourse with the Far East, and especially with the Indies. From the time of the Crusades eastern luxuries — spices, drugs, perfumes, gums, dyes, gems, porcelains, carpets, rugs, tapestries — had been brought overland or by water to Mediterranean ports, for distribution by Venetian and Genoese merchants throughout Europe. During the late fifteenth century Portuguese and Spaniards appeared as competitors for this lucrative Oriental trade. The Mediterranean being closed to them by the naval power of Venice, they tried to find an all-water route to the Indies, either around Africa or directly across the Atlantic. The Portuguese were the first in the field.

**Prince Henry the Navigator (1394–1460).** The genius of Dom Henriques, more familiarly known in history as Prince Henry the Navigator, opened the way oceanward for Portugal. The son of a Portuguese king, he relinquished a military career and for more than forty years devoted his wealth, learning, and enthusiasm to geographical discovery. Under his direction better maps were made, the astrolabe was improved, the compass was placed on vessels, and seamen were instructed in all the nautical knowledge of the time. Prince Henry then dispatched expedition after expedition southward to explore the African coast. It is improbable that he himself had definitely in mind the opening up of a trade route to the Far East; his spirit seems to have been that of a crusader rather than that of a merchant. By rounding the extremity of

---

[1] This chapter presents the "orthodox" story. Modern scholars disagree about the motives, personalities, and deeds of Columbus, Vespucci, Cabral, and Magellan.

Africa — then believed to extend not far below the equator —
he planned to effect a junction with the half-fabulous Christian
empire of "Prester John" and in alliance with that potentate to
crush the Turks and liberate Palestine.  But the religious motive
of explorations soon gave way to the commercial motive, and the
Portuguese, not long after Prince Henry's death, set out to seek
the wealth of the Indies.

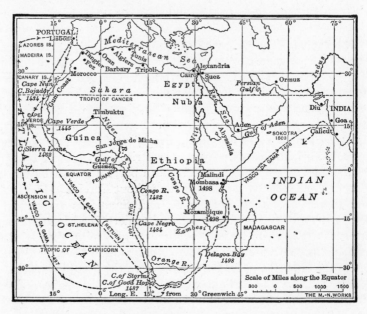

PORTUGUESE EXPLORATION OF THE AFRICAN COAST

**Exploration of the African Coast.**  The mariners of Portugal
began by rediscovering the Madeira Islands and the Azores, first
visited by Europeans in the fourteenth century but subsequently
forgotten.  Then they turned southward along the uncharted
African coast, toward waters which no keel had broken since the
time of the Phœnicians.  Cape Bojador, the previous boundary of
the unknown, was passed by one of Prince Henry's captains in
1434.  Eleven years later another daring sailor got as far as Cape
Verde, or "Green Cape," so called because of its luxuriant vegetation.  Later voyages brought the Portuguese to Sierra Leone, then
to the great bend in the African coast formed by the Gulf of

Guinea, then across the equator, and at length to the mouth of the Congo. In 1487 Bartholomew Díaz rounded the southern extremity of Africa. The story goes that he named it the Cape of Storms, and that the king of Portugal, recognizing its importance as a stage on the route to the Far East, rechristened it the Cape of Good Hope.

**Da Gama's Voyage (1497–1499).** The sea gates to the Indies were soon opened by Vasco da Gama. With four tiny ships he set sail from Lisbon in July, 1497, and after leaving the Cape Verde Islands made a wide sweep into the South Atlantic. Five months passed before Africa was seen again. Having doubled the Cape of Good Hope in safety, Da Gama skirted the eastern shore of Africa and then secured the services of an Arab pilot to guide him across the Indian Ocean. In May, 1498, he reached Calicut, an important port on the southwest coast of India. When Da Gama returned to Lisbon, after an absence of over two years, he brought back a cargo which repaid forty times the cost of the expedition. The Portuguese king received him with high honor and created him Admiral of the Indies.

VASCO DA GAMA

**Camoëns and the Lusiads.** The story of Da Gama's memorable voyage was sung by the Portuguese poet, Camoëns, in the *Lusiads*. It is the most successful of modern epics. The popularity of this work has done much to foster the sense of nationality among the Portuguese, and even today it forms a bond of union between Portugal and her daughter nation across the Atlantic — Brazil.

**Brazil (1500).** A companion of Columbus, Vicente Pinzón, discovered Brazil in 1500. He took possession of the country in the name of the Spanish sovereigns and carried home, as specimens of its productions, some drugs, gems, and brazilwood. As this region lay within the Portuguese sphere of influence, according to the line of demarcation agreed to in the Treaty of Tordesillas,[1] Pinzón's discovery proved fruitless for Spain. The claim of Portugal to Brazil rested on its discovery in the same year by Pedro Alvares Cabral, who, after Da Gama's return, had been intrusted by the Portuguese monarch with a commercial expedition to India. Probably by plan, possibly by accident, Cabral went so far out of his course that he reached the Brazilian coast in 16° S. latitude. Cabral landed, declared the country an appanage of Portugal, and set up a stone cross to commemorate the event. For many years after Cabral's discovery the kings of Portugal paid little attention to their newly acquired territory in America. A region inhabited only by savage tribes and apparently without mineral riches offered few attractions to the Portuguese government, into whose coffers poured the wealth of Africa and India. It was, in fact, not until Portugal, through her unfortunate connection with Spain,[2] had lost her empire in the East Indies, that the full importance of the magnificent regions of Brazil came to be appreciated.

**The Globular Theory.** Six years before Vasco da Gama cast anchor in the harbor of Calicut, another intrepid sailor, seeking the Indies by a western route, accidentally discovered America. It does not detract from the glory of Columbus to show that the way for his discovery had been long in preparation. In the first place, the theory that the earth is round had been familiar to the Greeks and the Romans, and to some learned men even in the darkest period of the Middle Ages. The revival of interest in Greek science, as a result of the Renaissance, called renewed attention to the statements regarding the sphericity of the earth by Ptolemy and other ancient geographers.

**Myth of Atlantis.** In the second place, men had long believed that west of Europe, beyond the Strait of Gibraltar, lay mysterious lands. This notion first appears in the writings of the Greek philosopher Plato, who repeats an old tradition about Atlantis. According to Plato, Atlantis had been an island continental in size, but more than nine thousand years before his time it had sunk beneath the sea. Medieval writers believed the story and found support for it in traditions of other western islands, such as the Isles of the Blest, where Greek heroes went after death, and the Welsh Avalon, whither King Arthur, after his last battle, was borne to heal his wounds. A popular legend also described the visit

[1] See page 64.    [2] Between 1580–1640. See page 51.

made by St. Brandan, an Irish monk, to the "promised land of the saints," an earthly paradise far out in the Atlantic. St. Brandan's Island was marked on early maps, and voyages in search of it were sometimes undertaken.

**Behaim's Globe.** The ideas of European geographers in the period just preceding the discovery of America are represented on a map, or rather a globe, which dates from 1492. It was made by a German navigator, Martin Behaim, for his native city of Nurem-

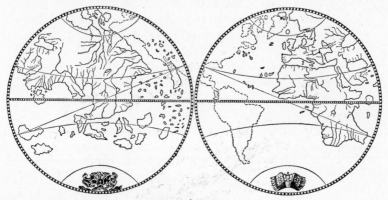

BEHAIM'S GLOBE

The outlines of North America and South America here shown do not appear, of course, on the original globe.

berg, where it is still preserved. Behaim shows the mythical island of St. Brandan, lying in midocean, and beyond it Cipango (Japan), the East Indies, Cathay (China), and India. It is clear that he greatly underestimated the distance westward between Europe and Asia. The error was natural enough, for Ptolemy had reckoned the earth's circumference to be about one sixth less than it is, and Marco Polo, the Venetian traveler who visited China toward the close of the thirteenth century, had given an exaggerated idea of the distance to which Asia extended on the east. When Columbus began his voyage, he probably believed that a journey of a few thousand miles would bring him to Cipango and Cathay. Had he known accurately the real distance between Europe and Asia, by the western route, he would never have undertaken a voyage for which neither the nautical knowledge nor the shipping of the period was considered equal.

**Columbus (1451?–1506).**   Christopher Columbus was a native of Genoa, where his father followed the humble trade of a weaver. He seems to have received some education in the schools of his native town, but at an early age he became a sailor.   Columbus knew the Mediterranean by heart;  he once went to the Guinea coast;  he visited the British Isles;  and he may have visited Iceland.   After settling in Lisbon as a map maker, he married a daughter of one of Prince Henry's sea captains.   As Columbus pored over his maps and charts and talked with Portuguese navigators about their voyages, the idea came to him that much of the world remained undiscovered and that the distant East could be reached by a shorter route than the one which led around Africa.   "It was in Portugal," his son afterward declared, "that the Admiral began to surmise that if men could sail so far south, one might also sail west and find lands in that direction."

C OLOMBVS LYGVRNOVIORBIS REPTOR

CHRISTOPHER COLUMBUS
Biblioteca Nacional, Madrid.

This is the so-called Yanez portrait, purchased in 1763 and named in honor of its former owner. It is the oldest canvas representation of Columbus known to exist in Spain. However, no one of the many portraits of Columbus that have come down to us is surely authentic.

**His Researches.**   Columbus was a well-read man, and in Ptolemy and other ancient authorities he found apparent confirmation of his grand idea.   Columbus also owned a printed copy of Marco Polo's book, and from his comments, written on the margin, we know how interested he was in Marco's statements referring to Cathay and Cipango.   Furthermore, Columbus brought together all the information he could get about the fabled islands of the Atlantic.   If he ever went to Iceland, some vague traditions may have reached him there of the Norse voyages to Greenland and Vinland.   Such hints and rumors strengthened his purpose to sail toward the setting sun in quest of the Indies.

**His Proposals.**   Columbus first applied to the king of Portugal for the necessary ships and equipment.   The Portuguese monarch, though engrossed in finding a southern route around Africa, listened with interest to his proposals and laid them before a geographical council. It reported adversely, and Columbus betook himself to Spain. The time was unpropitious, for Castile and Aragón were then in the thick of the struggle against the Moors. How Columbus triumphed over one obstacle after another and at length, through the intervention of faithful friends, found a patroness in Queen Isabella, who is said to have pledged her crown jewels to defray part of the cost of the expedition, is a familiar story. A few months after the fall of Granada an agreement was finally drawn up by which the Spanish monarchs promised that Columbus should have the rank of an admiral and the power of a viceroy over the islands and continents he might find or acquire in the ocean, together with one tenth of "all pearls, precious stones, gold, silver, spices, and all other articles and merchandise" which might be acquired from them. A crusading spirit animated Columbus, as also Prince Henry, and Columbus looked forward to the time when, with the vast resources of the Far East at his disposal, he might lead the chivalry of Europe in a new holy war against the Turk.

THE "SANTA MARIA"
FLAGSHIP OF
COLUMBUS

After the model reproduced for the Columbian Exposition at Chicago, 1893.

**First Voyage of Columbus (1492–1493).** Provided with a royal letter of introduction to the Great Khan of Cathay, Columbus set out from Palos on August 3. He first touched at the Canaries, and then turned westward, sailing for week after week over an unknown sea — the Sea of Darkness, "so called for the very reason that within it lies hid whatever land there may be beyond these islands." It was October 12 before the coral strand of one of the Bahamas [1] came into view. Cuba, which he identified with Cathay, and Haiti, which he similarly took for Cipango, were sighted soon afterward. Columbus now returned to Spain, confident that he had reached his goal. The name Indians, which he applied to the in-

[1] Named San Salvador by Columbus and usually identified with Watling Island.

BARTHOLOMEW COLUMBUS'S MONDO NOVO

habitants of the newly discovered regions, remains as a testimony to his error.

**Subsequent Voyages of Columbus.** The great Admiral made three other Atlantic voyages between 1493 and 1504. He visited Puerto Rico and Jamaica, besides a number of the Lesser Antilles, saw the northern coast of South America at the mouth of the Orinoco, and skirted the shores of Central America from Honduras to Panamá. But no glimpse of the long-sought empire of the Great Khan rewarded the explorer's efforts, and he died in 1506 without realizing that he had found, not Asia, but America.

> Nunc vero & heɛ partes funt latius luftrātæ/ &
> alia quarta pars per Americū Vefputium( vt in fe⁄
> ⟨or⟩ quentibus audietur)inuenta eft:quā non video cur
> Ame⁄ quis iure vetet ab Americo inuentore fagacis inge
> rico nīj viro Amerigen quafi Americi.terram/fiuɛ Ame
> ricam dicendam:cum & Europa & Afia a mulieri⁄
> bus fua fortita fint nomina.Eius fitū & gentis mo⁄
> res exbis binis Americi nauigationibus quɛ fequū
> tur liquide intelligi datur.

THE NAME "AMERICA"

Facsimile of the passage in the *Cosmographiæ Introductio* (1507), by Martin Waldseemüller, in which the name "America" is proposed for the New World.

**Naming of America.** The New World was named for a Florentine navigator, Amerigo Vespucci.[1] While in the Spanish service he undertook several western voyages and subsequently printed an account of his discovery of the mainland of America in 1497. Scholars now generally reject his statements, but they found acceptance at the time, and it was soon suggested that the new continent should be called America, "because Americus discovered it." The name referred at first only to South America, but in 1541 the great cartographer Mercator applied it to the northern continent as well. The Spaniards preferred "The Indies" as the official designation of the New World and did not use the name America on their maps until late in the eighteenth century.

**The Demarcation Line.** Shortly after the return of Columbus

[1] In Latin, *Americus Vespucius.*

from his first voyage, Pope Alexander VI, in response to a request
by Ferdinand and Isabella, issued in 1493 several bulls granting
to these sovereigns exclusive rights over the newly discovered
territory. In order that the Spanish possessions should be clearly
marked off from those of the Portuguese, the pope laid down an
imaginary line of demarcation in the Atlantic, one hundred leagues
west of the Azores and the Cape Verde Islands. All new discoveries
to the west of this boundary were to belong to Spain; all those east

THE STRAIT OF MAGELLAN

of it, to Portugal.[1] In 1494 Spain and Portugal agreed, by the
Treaty of Tordesillas, to shift the dividing meridian two hundred
and seventy leagues farther to the west. This agreement proved
to be a fortunate one for Portugal, as it gave her title to
Brazil.

**Ferdinand Magellan (1480?-1521).** The demarcation line had
a good deal to do with bringing about the first voyage around the
globe. So far no one had yet realized the dream of Columbus to
reach the Indies by sailing westward. Ferdinand Magellan,[2] a
Portuguese navigator in the service of Spain, believed that the
Moluccas, or Spice Islands, lay within the Spanish sphere of influence and that an all-Spanish route to them, through some strait
at the southern end of South America, could be found.

[1] See the map on page 81.    [2] In Portuguese Fernão de Magalhães.

**Circumnavigation of the Globe (1519-1522).**  Charles I, king of Spain (not yet the emperor Charles V), looked with favor upon Magellan's ideas and provided a fleet of five vessels for the undertaking.  After exploring the eastern coast of South America, Magellan reached the strait that now bears his name.  Its passage took twenty-eight days.  The new ocean upon which he emerged was so peaceful that Magellan called it the Pacific (*Mare Pacificum*).  The sailors now begged him to return, for food was getting scarce, but the navigator replied that he would go on "if he had to eat the leather off the rigging."  He did go on, for ninety-eight more days, until he reached the Ladrone Islands.[1] By a curious chance, in all the long voyage across the Pacific, Magellan came upon only two islands, both uninhabited.  He then proceeded to the Philippines and took possession of them in the name of Spain.  Magellan was killed in a fight with some of the natives, but his men managed to reach the Moluccas, the goal of the journey.  Afterwards a single ship, the *Victoria*, carried back to Spain the few sailors who had survived the hardships of a journey lasting nearly three years.

FERDINAND MAGELLAN

From a portrait formerly in the Versailles Gallery, Paris.

**Results of the Circumnavigation.**  Magellan's voyage forms a landmark in the history of geography.  It proved that America, at least on the south, had no connection with Asia, and that the western sea route to the Indies, of which Columbus dreamed, really existed.  Furthermore, it revealed the enormous extent of the Pacific Ocean.  Henceforth men knew of a certainty that the earth is round, and in the distance covered by Magellan they had a rough approximation as to its size.  The circumnavigation of the globe ranks, with the discovery of America, among the most significant events in history.  Magellan stands beside Da Gama and Columbus in the company of great explorers.

[1] Also known as the Marianas Islands.  Magellan called them the Ladrones (Spanish *ladrón*, a robber) because of the thievish habits of the natives.

**The Spaniards in the West Indies.**   The discoverers of the New World were naturally the pioneers in its exploration and conquest. The Spaniards soon occupied the four islands of the Greater Antilles, which Columbus had found.   Columbus himself began the work of colonization in 1493 by building a fort on the island of Haiti [1] and leaving there some forty men.   This garrison was exterminated by the Indians.   A better fate attended the colony of Santo Domingo, founded in 1496 by the explorer's brother, Bar-

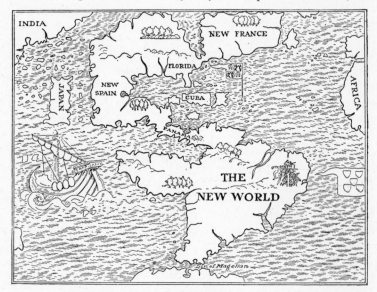

MÜNSTER'S MAP OF THE NEW WORLD (1540 A.D.)

tholomew Columbus.   Santo Domingo, now the capital of the republic named after it, is the oldest existing European settlement in the New World.   It formed the center from which the Spaniards, during the next twenty years, extended their authority to Puerto Rico, Cuba, and Jamaica.

**Ponce de León and Florida (1513).**   The Spaniards were now familiar with the West Indies and the Caribbean edge of that southern continent which on the earliest maps is termed *Mondo Novo* (New World).   The Spanish discovery of the northern continent was made by Juan Ponce de León (John of the Lion's

[1] Called by Columbus Española, whence the English name Hispaniola.

## SPANISH DISCOVERIES, EXPLORATIONS, AND CONQUESTS

| NAME | DATE | PLACE |
|---|---|---|
| Columbus (I) | 1492–1493 | Bahama Islands, Cuba, Haiti |
| Columbus (II) | 1493–1496 | Lesser Antilles, Puerto Rico, Jamaica |
| Columbus (III) | 1498–1500 | Island of Trinidad; estuary of Orinoco River |
| Alonso de Ojeda | 1499 | Gulf of Maracaibo, Venezuela |
| Vicente Pinzón | 1499–1500 | Brazil, at about 8° S.; mouth of the Amazon |
| Diego de Lepe | 1500 | Brazil, to about 10° S. |
| Bastidas and La Cosa | 1500–1502 | Coast of Venezuela, Colombia, and Isthmus of Panamá |
| Columbus (IV) | 1502–1504 | Atlantic coast of Central America from Cape Honduras to Gulf of Darién |
| Sebastián de Ocampo | 1508 | Circumnavigation of Cuba |
| Pinzón and Solís | 1508–1509 | Brazil, to about 40° S. |
| Juan Ponce de León | 1513 | Florida |
| Vasco Núñez de Balboa | 1513 | Pacific Ocean |
| Díaz de Solís | 1516 | Rio de la Plata |
| Hernández de Córdoba | 1517 | Yucatán |
| Juan de Grijalva | 1518 | Gulf coast of Mexico |
| Alonso de Pineda | 1519 | Gulf coast of the United States |
| Hernando de Cortés | 1519–1521 | Plateau of Anáhuac; city of Tenochtitlan |
| Magellan and Elcano | 1519–1522 | Circumnavigation of the globe |
| Gil González Dávila | 1522 | Nicaragua |
| Pedro de Alvarado | 1523–1524 | Guatemala, Salvador |
| Cristóbal de Olid | 1524 | Honduras |
| Esteban Gómez | 1525 | North American coast between Nova Scotia and Florida |
| Vásquez de Ayllón | 1526 | Carolina shore of the United States |
| Narváez and Cabeza de Vaca | 1528–1536 | Florida, Gulf coast of the United States, Texas, northern Mexico |
| Francisco Pizarro | 1531–1533 | Perú; city of Cuzco |
| Sebastián de Benalcázar | 1533–1538 | Ecuador, Colombia |
| Diego de Almagro | 1535–1536 | Chile |
| Juan de Ayolas | 1535–1537 | Paraguay |
| Jiménez de Quesada | 1536–1537 | Plateau of Bogotá |
| Francisco de Ulloa | 1539 | Gulf of California |
| Friar Marcos de Niza | 1539 | Arizona |
| Hernando de Soto | 1539–1543 | Southern United States |
| Francisco de Orellana | 1540–1541 | Amazon Valley |
| Francisco Vásquez de Coronado | 1540–1542 | Southwestern United States |
| Juan Rodríguez Cabrillo | 1542–1543 | Coast of Baja and Alta California |
| Juan de Oñate | 1598–1604 | Southwestern United States |
| Sebastián Vizcaíno | 1602–1603 | Coast of Baja and Alta California to Cape Mendocino |
| Francisco Garcés | 1768–1776 | Arizona and New Mexico |
| Gaspar de Portolá | 1769 | San Francisco Bay |

Paunch), a blue-blooded and wealthy colonist of Haiti, who had
subdued Puerto Rico and added it to the territory under Spanish
occupation. He now sought fame and wealth in another field. In
the unexplored seas to the north of the Antilles rumor told of a
great island called Bimini, where lay a wonderful spring or river
whose waters would restore youth to the aged. Ponce de León secured a patent from the Spanish king, authorizing him to find and
settle Bimini. Having equipped three vessels at his own expense, he
set out from Puerto Rico, and after winding through the Bahamas
and touching at San Salvador, sighted the land which he named
La Florida, because of its verdant beauty and because of its discovery during *Pascua Florida*, the Easter season. At length he
landed near the mouth of the St. John's River, and took possession of the country, which was supposed to be an island. He
followed much of the Florida coast, both east and west, before
returning to Puerto Rico, but came upon no traces of Bimini. His
voyage was not fruitless, however, for it resulted in the finding of
the Bahama Channel, which became the route of the treasure ships
from the New World to Spain. The need of protecting this channel
led subsequently to the Spanish colonization of Florida.

**Balboa and the Pacific (1513).** Almost at the same time that
Ponce de León reached the mainland of North America, another
Spaniard discovered the Pacific. He was Vasco Núñez de Balboa,
a bankrupt planter of Haiti. To evade his creditors, Balboa went
as a stowaway in a ship sailing from Santo Domingo to a Spanish
settlement on the Gulf of Darién. A man of great resourcefulness
and courage, Balboa soon became a leader among his fellows. It
was at his suggestion that the colonists moved over to the southeastern margin of the Isthmus of Panamá and founded there a
town (no longer existing) called Darién. The Spaniards, scouring
the neighborhood for gold, heard from the Indians that beyond the
mountains of the interior lay "another sea" and that the land about
it abounded in the precious metals. To find this sea Balboa led
one hundred and ninety armed men for eighteen days through the
jungle and swamps of the isthmus, until at length from the crest
of the Cordilleras he looked out southward on the boundless expanse of an ocean which he called the *Mar del Sur* — the "South
Sea." A few days later he entered its waters, sword in hand, and
took formal possession for Spain. The expeditions of the Spaniards

henceforth included both the eastern and the western shores of the New World. On both shores they were now on the eve of finding a vast continental region rich in gold and silver. They were about to discover and conquer Mexico and Perú.

**Hernando Cortés (1485–1547).** One of the many ambitious Spaniards who went out to Haiti seeking their fortunes was Hernando Cortés. His parents were of noble descent, though poor. Cortés studied for a time at the University of Salamanca, but soon threw aside books and entered upon the life of adventure for which his stout heart, military skill, and powers of leadership so well fitted him. Having accompanied the governor of Cuba to that island, he rose to be a judge (*alcalde*) of Santiago de Cuba and at length received command of an expedition for the exploration of Mexico. This was in 1519. The Maya and Aztec land had only just come to the knowledge of the Spaniards, as the result of two voyages of discovery from Cuba across the Gulf of Mexico. The inhabitants, it was learned, wore clothes, erected stone temples and idols, and possessed gold in abundance. They were pueblo or "town" Indians, far superior to the natives of the Antilles, with whom the Spaniards had so far been familiar.

**The Expedition of Cortés.** Eleven vessels, carrying some six hundred Spaniards (soldiers and marines), two hundred Indians, several cannon, and a number of mail-clad horses, formed the armada which sailed from Santiago de Cuba and landed on the peninsula of Yucatán. The natives, though hostile, could not resist the god-like strangers, whose guns belched forth lightning and whose cavalry, half man and half beast, seemed a greater marvel still. Cortés occupied the town of Tabasco and then coasted along the Gulf as far as the island of San Juan de Ulúa. It was here that he first learned definitely of the existence of Montezuma. Embassies from that Aztec ruler brought rich presents, including two great plates, one of gold and one of silver, and a helmet filled to the brim with gold dust. These gifts aroused the cupidity of the Spaniards as never before. Cortés, who had started out simply as an explorer, determined to invade and conquer the Aztec realm. The superiority of the Spaniards in arms and discipline made for the success of this bold enterprise; moreover, Cortés had the support of native troops, whom he persuaded or compelled to accompany his little army.

**Anáhuac Invaded.**   After founding the town of Vera Cruz to serve
as a base and scuttling his ships to cut off the possibility of retreat,
Cortés began the ascent of the mountains which rim the plateau of
Anáhuac.   The Indians of Tlaxcala, who were hostile to the Aztecs,
opposed him, but he routed their forces, dictated peace on moderate
terms, and converted them into powerful auxiliaries.   Upon the
inhabitants of Cholula, who plotted to destroy him, Cortés turned
his guns.   One obstacle after another was surmounted, until at

AN AZTEC PICTOGRAPH

Represents the arrival of Cortés, on horseback, with sword and cross.
Montezuma brings him gold.   From the *Codex Vaticanus.*

length the Spaniards and their native allies came in sight of the
lake on which rose the Aztec capital.

**Cortés at Tenochtitlan.**   Montezuma at first believed that these
mysterious, white-faced strangers were priests or heralds of the
fair god and culture hero Quetzalcoatl,[1] who in an earlier age had
gone away over the distant ocean, but who would some time
return from the east and resume his beneficent rule.   Accordingly, the Spaniards were received with great pomp and assigned
lodging in a council house.   Here Cortés made himself secure
by placing cannon to command the approaches.   It was a wise

[1] See page 27.

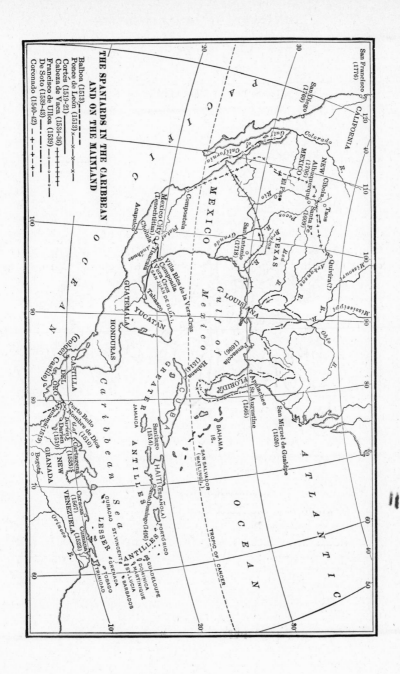

THE SPANIARDS IN THE CARIBBEAN
AND ON THE MAINLAND

Balboa (1513) ——————
Ponce de León (1513) x—x—x—x
Cortes (1519-21) ——————
Cabeza de Vaca (1534-36) ++++++++
Francisco de Ulloa (1539) —o—o—o—
De Soto (1539-43) —o—o—o—o
Coronado (1540-42) —+—+—+—+

San Francisco
(1776)

San Diego
(1769)

CALIFORNIA

120

40

110

PACIFIC

OCEAN

Acapulco

100

90

Compostela

Mexico City
(Tenochtitlan)

Cholula Tlascala
Vera Cruz
Villa Rica de la Vera Cruz
Campoalla
SAN JUAN DE ULÚA
Tabasco

GUATEMALA

HONDURAS

YUCATAN

MEXICO

Colorado R.

NEW CIBOLA
(1540)
Albuquerque
(1706)
Santa Fé
(1609)
MEXICO
(?)

Taos

El Paso
Pecos
Rio Grande

San Antonio
(1718)

TEXAS

Quivira (?)

Red R.

Arkansas R.

LOUISIANA

Gulf of Mexico

Habana
(1514)

CUBA
GREATER
Santiago
(1514)

HAITI (Española)
Santo Domingo (1496)
PORTO RICO

JAMAICA

ANTILLES

SAN SALVADOR
(WATLING)

BAHAMA
IS.

Pensacola
(1696)

Appalachee
(1528)

FLORIDA
St. Augustine
(1565)

San Miguel de Gualdape
(1526)

Missouri R.

Ohio R.

Mississippi R.

100

90

80

ATLANTIC

OCEAN

80

70

TROPIC OF CANCER

60

50

40

Caribbean Sea

CASTILLA
DEL
ORO
(Golden Castile)

Porto Bello
Nombre de Dios
Darien
(1510)
Panama (1519)

Cartagena
(1533)

Gulf of
Darien

NEW
GRANADA

Bogotá

VENEZUELA
(1528)

Caracas
(1567)
Cumaná
(1523)

Orinoco R.

CURACAO
ST. VINCENT
GRENADA
TOBAGO
TRINIDAD

LESSER
ANTILLES

GUADELOUPE
DOMINICA
MARTINIQUE
ST. LUCIA
BARBADOS

20

10

20

30

precaution, for the Aztecs, having soon learned that their visitors were not divinities but mortal men, prepared to offer them up as sacrificial victims. Cortés discovered the plot and checkmated it by boldly seizing Montezuma and conducting him to the Spanish quarters. The Aztec monarch had to issue an official declaration recognizing the supremacy of the king of Spain. Montezuma was also obliged to present his captors with a prodigious quantity of pure gold and precious stones.

**Fall of Tenochtitlan.** Fresh complications now arose. The suspicious governor of Cuba, anxious himself to have the glory of conquering Mexico, sent out a formidable expedition to deprive Cortés of the command. Leaving a part of his force in the Aztec capital, Cortés hastened to the coast, defeated the Spanish soldiers who had been sent to attack him, and then persuaded them to enlist under his standard. He returned to Tenochtitlan only to find that the inhabitants had revolted against both their ruler and the Spaniards. Montezuma perished while attempting to pacify his rebellious subjects, and the Aztecs, under a new and braver war chief, attacked the Spaniards with the utmost fury. Cortés found it necessary to withdraw from the city. The retreat cost him dear, for in the "doleful night" (*noche triste*) of July 5, 1520, the entire Spanish rear guard was cut to pieces. The survivors then retreated to friendly Tlascala, where Cortés, nothing daunted by his terrible reverse, gathered reinforcements from the West Indies and among his Indian allies for a fresh attack upon Te-nochtitlan. The city fell in 1521, after a siege of several months, and the Aztec Empire did not long survive the collapse of its capital.

**New Spain.** The victor was not only the most heroic, but he was also the most statesmanlike, of the Conquistadors. As governor of Mexico by royal appointment, Cortés devoted himself to the organization of the wide territories which his sword had won. Mexico City, a new and Christian capital, rose upon the ruins of Tenochtitlan. Anáhuac, long desolated by warfare and slave raids, entered upon an era of peace and prosperity. European plants and animals were introduced, and Spanish settlements were established at favorable points as centers of civilization for the Indians. Cortés also pushed forward the work of exploration, both personally and through lieutenants, so that the whole of the west coast of Mexico, together with the Peninsula and Gulf of California, soon became known to Europeans. All the former provinces of the Aztec Empire, as well as the other civilized Mexican states, were thus brought under one government, which received the proud title of New Spain.[1] The boast of Cortés to Charles I, "I am a man who has given you more provinces than your ancestors left you cities," had indeed ample justification. Cortés was completely displaced as the head of New Spain by creation of an audiencia (1527) and of a viceroyalty in 1535. By

THE CITY OF MEXICO UNDER THE CONQUERORS
From the engraving in the *Niewe Wereld* of Montanus.

his and other men's efforts Spanish settlements expanded rapidly in all directions, until practically all of present-day Mexico had been occupied by 1590.

**Central America.** The area between Panamá and Mexico was conquered from three directions, beginning in 1522. Pedrarius Davila, having founded Panamá City (1519), used it as a base for explorations to north and south along the Pacific coast, and sent lieutenants into Central America. These conquered Costa Rica and Nicaragua without serious difficulty and moved on to Honduras. About the same time, Cortés sent lieutenants south from Mexico. The chief man, Pedro de Alvarado, won hard but fairly quick victories in Salvador and Guatemala. Others advanced on Honduras. That region, having been entered also direct from the

---

[1] Eventually, New Spain in the broadest sense comprised all the Spanish possessions in North America and the West Indies, together with the Philippine Islands.

Antilles, became a cockpit for Spanish contestants. Cortés himself came in 1524, to repress the treachery of his agent Olid, and on the whole Honduras must be regarded as conquered from the north. Meantime Chiapas and Yucatán had escaped subjection. The Chiapan Indians, after defeating several warlike expeditions, were peacefully converted by the great missionary Las Casas and his aid Luis Cancer, 1540–1545. Francisco de Montejo, formerly a

FRANCISCO PIZARRO

A portrait in the Palace of the
Viceroys, Lima, Perú.

companion of Cortés, came to Yucatán in 1527 with a separate grant from Spain. He struggled for twenty years before he subdued the natives. Many outlying regions in Yucatán and elsewhere long remained beyond real control by Spain. But the important parts of the present five states were conquered and made provinces by 1530. They acquired a bond of unity by the creation of an audiencia or supreme court (1543) whose president and captain-general had powers over the whole area. The location before long of the tribunal in Guatemala City accompanied the rise of the major center of Central American life in that place. The other provinces retained frontier conditions much longer, though all had one or more real cities. Panamá was part of the viceroyalty of Perú during the colonial era. Use of the isthmus for all the trade of Perú gave life to the terminal ports of Panamá and Puerto Belo, but the province had little other importance.

Francisco Pizarro (1471?–1541). The reports of flourishing empires and boundless wealth on the Pacific side of the southern continent stirred the imagination of Francisco Pizarro, who had been one of Balboa's associates in the discovery of the South Sea and later became a cattle farmer at Panamá. Here he entered into partnership with a soldier named Diego de Almagro and a priest named Fernando de Luque for the purpose of exploring and conquering Perú. Luque agreed to advance the funds for the expedition, but the conquered territory and treasure were to be divided equally among the three associates. Pizarro then made two explorations down the west coast of South America, getting as far south as the Gulf of Guayaquil and bringing back llamas, ornaments of gold, and several Peruvian Indians. The governor of Darién showed little disposition to encourage the adventurers in further discoveries, so Pizarro sailed for Spain and appealed directly to the Spanish monarch for help. Charles I was won over by Pizarro's story of his exploits and by the prospect of finding in Perú another golden realm comparable to Mexico. The agreement, now drawn up, provided that Pizarro should be governor and captain-general for life of the province of New Castile, for a distance of two hundred leagues along the newly discovered coast. Almagro and Luque were left in wholly secondary positions as the result of this contract with the king.

**Pizarro's Expedition.** Pizarro gathered some recruits in Spain, including his three brothers, and then returned to Panamá to make ready for the invasion of Perú. Volunteers came in slowly, and the expedition which set forth in December, 1531, consisted of only one hundred and eighty men, besides a number of horses. After landing at Tumbés, on the Gulf of Guayaquil, the invaders were joined by one hundred soldiers under the command of Hernando de Soto. Pizarro founded the town of San Miguel, to serve as a base of operations, and then with the remainder of his little army started boldly on the march into the interior.

**Perú Invaded.** Cortés, entering Mexico, was welcomed as a god, or the messenger of a god, by Montezuma. Pizarro had a similar reception by the Inca ruler, Atahualpa. After news came of the white and bearded strangers who had arrived from the sea, strangers riding upon unearthly monsters and wielding deadly thunderbolts, Atahualpa sent envoys to Pizarro with gifts and an invitation for a meeting at Cajamarca. The Spaniards arrived there, after a toilsome climb of the snow-capped Andes, to find Atahualpa and thousands of dusky warriors encamped in the neighborhood.

The Indians were plainly impressed by the sight of the Spanish soldiers and horses. Pizarro, who realized that no delay must elapse in taking advantage of their superstitious fears, determined to imitate the exploit of Cortés at Tenochtitlan and secure the person of the Inca monarch. When, therefore, the unsuspecting Atahualpa came to visit his guests, he was promptly seized and his bodyguard butchered in cold blood.

THE CONQUEST OF PERÚ,
1531–1533

**Fall of Cuzco.** Pizarro's *coup* met instant success. The Indians, at first, were too dazed by the capture of the Child of the Sun for any organized resistance. When Atahualpa offered as ransom enough gold nearly to fill the room in which he was confined, his faithful subjects everywhere stripped the temples of ornaments and utensils, and a golden stream poured into Cajamarca from all parts of the Inca realm. The treasure, equivalent to more than $15,000,000 in modern reckoning, besides a vast amount of silver, was divided among the conquerors, who were careful to reserve for the Spanish sovereign a share of the plunder. Pizarro, however, did not free his captive; instead, he brought Atahualpa to trial on sundry trumped-up charges, even including idolatry and polygamy, and upon conviction had the unfortunate monarch strangled. From Cajamarca Pizarro, who in the meantime had been joined by Almagro, set out for distant Cuzco, the goal of the expedition. The Spaniards were much harassed on the march by the Indians, who now became bold enough to attack the invaders. Pizarro's triumphal entry into Cuzco in November, 1533, completed the first and most dramatic stage in the conquest of Perú. Fighting went on for several years, however, before the Indians were completely subdued.   Pizarro founded the city of Lima, which became the capital of the viceroyalty of Perú.  Civil wars among the conquerors, and rebellions against efforts to establish royal control, kept Perú in turmoil for much of the next generation.   But a viceroyalty was created in 1542, and the stern but wise rule of Viceroy Francisco de Toledo (1569–1581) is generally regarded as the start of peace and prosperity.

**Chile and Upper Perú.**   The Spaniards soon turned their attention to the outlying provinces of the Inca Empire.   Almagro, who had received from the Spanish Crown a grant of territory for two hundred and seventy leagues south of Pizarro's grant, reached the green valleys of Chile in 1535, but no gold rewarded his search, and he returned empty-handed to Cuzco.   Pizarro then sent Pedro de Valdivia to make a regular conquest of the country.   Santiago de Chile, the first permanent settlement, was founded in 1541. The Araucanian Indians, who refused to be Christianized, offered a stern resistance to the invaders of their land.   The Spaniards, in fact, never conquered the Araucanian territory below the Bio-bio River, which was not annexed to Chile until the close of the nineteenth century.   Spanish Chile formed a part of the viceroyalty of Perú, but had become a semi-autonomous captaincy-general by the seventeenth century.   Upper Perú, the Bolivia of later days, had also been included in the Inca Empire.   Almagro, on his way to Chile, subjugated the district around Lake Titicaca, and the discovery of the rich mines of Potosí (1545) caused rapid settlement.   In 1559, creation of the audiencia of Las Charcas gave Upper Perú a partially distinct existence within the viceroyalty of Perú.

**Quito.**   Sebastián de Benalcázar, another of Pizarro's lieutenants, conquered in 1533–1534 the Indian kingdom of Quito, which had been incorporated in the Inca realm.   Benalcázar soon moved on to explorations and conquests in the north, but was succeeded by other governors under Pizarro or the Crown.   Like Upper Perú, the region acquired a somewhat distinct character within the viceroyalty by creation of its own audiencia (1563), and the city of Quito was famous as a center of colonial culture.   But the region's history was, on the whole, the history of the viceroyalty of Perú until the eighteenth century, when it was attached to the new viceroyalty of New Granada.

**New Granada.**  The country now known as Colombia was opened to settlement by exploring parties from the northern coasts, from Quito, and from Venezuela.  The first cities, Santa Marta (1525) and Cartagena (1533), were established on the Caribbean lowlands and became the base for explorations in that vicinity. From the former, in 1536, Gonzalo Jiménez de Quesada led an expedition up the Magdalena River.  Ascending the river and scaling the mountains during an arduous year, he reached the plateau of Bogotá just in time to forestall adventurers coming from the other directions.  Taking advantage of the Chibcha Indian rivalries, Quesada conquered them, seized their treasures of gold and emeralds, and founded Santa Fé de Bogotá in 1538.  The area was so rich and so isolated from other centers of government that it soon became independent of the viceroyalty of Perú under its own audiencia (1548) and captain-general.  Despite its isolation, it became a center of Spanish culture, and in the eighteenth century became the nucleus of the viceroyalty of New Granada.

**Venezuela.**  Columbus on his third voyage (1498) beheld for the first time the mainland of South America at the mouth of the Orinoco.  During the following year one of his companions reached the Gulf of Maracaibo.  The Spaniards, seeing the native huts raised on piles above the swampy ground, called the region Venezuela (little Venice).  The rich pearl fisheries and the possibility of enslaving the Indians legally (as reputed cannibals) caused the establishment of the cities of Cumaná (1523) and Coro (1527).  In 1528 the Crown turned the province over to the great Augsburg banking house of Welser, as security for a loan.  The Germans soon demonstrated that the Spaniards had no monopoly on brutality to the Indians, and did less than the Spanish to develop the settlements.  About the only result of their activities having been exploration of the back country, in 1545 the Crown rescinded the contract.  Full royal control was delayed until 1556 by the resulting lawsuit, and Venezuela had few attractions for the Spaniard of the day, but expansion advanced slowly along the coasts. Caracas, founded in 1567, became the capital a few years later, due to its better location.  The province was part of the captaincy-general of Santo Domingo until 1731, when it was joined to the new viceroyalty of New Granada.  Late in the eighteenth century it became independent of that region with an audiencia and captain-general of its own.

**El Dorado.**  As early as 1539, Gonzalo Pizarro crossed the Andes from Quito, seeking what might be found in one of the few regions still totally unknown.  Coming to the headwaters of the eastward flowing rivers, he sent his aid, Francisco de Orellana, to explore ahead.  Orellana seized the chance to discover for himself, and abandoning one man who objected, passed completely down the rivers to the Atlantic, arriving there in 1541.  Having found Indian women fighting beside their men during his passage, he called the waterway the "River of Amazons," and the name has persisted to this day.  Belief in the existence of Amazons was only one of many semimythical stories that lured men into the forbidding interior of South America.  The Spaniards had been first attracted toward New Granada in consequence of the legend of El Dorado.  This name (Spanish for "the gilded one") applied originally to the king or high priest of a Chibcha tribe, who was said to smear himself with gold dust at an annual religious ceremony near Bogotá.  El Dorado next referred to a legendary city and lastly to a mythical country of South America, marvelously rich in gems and precious metals.  Such stories stirred the imagination of the Spaniards, who fitted out many expeditions to find the gilded man and his gilded realm.  The quest for El Dorado, though never successful, opened up the valleys of the Amazon and Orinoco and the extensive forest region east of the Andes.

**La Plata Colonies.**  The eminent Spanish navigator, Díaz de Solís, while exploring the coast of South America in search of the strait which Magellan afterward found, in 1516 came upon a wide expanse of fresh water (later proven to be the Plata Estuary), which he named the *Mar Dulce* (Fresh Sea).  Reports of the mineral wealth supposed to be found hereabouts gained for the estuary the name of the Rio de la Plata (Silver River).  The conquest of this region was soon undertaken by Pedro de Mendoza, who expected to repeat in the southern part of the continent the wonderful exploits of Pizarro in Perú.  Having secured from Charles I a grant of two hundred leagues from the boundary of the Portuguese possessions southward toward the Strait of Magellan, Mendoza set forth in 1535 at the head of the largest and best equipped expedition that had ever left Europe for the New World.

His fleet of fourteen ships carried no less than twenty-five hundred men, who became the progenitors of the Spanish population of the Argentine provinces. Mendoza founded Buenos Aires, but cease-less attacks by the Indians soon led to its abandonment. Mean-while, one of his lieutenants, Juan de Ayolas, followed the rivers inland, and at the junction of the Paraguay and the Pilcomayo built in 1537 a fort called Asunción. This proved to be the first permanent Spanish settlement in the interior of South America. The mouth of the river remained unpeopled for the next forty years. Meanwhile settlements crept into the Plata Valley from north and from west. Chileans crossed the Andes in 1553 to establish towns in the vicinity of present-day Mendoza. About the same time, men from Perú worked south along the foothills, founding such cities as Tucumán and Córdoba. Finally colonists from Asunción went south down the river to locate Santa Fé (1573) and then Buenos Aires once more in 1580. The whole movement from the north depended largely upon the "pull" of one of the world's greatest natural waterways, and Buenos Aires grew at last into an important port city in spite of the Spanish trade restric-tions. In 1617 the Crown created separate provinces for Buenos Aires, Asunción, and Mendoza or Cuyo. The last was part of Chile. Asunción — present-day Paraguay — and Buenos Aires were under the audiencia of Las Charcas and therefore part of the viceroyalty of Perú until 1776. In that year they, along with Cuyo province and Upper Perú itself, were amalgamated into the new viceroyalty of Buenos Aires of the Plata.

**Spanish America.** The Spanish had practically completed the conquest of the New World by 1545. Lust for gold, martial spirit, and religious enthusiasm had carried them from island to island of the West Indies, over Mexico and Central America, all along the Pacific coast of South America, across the mighty barrier of the Andes, down the Amazon to the ocean, and up the Plata tributaries into the very heart of the southern continent. Their discoveries, explorations, and conquests formed a remarkable achievement, all the more remarkable considering the brief period within which it was accomplished. They created for Spain an empire more ex-tensive than any ever known before.

**Spanish Borderlands.** What the Spanish conquered and settled in the first half century is still Spanish America, though no longer

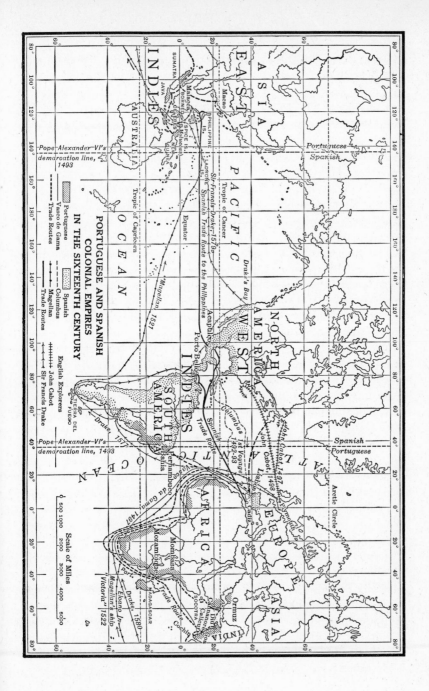

PORTUGUESE AND SPANISH
COLONIAL EMPIRES
IN THE SIXTEENTH CENTURY

Portuguese
Spanish

████ Portuguese
∙∙∙∙ Spanish

——— Vasco de Gama
∙∙∙∙∙∙ Columbus
+++++ Magellan
←←← Sir Francis Drake

Trade Routes

English Explorers
+++++ John Cabot
←←← Sir Francis Drake

Trade Routes

Scale of Miles
0  500 1000   2000   3000   4000   5000

Spain's. Any map shows the interesting fact that, with slight extensions into near-by Paraguay, Chile, and central Mexico, all those areas were in the tropics. Expansion outside the tropics was handicapped, not by insistence on a mild climate, but by other problems. Temperate-zone Indians were less numerous, less sedentary, and less acquainted with mineral resources, and therefore harder to conquer with profit, than were those of the semi-civilizations of the tropics. Life in most temperate-zone lands offered only the rewards of agriculture and ranching, and so furnished less incentive to leave Spain than did the dazzling chances of the tropical highlands. Nevertheless, some expansion into the temperate zone occurred. Mines were found in northern Mexico and Chile, the Church was eager to extend Christianity to the most scattered heathen, and men late for the glories of the great conquests could advance in social standing merely by becoming landholders. If as *adelantados* they spent their own funds in conquering new lands, they could expect political power and often a title of nobility as well.

**Northern Expansion.** Settlement of those borderlands which have remained part of Hispanic America has already been recounted. An enormous other territory to the north, since become part of the United States, shows to this day that its pioneers were Spanish missionaries, soldiers, and settlers. Six of the states of the Union [1] have names of Spanish origin; scores of rivers and mountains and hundreds of towns and cities bear the designations given to them by Spaniards. Spanish is still spoken by the southwestern Indians in preference to English, as well as by the descendants of Castilian hidalgos. The architecture of churches and missions, and even of many secular buildings, is prevailingly Spanish. Everywhere social, economic, and legal customs reflect their Spanish origin. The rule of Spain in this part of North America has passed, but the imprint of her culture remains indelible.

**Early Expeditions to Florida.** The Spaniards soon found Florida to be a part of the mainland, and not, as Ponce de León supposed, an immense island. On the Spanish maps of the period "Florida" signified the entire eastern half of North America, from Mexico to Canada. The first attempts of the Spaniards to occupy this

[1] Florida, Colorado, Nevada, California, New Mexico, and Texas.

region failed completely. Ponce de León, who led a colonizing expedition to the Florida peninsula in 1521, was mortally wounded by the Indians. Five years later Vásquez de Ayllón sailed from Haiti with five hundred men and women — a force larger than that of Cortés — and began a settlement called San Miguel de Gualdpe, somewhere on the Carolina coast. This first Spanish colony within the territory of the present United States had a miserable end. Ayllón died, provisions gave out, an exceptionally cold winter occurred, the Indians attacked, and at length the survivors, less than a third of the original company, returned to the West Indies. Still more disastrous was the enterprise undertaken by Narváez, who, having obtained permission to conquer and govern all the northern shores of the Gulf of Mexico, started from Cuba and in 1528 landed on the Florida coast. He and his men remained for six months in the country, suffering terribly from exposure, hunger, and fierce Indian attacks. Finally, the Spaniards built a fleet of horsehide boats and tried to follow the Gulf coast to Mexico, which they believed to be not far away. But Narváez lost his life in a storm, most of his men were drowned or murdered by the natives, and only four survivors, after eight years of captivity and of long and weary wanderings in the wilderness of Louisiana and Texas, at last reached the city of Mexico.

**De Soto's Expedition (1539–1543).** One of the four survivors of this ill-fated enterprise, a certain Cabeza de Vaca, brought back wild and fantastic reports of the wealth to be secured in the interior of the continent. His stories aroused the ambition of Hernando de Soto, a former associate of Pizarro, to find and conquer another Perú. Having secured from Charles I a commission as "*adelantado* of the lands of Florida," De Soto set out from Havana with over six hundred men, magnificently equipped, and landed at Tampa Bay. In the course of the next three years he and his men wandered up and down the southeastern part of the present United States, reached the Mississippi — the first Europeans to approach it from the land — and even penetrated to some distance beyond the great river. They came upon neither gold nor jewels, but everywhere encountered numerous and warlike Indians. At length the indomitable De Soto died of a fever and found a grave in the river which he had discovered. The Spaniards now decided to abandon the search for El Dorado. Building boats, they floated down the Mississippi to its mouth and followed the coast to Mexico. Scarcely half of the band which had set out with such high hopes survived the hardships of this remarkable expedition.

**Florida under Spain.**   After one or two further projects, Spain abandoned the effort to occupy Florida, but was soon forced to move in for strategic reasons.   Hostile Frenchmen having settled there, a royally supported garrison (*presidio*) was placed at St.

CITY GATE OF ST. AUGUSTINE, FLORIDA

This gate is all that remains of a wall which once reached from Fort Marion on the seashore to the San Sebastian River at the western side of the city.   It was erected during the Spanish period.

Augustine, in 1565.  This eventually became a civilian town. Missionaries also moved in, though never in large numbers. Pensacola, the other Spanish settlement in Florida, was not founded until the close of the seventeenth century.  By this time Spanish Florida included only the peninsula, with a strip of Gulf coast reaching to the Mississippi.  It was hemmed in on the north by the English colonies and on the west by the French possession of Louisiana.  The Treaty of Paris, at the close of the Seven Years' War in 1763, assigned Florida to Great Britain, in return for Cuba and the Philippines.  The British formed the region into two provinces, called East Florida and West Florida. Both provinces reverted to Spain twenty years later by the second Treaty of Paris.  Their cession to the United States in 1819 ended Spanish dominion in this part of the North American continent.[1]

**Louisiana under Spain.**   In spite of De Soto's discoveries, Spain set up no claim to the Mississippi Valley.  When, therefore, the most illustrious of French explorers, Robert de La Salle, in 1682

[1] Spain by the treaty of 1819 also relinquished to the United States all claim to territory on the Pacific north of the 42d parallel.  The Spaniards had never made any effort to colonize the Oregon country or to develop its trade with the Indians.  See the map on page 106.

descended that river to its mouth, he was able to take possession for France and to name all its drainage area Louisiana, in honor of Louis XIV. A secret treaty between the French and Spanish governments, signed before the conclusion of the Seven Years' War, subsequently transferred Louisiana to Spain, in order to save it from Great Britain. There followed a brief period of Spanish rule, during which the Castilian language and Hispanic law became official in New Orleans and. other French settlements. Many Americans settled in the country during this time. Napoleon, needing Louisiana for his own purposes, took it from Spain without ceremony in 1800, but three years later sold it to the United States for the paltry sum of $15,000,000. All the vast territory between the Mississippi and the Rocky Mountains thus passed to the North American republic, while Spain had to fall back again on her old frontier in Texas and New Mexico.

**Texas under Spain.** The explorations of La Salle in the territory north of the Rio Grande and his attempt to plant a colony there led the Spaniards, during the last decade of the seventeenth century, to establish several settlements beyond the Mexican boundary, in order to forestall the threatened French occupation. This region, previously neglected by them, was formed into a province and called Tejas, or Texas, after an Indian confederacy. The mission and presidio of San Antonio, founded in 1718, became the center of Spanish operations in Texas. The subsequent history of the country as a Mexican province, and afterward as an independent republic, will be treated in another chapter.

**Coronado's Expedition (1540–1542).** The Spaniards first learned something about the region now included in the states of Texas, Oklahoma, New Mexico, and Arizona through Coronado's famous expedition. Like De Soto's it was directly inspired by the marvelous tales of Cabeza de Vaca concerning the riches to be found in the interior of North America. Here too, Indian storytellers located the Seven Cities, supposed to abound in gold and silver and precious stones. Indeed, a Spanish missionary, Friar Marcos, whom the viceroy of Mexico sent out to ascertain the truth concerning these cities, declared that he had seen one of them from a distance and that it appeared actually as large as the Mexican capital. Preparations were at once begun to invade the new land of wonder and to repeat, if possible, the epic story of Cortés and

Pizarro.   The enterprise was placed in charge of Francisco Vásquez
de Coronado, governor of the northern frontier province of New
Spain.   Leaving Compostela in 1540, Coronado and his horsemen
made their painful way through the wilderness, reached Cibola,
the first of the Seven Cities, which turned out to be simply a
pueblo of the Zuñi Indians, visited still other pueblos, all of them
small, poor villages, built of sun-dried brick, and then, still eager
for gold, pushed northward over the boundless plains as far as the
rude Indian settlement of Quivira, probably in what is now central
Kansas.   A few hundred miles to the southeast De Soto was exploring Arkansas at the same time.   The great expedition at length
returned empty-handed to Mexico.   It had failed of its immediate
object, but it revealed the character of the American Southwest
and so prepared the way for the Spanish occupation of that region.

   **The Spaniards in New Mexico.**   Not quite forty years after
Coronado's return soldiers and missionaries began once more to
push northward into the country which, from the resemblance of
the pueblos to the Aztec dwellings, received the name of New
Mexico.   The Spanish occupation dates from 1598, when Juan de
Oñate arrived with several hundred colonists at the Rio Grande
(near the present El Paso), and took formal possession "of all the
kingdoms and provinces of New Mexico, on the Rio del Norte, in
the name of our Lord King Philip."   Santa Fe, the second oldest
town within the borders of the United States, was founded in 1609
on the site of a deserted Indian village.   It has ever since been
the seat of government of New Mexico.   Toward the end of the
seventeenth century the Indians, resentful at being compelled to
work for their conquerors and at the zeal of the Church in stamp-
ing out their religious rites, revolted, massacred many Spaniards,
and drove the remainder entirely out of the country.   The reconquest was effected by Diego de Vargas, who, after hard fighting
and much bloodshed, secured the submission of all the pueblos.
New Mexico continued under Spain until 1821, when it became a
province of Mexico with a northern boundary at the forty-second
parallel.   It thus included, not only the present American state of
that name, but also Colorado, Utah, and Nevada, together with
most of Arizona.

   **The Spaniards in California.**   The name California seems to
have been taken by Cortés from a popular Spanish romance of

Photo by School of American Research

### THE PUEBLO OF TAOS, NORTH GROUP

The pueblo lies at the foot of the Sierra de Taos about ninety miles north of
Santa Fe. It consists of two large communal houses, in which live about four
hundred Indians. The pueblo was first visited by the Spaniards in 1541.

### SANTA BARBARA MISSION

The Franciscan mission at Santa Barbara, California, was founded in 1786 by
Padre Lasuen, the successor of Junípero Serra. It is the best preserved of all the
California missions. The walls of the monastery are of sun-dried brick (*adobe*);
the roofing consists of heavy rafters covered with tiles. The church, dedicated in
1820, is a solid structure of sandstone and cement.

chivalry, in which it referred to a fabulous island "to the right of the Indies," peopled by black Amazons, and abounding in gold. Cortés in 1539 sent out an exploring expedition, which reached the head of the Gulf of California, rounded the peninsula, and returned with news that it was not after all an island but a part of the mainland. Three years later the Portuguese mariner Cabrillo, then in the Spanish service, followed the coast of the peninsula northward, discovered San Diego Bay, and finally reached a latitude some distance beyond the Golden Gate. Vizcaíno, another daring mariner, in 1602–1603 discovered Monterey Bay and got as far north as Cape Mendocino. These and other voyages resulted in considerable knowledge of the entire California coast, with the striking exception of San Francisco Bay. Missionaries working up the west coast of Mexico added Sonora to the Spanish zones by the later seventeenth century, and this was followed by Jesuit expansion into Lower California and Arizona. Upper California remained unsettled until English and French voyages, and Russian expansion across Behring Straits, had alarmed Spain. In 1769 Father Junípero Serra established a Franciscan mission at San Diego, and his soldier associate Gaspar de Portolá discovered the Golden Gate. Before independence, twenty-one missions had reached to Sonoma, north of present San Francisco. Two small towns, San José and Los Angeles, presidios at San Diego, Santa Barbara, Monterey, and San Francisco, and a few ranches, also existed. The Nootka Sound controversy with Britain (1789–1794) had limited northern expansion.

**Area and Population of Spanish America.** The Spanish dominions had reached their widest bounds near the close of the eighteenth century. They then included the islands of the West Indies except Jamaica, which had been ceded to Great Britain, and Haiti, ceded to France. On the North American continent, what are now Florida, southern Alabama and Mississippi, the entire area of the United States west of the Mississippi River, Mexico, and Central America belonged to Spain. All South America, except Brazil and the Guianas, acknowledged Spanish sway. The population of this enormous region may have reached 17,000,000. Between one fourth and one fifth of the inhabitants came of European stock, including not only Spaniards, but also English-speaking folk in the Floridas and the French in Louisiana. The viceroyalty of New Spain ranked first in population, and then, in order, the viceroyalties of New Granada, Perú, and La Plata.

\*    \*    \*

**Settlement of Brazil.**  Cabral, who reached Brazil in 1500,[1] believed it to be another island of the Antilles and called it, accordingly, *Ilha da Vera Cruz*.  This name, after the Portuguese learned that the supposed island formed part of a great landmass and that it contained a dyewood similar to the valued brazil-wood of the East, was changed to Brazil.  At first Portugal, busy in India, neglected its American territory, but a few sugar growers, traders, or marooned seamen arrived early.  Planned occupation of the country began with the colony which Affonso de Souza set up in 1532 at São Vicente, in the southern part of the present state of São Paulo.

**The Captaincies.**  The king of Portugal, in order to stimulate colonization, divided Brazil into twelve captaincies, each extending along fifty leagues of coast and, in theory, running inland to the demarcation line.  Their size varied from 6000 to 12,000 square leagues.  The captains-donatory, who ruled them, exercised almost absolute authority as owners of the soil.  This attempt to fasten a semi-feudal system upon a virgin country met with little success.  Few colonists went to Brazil during the first half of the sixteenth century.  Permanent settlements were made in only six of the captaincies.  Finally, the Portuguese monarch decided to limit the extensive powers of the captains-donatory, while leaving them their grants, and to establish a common government under a governor-general.  In 1549 Thomé de Souza came over in this capacity and founded the city of São Salvador, later known as Bahía.  It remained the most important city of Brazil until well into the eighteenth century and the seat of colonial administration until 1763.

**French Aggressions.**  The mariners of France visited the Brazilian coast from the time of its discovery.  After the middle of the sixteenth century French Huguenots, persecuted in their own country, began to look to Brazil as a place of refuge.  The Huguenots made the first settlement at Rio de Janeiro, naming their

[1] See page 58.

colony there "Antarctic France." A Portuguese expedition from
Bahía expelled the intruders in 1567. To safeguard the excellent
harbor, the Portuguese then founded their own city. By 1763 this
had grown so outstandingly that it was chosen as the viceregal
seat.

**Dutch Aggressions.** The Dutch were more formidable rivals.
Not contented with stripping Portugal of her choicest possessions
in the East Indies, they sought the conquest of Portuguese
America. One of the main objects of the Dutch West India
Company, charted in 1621, was the annexation of Brazil. The
city of Pernambuco and six provinces in northern Brazil fell for a
time under the sway of the energetic Netherlanders. Holland
subsequently relinquished her Brazilian possessions by treaty
(1661), but kept her colonies in Dutch Guiana, or Surinam.

**The Paulistas.** Brazil, which contained no rich native states
like those of the Aztecs and the Incas, did not attract empire-
builders. The nearest approach to the Spanish Conquistadors was
furnished by the Paulistas, the name applied to the half-caste
descendants of Portuguese settlers within the area of São Paulo.
The Paulistas fought their way into the interior of the continent,
capturing Indians to be sold as slaves and opening up the gold
mines and diamond mines of Minas Geraes and Matto Grosso.
These adventurers carried the frontiers of the Portuguese domain
right up to the slopes of the Andes.

**The Jesuit Missions.** The pioneering activities of the Paulistas
were supplemented by those of the religious orders who planted
numerous mission stations in the Paraná basin and along the
Amazon and its chief tributaries. By the middle of the eighteenth
century no hostile tribes remained on the banks of the Amazon
throughout its entire course. The Jesuits performed truly her-
culean labors among the natives, winning them by thousands to
Christianity and protecting them from the rapacity of the slave-
hunters. Due partly to the activity of the missionaries, Brazil did
not suffer from the Indian wars so common in the colonization of
America. The civilizing work of the Society of Jesus ended
abruptly in 1759, when the king of Portugal decreed its expulsion
from Brazil and other Portuguese colonies. The property of the
order was confiscated, the missions were neglected or abandoned,
and the Indian converts were allowed to relapse into barbarism.

**Expansion of Brazil.** As a result of the pioneering of the missionaries and the Paulistas, and of the finding of mines in the interior, an enormous increase of immigration and a westward shift of population occurred in Brazil in the eighteenth century. A thousand miles of coast remained unsettled by white men between São Paulo and Rio de Janeiro in the south and Bahía and Pernambuco in the north, but the populous province of Minas Geraes grew up on the southern and central plateau. Even earlier, some pressure from land hunger and much governmental encouragement caused a movement along the coasts to north and south of the older cities, so that by the end of the seventeenth century a string of Portuguese missions or forts had reached Pará on the southern outlet of the Amazon, and contraband traders and frontiersmen had established themselves in Uruguay.

**Boundaries between Portuguese and Spanish America.** The Treaty of Tordesillas in 1494 had separated the Portuguese and Spanish possessions in the New World by a line of demarcation supposed to be drawn three hundred and seventy leagues west of the Azores and the Cape Verde Islands. This league line was never surveyed. As the Paulistas, Jesuits, and other Portuguese colonists pressed inland, the determination of the exact frontiers became an urgent matter. An agreement between Portugal and Spain was not reached until 1777, when, by the Treaty of San Ildefonso, the former power obtained a clear title to an enormous territory in the interior of Brazil, but recognized the Spanish claim to the Uruguay region. This treaty, so favorable to Portugal, explains the fact that South America is now partitioned in such nearly equal proportions between the two Hispanic peoples.

**Brazilian Population.** By 1800 the area of Brazil was practically the same as it is today, but the population was much smaller even than that of the Spanish colonies. It may have equaled three million. About one third were Negroes, perhaps eight hundred thousand were white or "passed for white," three hundred thousand were Indians, and the rest were half-castes of some type. Foreigners were exceedingly few. The captaincies of Minas Geraes, Bahía, Pernambuco, and Rio de Janeiro accounted for at least two of the three millions.

## Words and Phrases You Should Know

| | | |
|---|---|---|
| Atlantis | Indies | pueblo |
| Cape Verde | Ladrones | Seven Cities |
| Cathay | line of demarcation | Saint Brandan |
| Cipango | Moluccas | Treaty of Paris |
| El Dorado | New Granada | Treaty of San Ildefonso |
| globular theory | papal bull | Treaty of Tordesillas |
| Great Khan | Paulistas | viceroyalty |

## Questions You Should Be Able to Answer

1. Why were Portuguese navigators so persistant in their efforts to get around Africa?
2. Of what value to explorers was the work of Prince Henry?
3. Why was the cargo which Da Gama brought back to Europe so valuable?
4. Although Brazil was first claimed for Spain it became a Portuguese colony. Why?
5. From what sources do you think Columbus obtained his ideas about the shape of the earth? about the Atlantic Ocean? about the Indies?
6. What were the terms of the agreement between Columbus and Ferdinand and Isabella?
7. Why did Columbus die a disappointed man?
8. How did America get its name?
9. How did Spain and Portugal come to an agreement in regard to the division of the newly discovered lands?
10. What practical results did the Spanish king hope would come from Magellan's voyage? What did his voyage actually prove?
11. Cortés ". . . was not only the most heroic, but he was also the most statesmanlike of the Conquistadors" (page 72). Give some evidence to prove this statement.
12. Do you think Pizarro's conquest of Perú was a more or less difficult task than Cortés's conquest of Mexico?
13. What was the legend of El Dorado?
14. Why were the explorations of de Solís and Mendoza less rewarding than those of Cortés and Pizarro?
15. In what ways is Spanish influence still in evidence in our Southwest?
16. Who were some of the Spanish adventurers who explored in what is now our South and Southwest? How do you account for their lack of great success?

17. What difficulties did the Spanish encounter in their early attempts to conquer and settle New Mexico and California?
18. How did the Paulistas and Jesuits contribute to the settlement and control of Brazil?

## Projects and Activities

1. Using a wall map of the world, tell the story of the voyages of Díaz, Da Gama, Pinzón, Cabral, Columbus, Vespucci, and Magellan. Be sure to emphasize the significance of each voyage.
2. Give a brief talk on the world as it was known in Columbus's time.
3. Be prepared to explain, using a wall map, how the Treaties of Tordesillas and San Ildefonso affected the colonial possessions of Spain and Portugal.
4. List several arguments that Columbus might have used to obtain support from Ferdinand and Isabella.
5. Make a chart of Spanish explorations in territory that is now included in the United States. Use these headings: Name of Explorer; Dates of Explorations; Regions Explored; Results of Explorations.
6. On a map of the United States indicate by brief legends some of the explorations noted in Project 5.
7. Construct a time line showing ten outstanding events in Spanish and Portuguese exploration.
8. Write a short play based upon incidents in the career of Ponce de León or some other explorer.
9. Imagine that you are a follower of Cortés. Write in diary form some of the happenings in which you took part or witnessed when you were with him in Mexico.
10. Make a chart of Spanish explorations in South America. Use the headings suggested in Project 5.
11. Prepare an outline of the history of Florida to 1819.

# CHAPTER IV

# Spanish and Portuguese Colonies in Latin America

**Racial Contact.** Spanish colonization of the New World brought together two great races hitherto unknown to each other. The Spaniards came to America with their Christian religion, European civilization, and special Hispanic characteristics, as developed during more than ten centuries of history. They found in America a large aboriginal population, whose culture ranged from the lowest grade of savagery to upper barbarism. The colonists, though almost everywhere far less numerous than the natives, quickly assumed and always maintained the mastery, so that racial contact involved the domination of one race by another. The Spaniards started out, of course, with no conception of what they actually found in America; they expected to encounter advanced Oriental peoples, whose material goods might be gained by trade and whose spiritual welfare might be secured by conversion to the true faith. The real truth soon dawned upon the minds of the avaricious, unscrupulous adventurers who founded Spanish power in America. The Indians were a race who might be subjugated, sold into slavery, exploited for the benefit of their conquerors, and, if necessary, exterminated.

**Subjugation of the Indians.** The conquest of the Arawaks in the Greater Antilles, mostly a harmless and gentle people, formed no difficult matter for the Spaniards, with their swords of tempered steel, crossbows, firearms, armor, horses, and bloodhounds. How easily the Spaniards overcame the more civilized inhabitants of Mexico, Central America, and Perú has already appeared. Indian revolts were later very common, but usually easily crushed. Only the Araucanians of Chile, some of the Caribs of northern South America, and the Mexican Yaqui, peculiarly warlike and independent peoples, offered really successful resistance.

**Indian Slavery and Serfdom.** The Spaniards, as spoils of conquest, pillaged the Indians of their wealth and then proceeded to
reduce them to slavery. Columbus himself captured six hundred
natives and sent them to Spain as slaves. Spanish law, in the time
of Ferdinand and Isabella, made it permissible to enslave cannibal
tribes and prisoners of war. Thus began the terrible slave raids
through the West Indies, ending in the wholesale deportation of
entire tribes to the gold mines of Haiti. This rough-and-ready
method of forcing the natives to work for their conquerors soon
gave way to a system of compulsory labor resembling the serfdom
which still prevailed on the estates of Spanish nobles in the Peninsula. Grants of land to discoverers, conquerors, and founders of
settlements included also the Indians living on the land, for service
both on the plantations and in the mines. Their personal freedom
was recognized under this arrangement, inasmuch as individuals
might not be bought or sold; they were bound to the soil as were
the serfs of medieval Europe. An estate with servile Indians on it
received the name of *encomienda*, because they lived under the
protection of their lord and patron. Indeed, he was supposed to
look after their souls as well as their bodies, to train them in
civilization, and to teach them Christianity. But human nature
is weak, and the *encomenderos* too often neglected the welfare of
the Indians, while exploiting their labor to the utmost. After 1542
Indians under *encomienda* owed tribute and not labor, but another
system of forced labor, the *mita*, became general throughout
Spanish America. It did not entirely disappear until the end of
Spanish control.

**The Indian Population.** The enslavement of the Indians and
the serfdom which supplanted it account in part for the marked
decline of the native population during the earlier period of Spanish
rule. More stress should be laid, however, upon the disastrous
effect of European diseases (above all, smallpox), which raged
irresistibly among the Indians, their excessive indulgence in intoxicating liquors, and the famines that followed warfare and
failure of crops. Depopulation proceeded rapidly in the Antilles;
there the aborigines, who seem to have been very numerous,
melted away altogether in less than fifty years after their discovery.
The fate of the Indians upon the mainland was not so swift or so
sweeping. Those in the mining regions appear always to have

been the greatest sufferers. Certain it is that entire tribes and peoples sometimes perished. Conditions improved soon and, probably in the middle of the seventeenth century, the natives began to increase in number. At the end of the colonial era they probably amounted to 7,500,000 out of a total population of perhaps 17,000,000. Indians thus constituted about 45 per cent of the inhabitants of Spanish America.

LAS CASAS

A portrait in the Bibliothèque
Nationale, Paris.

**Protective Legislation.** The ill-treatment of the aborigines was never for a moment countenanced by the Spanish rulers. The Crown tried from the start to interpose between the conquerors and the conquered. It limited and finally abolished slavery; appointed protectors of the Indians; required the Indians to live by themselves in villages under freely elected native chiefs; and, as already pointed out, ordered the *encomenderos* to educate, civilize, and convert their charges. These and other regulations were set forth long before the so-called "New Laws" of 1542 and they fill many pages of the Laws of the Indies as published in 1680. The benevolent purpose of all this legislation deserves the highest praise. Doubtless the laws were often defeated by the greed of the colonists, especially in the viceroyalty of Perú, which was not so well governed as New Spain. No other result could be anticipated, considering how isolated were the colonies, and how generally inefficient, even when not corrupt, was their administration.

**Bartholomew de Las Casas.** An account of Spanish relations with the Indians ought not to omit some mention of Las Casas, the "Apostle of the Indies." Las Casas accompanied his father on one of the expeditions of Columbus to the West Indies and there received holy orders, being the first priest ordained in America. He became convinced that Indian slavery was wrong, preached against it, and finally persuaded Charles I to issue the royal prohibition of it in the "New Laws." His success came too late to help the inhabitants of the West Indies, who by this time had become practically extinct, but those on the mainland were saved from the fate of the unfortunate islanders. Some years later Las Casas published his famous work on the *Destruction of the Indies*,[1] which was soon translated into all the principal languages of Europe. The account there given of Spanish inhumanity toward the natives was not justified even at this period, when the Spaniards had been scarcely fifty years in the New World; and its lurid pictures of cruelty and oppression ought not to throw into the background the persistent efforts of the government, throughout the two centuries following, to better the lot of the aborigines. Las Casas worked diligently among the Indians, and by his tact and kindliness many of them in southern Mexico were won to Christianity.

**Conversion of the Indians.** The Church found in the New World abundant opportunity to display missionary zeal. Preaching, praying, and baptizing went hand in hand with the work of conquest. As Spanish influence extended over the more civilized Indians, each town, Indian as well as Spanish, was required to have a church, hospital, and school for native children. Sometimes converts, having learned to read in their own language and later in Spanish, were admitted to the priesthood and to the monastic orders. The Church took a very paternal attitude toward the Indians, "on account of their ignorance and their weak minds." It indulged them, as no Spaniard would have been indulged, respecting confession, penances, fasts, and masses. It did not require them to give up immediately all their primitive superstitions. It provided for them numerous holidays in the ecclesiastical festivals (*fiestas*) and pilgrimages (*romerias*). This policy of lenience and forbearance goes far to explain the remarkable ascendancy which the clergy soon gained over the Indians.

---

[1] *Brevissima relación de la destruyción de las Indias.*

**Missions.** Missionary enterprise among the less civilized tribes of the interior did not really begin on a large scale until about the middle of the seventeenth century. When such work proved successful, the Indians were gathered together in a village called a mission, which often lay far distant from any considerable Spanish settlement. Scattered about the surrounding region might be a number of isolated *haciendas*, or ranches, generally devoted to cattle raising. For the protection of several missions *presidios*, or small forts, with a garrison of soldiers, were established at intervals. Then, as the country opened up and white settlers came in, the little Indian village would be gradually transformed into a thriving Spanish town. The missions thus formed outposts of civilization, and the friars who directed them became the pioneers of civilization.

**The Missionary Orders.** The missions were a major work of the various orders of monks and friars. The Franciscans, the Dominicans, the Mercedarians, the Augustinians, and other groups all had widespread and successful accomplishments, but discussion of some of the work of the Jesuit priests must suffice as a sample for all. Many Jesuits became famous in Florida and northern Mexico. The life of Eusebio Kino, who led the Spanish advance into what is now Arizona and who made over fifty missionary journeys, varying in length from one hundred to a thousand miles, in that region, deserves to be held in grateful memory. "No one ever saw in him any vice whatsoever, for the discovery of lands and the conversion of souls had purified him." Father Salvatierra, who labored successfully among the Indians of Lower (Baja) California, was another heroic figure. After Charles III in 1767 expelled the Jesuits from the Spanish dominions, Lower California was assigned to the Dominicans and Upper (Alta) California to the Franciscans. Reference has already been made to the Franciscan missions in the Golden State.[1] They stretched all the way from San Diego northward to beyond San Francisco. Some of the mission buildings now lie in ruins and others have entirely disappeared. But such a well-preserved structure as the mission of Santa Barbara recalls a Benedictine monastery, with its shady cloisters, secluded courtyard, and timbered roof covered with red tiles. It is a bit of the Old World transplanted to the New.

[1] See page 88.

**Jesuit Missions in Paraguay.** The missions established by the Society of Jesus among the Guaraní Indians in what is now Paraguay numbered as many as forty by the end of the seventeenth century. Each one was organized upon a communistic pattern. The Indians worked two days a week on the common land, under the direction of a *padre*, who also taught them simple mechanic arts. Their hours for meals, food, dress, and amusements were all regulated for them by the friars. Such foreign necessities as had to be imported were paid for by the sale of "Paraguay tea," which the order managed. Every effort was made to maintain the exclusiveness of the missions, so that the morals of the innocent natives might not be contaminated by contact with outsiders. Here aloof from the world the Indians lived peaceful and industrious, if also circumscribed and narrow, lives. With the suppression of the Jesuit order the missions in Paraguay decayed and the neophytes relapsed into the barbarism of former days.

**Mestizos.** Spanish immigrants to America brought few women with them and hence had to find wives or concubines among the Indians. Intermarriage between the two races became common; the government on the whole encouraged it; and the Spaniards, like the French in Canada but unlike the English in the Thirteen Colonies, felt no repugnance to mingling their blood with the natives. The result was the formation of the mestizos, or half-breeds, who are still found throughout the greater part of Spanish America. Mestizos probably numbered about 5,000,000, or 30 per cent of the total population, by the close of the colonial period.

**Negro Slavery.** The introduction of Negro slavery into the New World dates from 1502, only a decade after the Columbian discovery. Negroes were more efficient than Indians, and their labor seemed indispensable to the Spaniards for the development of the mines and the plantations. The Spanish authorities also favored Negro slavery, not only on economic grounds, but also as a means of sparing the Indians. Even the noble Las Casas advocated this policy, though he lived long enough to express his regret at being so slow to realize that Africans were as much entitled to freedom as the American aborigines. The method of procuring Negroes was by letting out contracts, or *asientos;* these were granted at first to the Portuguese, who controlled the sources of supply in Africa.

Other nations received contracts later, the British having an exclusive one from 1713 to 1750.

**The Negro Population.**  African slavery flourished in the West Indies and along the Caribbean shores of South America, where the tropical climate suited the Negroes and where their labor could be most profitably employed on the sugar plantations. It never became widespread elsewhere in the Spanish colonies, for much the same reasons which limited its prevalence in the English colonies. The total number of Negroes, slave and free, in Spanish America is estimated to have reached 776,000 at the beginning of the nineteenth century. This would be less than 5 per cent of the total population.

**Emancipation of Slaves.**  The Spanish slave code, more humane than the laws respecting slaves in the French and English colonies, made emancipation easy. Slaves were often freed by the master's will. The law also allowed them to accumulate property, with which they might buy their liberty, and that of wives and children, at the lowest market rate. The consequences of this legislation appeared in the large number of free Negroes everywhere in Spanish America.

**Zambos and Mulattoes.**  The Negroes intermarried more or less with Indians, forming the racial type called zambos. The government, however, did not look with favor upon such unions and tried to prevent them by legislation. Ranking higher in the social scale than zambos, but lower than mestizos, were mulattoes, the offspring of Negroes and whites.

**Spanish Immigration to America.**  Comparatively few Spaniards went to America throughout the three centuries of Spanish rule. In contrast to the English government, which stimulated emigration and so built up a colonial market, Spain restricted the free movement of its peoples to the colonies. No Spaniard could go to the Indies without first securing a license and satisfying the authorities as to his morals and his orthodoxy. The Crown sought in this way to preserve the purity of the Spanish stock in the New World, and at the same time to protect the colonies from being overrun with idle and turbulent adventurers, anxious only to get rich. During the sixteenth century the entire emigration from Spain to America is believed not to have much exceeded one thousand or fifteen hundred persons a year; probably these figures also represent the maximum for the two centuries following. More Spaniards would have emigrated in spite of harassing restrictions, if the colonies had offered attractive economic opportunities for people of limited means. But in Spanish America the manual labor was performed by Indians, Negroes, and half-castes; commerce was hampered by governmental regulations; and manufactures were insignificant. As for farming, stock raising, and mining, these were large-scale industries which required a heavy investment of capital. A prosperous middle class of small farmers, traders, and handicraftsmen never developed in the colonies.

**The White Population.** Such a class might have arisen, had foreigners been allowed to settle in Spanish America. But the non-Spaniard was unwelcome there. The Crown, so zealous in extirpating heretics at home, naturally did not wish its American dominions to become a hotbed of heresy. There was also the purpose of preventing the diffusion of knowledge in foreign countries of the wealth and resources of the Spanish possessions. Though this exclusion policy weakened in the eighteenth century, Europeans not of Spanish stock were exceedingly rare in the colonies. The total number of whites, or of those who passed for whites, at the end of the eighteenth century was between 3,000,000 and 4,000,000, or about 20 per cent of the entire population.

**Peninsular Spaniards and Creoles.** The whites were divided into two social classes, according as they had been born in Spain or in the colonies. To American-born Spaniards the word Creole was usually applied. The peninsular Spaniards, though much less numerous than the Creoles, enjoyed governmental favor and monopolized the higher offices in Church and State. Of the 754 viceroys, captains-general, governors, and presidents who ruled in the colonies, only 18 were Creoles. The latter held the lower offices; they also constituted the majority of the planters, cattle raisers, mineowners, professional men, and merchants. A good deal of friction developed between these two social classes. Peninsular Spaniards treated the Creoles as inferiors; the Creoles, becoming wealthy and ambitious, naturally resented this contemptuous attitude. Thus, in addition to racial antipathy between Indians, Africans, Europeans, and the mixed breeds produced by their crossings, there was also social antagonism between the two classes of dominant whites. The government made no effort to lessen these currents of aversion, for it saw in them the chief means of preventing any union of all the people against Spanish rule. Spain, as other imperial powers have done, followed the policy of *divide et impera* — "divide and rule."

**Conquistadors *versus* Royal Agents.** The expeditions of the Conquistadors, as we have seen, were usually private undertakings, rather than state-assisted enterprises. Columbus, Cortés, Pizarro, and their lesser imitators must be regarded as essentially adventurers, who at their own risk provided the tiny fleets and little armies with which they won such amazing triumphs. Spanish predominance once established, it became the prime object of the Conquistadors to appropriate by any means the wealth that they had found. Conquest for exploitation thus characterized the earlier activities of the Spaniards in the New World. But this phase did not last long. The Spanish Crown, through its own agents, soon began to extend its authority to the New World. Columbus, for alleged mismanagement in Haiti, lost all the privileges which had been conferred upon him as ruler of an island-empire. Cortés, before completing the pacification of Mexico, found himself thwarted at every step by royal commissioners and finally had to relinquish the conduct of civil affairs to a viceroy sent from Spain. The Pizarro brothers, who had well-nigh established an independent dynasty in Perú, were also eventually superseded by a Spanish viceroy.

**Colonial Administration.** The Spaniards devised for their colonial dominions an administrative system which followed, as closely as possible, the political institutions of Spain. Necessarily, it was absolutist in character. The sovereign, now supreme at home, intended to be equally supreme abroad. Just as the laws of Spain were made by the king, with the advice of his councilors, so the laws of Spanish America were made by the king in council. The question of parliamentary supremacy over the colonies, through the Cortes,[1] never was even raised.

**The Council of the Indies.** The agency of colonial administration was the *Consejo de Indias*, the "Royal and Supreme Council of the Indies." Formally organized as early as 1524, the council for more than two centuries directed the affairs of Spanish America. The members were appointed by the Crown from officials of noble

[1] See page 44.

birth, preferably those who had served in the colonies. The
council met daily, except on Church holidays. Meetings were
always in the neighborhood of the court, so that the king, if he
desired, might be present. A two-thirds majority was required
for any decision. This body virtually drew up all legislation for
the colonies and was a high tribunal of appeal from the colonial
courts. It also became the fountain of patronage, since the king
listened to its advice as to all appointments for civil and ecclesiastical offices. The Spanish monarch, it has been well said, saw
his American domains only through the eyes of his council.

**The Laws of the Indies.** A worthy monument to the council
is the Laws of the Indies,[1] promulgated in 1680. This code brought
together all the scattered legislation on every aspect of colonial
life. It exhibits throughout a consideration for the welfare of the
Spanish Americans, whether whites, Negroes, or Indians, far more
humane and liberal than anything to be found in the regulations of
France or England for their dependencies overseas. Unfortunately,
the code was too often neglected by the officers charged with its
enforcement.

**The Viceroy.** The most important official nominated by the
Council of the Indies and appointed by the Crown was the viceroy.
Over seventy laws in the *Recopilación* are devoted to specifying
his duties. He maintained a court, modeled after that of Madrid,
and performed all the royal functions, as though the king were
present and reigning in person. His term of office was regularly for
three years, extended in the eighteenth century to five years. New
Spain had sixty-two viceroys between 1534 and 1821. The viceroyalty of Perú outranked that of New Spain until the eighteenth
century; successful rulers in the latter province were often promoted to Perú. A viceroy necessarily enjoyed much independence,
because of the remoteness of the colonies from the mother country.
To hold him in check royal "visitors" were sent out, with a power
of inspecting all branches of the colonial service. Moreover, every
viceroy, when his term ended, had to undergo an inquest, or inquiry, into his official conduct. The justice of any charges against
him was decided by the Council of the Indies. Unless favoritism
at court exempted him from investigation, or bribery corrupted the
investigator, this method of securing accountability worked well.

[1] *Recopilación de leyes de los reinos de las Indias.*

**The Audiencia.** The only other important check on the arbitrary power of a viceroy was that exercised by the body of magistrates known as the *audiencia*. It formed the viceroy's advisory council and at the same time the highest colonial court. Persons who felt wronged by viceregal acts or decisions might appeal to the *audiencia*, from which, in turn, important questions could be carried to the Council of the Indies. The *audiencia* acted in place of the viceroy in case of his absence or disability, and each, without informing the other, might communicate directly with the Crown. The members of this body made regular visits to the different towns and cities within their jurisdiction; their thorough inspection extended, it is said, even to the testing of the purity of drugs in apothecary shops. The high rank and good salary of these magistrates placed them in an independent position, though naturally they were overshadowed by the viceroy, who presided over their meetings. The *audiencia*, in short, was for its special district what the Council of the Indies was for the whole of Spanish America.

**The Captain-General.** To provide better government and especially defense in important but distant areas, the authority of the viceroy was practically nonexistent in certain "captaincies-general." These were ruled by a man called "Governor, captain-general, and president of the audiencia." Santo Domingo, Guatemala, Bogotá, and Manila enjoyed such a status from the sixteenth century. Panamá and Chile were then only semi-independent of the viceroy of Perú, but they, Venezuela, and Cuba acquired the same autonomy in the later eighteenth century. The captains-general corresponded directly with the Crown.

**Political Divisions.** Four viceroyalties had been established by the eighteenth century: New Spain (1534), Perú (1542), New Granada (1739), and La Plata (1776). The number of districts with supreme courts (*audiencias*) reached fourteen at the period under consideration.[1] In addition, there were the eight captaincies-general. These political divisions, as established during the colonial era, furnished lines of cleavage for the independent states which afterward arose in Spanish America.

---

[1] Santo Domingo, Guadalajara, Mexico, Guatemala, Panamá, Caracas, Santa Fé de Bogotá, San Francisco del Quito, Lima, Cuzco, Charcas, Santiago de Chile, and Buenos Aires.

**Local Administration.** The viceroys, *audiencias*, and captains-general had under their direction various executives, such as governors and alcalde mayors, for the provinces, Spanish towns and cities, and the adjacent Indian villages. These minor officials were also selected by the Crown, though *ad interim* appointments might be made by the viceroy. In the second half of the eighteenth century the local administration was reorganized, and the provinces were divided into districts called intendancies, each with its intendant, a royal officer specially charged with military and financial matters. It was only in the municipalities that some degree of self-government existed. A municipal council (*cabildo*) conducted civic affairs, subject, however, to the oversight and constant regulation of the provincial governor or of the intendant. Membership of the *cabildo* was, of course, confined to Spaniards, either emigrants from Spain or born in the colonies. In some Spanish American cities resident householders enjoyed the right of freely electing representatives on the *cabildos;* in other cities the governor exercised the privilege of appointing them. It should be noted, as characteristic of the administrative system, that public offices were regularly bought and sold to the highest bidder. This practice, so repugnant to present-day ideas, was in accord with the custom in Spain. As might be expected, it took away from office-holding all idea of civic patriotism or devotion to the good of the community. Politics became entirely a business matter, a private business matter.

**Defects of the Administrative System.** The proper treatment of conquered territories is always a difficult problem for the best-intentioned state. That Spain's intentions in America were good the Laws of the Indies amply evidence. She faced, however, a tremendous task in trying to rule justly, wisely, a realm so vast and so distant as Spanish America. The absence of any means of quick transportation and communication, such as modern colonial nations enjoy, itself proved an almost fatal obstacle to efficient management of her dependencies. Hence, we are not surprised to learn that justice was slow and uncertain, that many officials enriched themselves in illegal ways, and that, in general, the administrative system was cumbersome, even when not actually oppressive. Furthermore, it failed to develop either local or national institutions through which the colonists could have

LATIN AMERICA
AT THE END OF THE
18th CENTURY (1796)

learned how to manage their own affairs. There were no town meetings of all the citizens and no deliberative assemblies corresponding to the legislatures of the Thirteen Colonies. Even the *cabildos*, or municipal councils, had little initiative and power of self-direction. But since free political institutions did not exist in Spain at this period, they naturally did not arise in Spanish America.

**Commercial Policy: Mercantilism.** The government of Spain, in its economic relations with the colonists, adopted the principles of mercantilism. The mercantile theory, generally accepted throughout the sixteenth, seventeenth, and eighteenth centuries, emphasized the importance of commerce as a source of national wealth. Extreme mercantilists even argued that the prosperity of a nation is in exact proportion to the amount of money circulating within its borders. They urged, therefore, that each country should so conduct its business with other countries as to attract to itself the largest possible share of the precious metals. If the country sold more to foreigners than it bought of them, then there would be a "favorable balance of trade," and this balance the foreigners would have to make up in coin or bullion. Mercantilists also believed that a colonial power ought by all means to prevent the subjects of other powers from trading with its dependencies. It should keep their profitable commerce for its own people. Spain and Portugal, and later Holland, France, and England, all followed this policy. But Spain, to whose shores soon flowed the enormous wealth of Mexico and Perú, was obviously the best situated of all European states for putting into effect the theory of mercantilism.

**The House of Trade.** The instrument for commercial dealings with the colonies was the *Casa de Contratación*, established at Seville as early as 1503. It had charge of emigration and immigration, for a Spaniard could go to the colonies only from Seville and could come back from them only to that city. It also regulated commerce, since Seville formed the sole port from which ships might sail to America and through which colonial products might enter Spain in return.[1] In short, the House of Trade enabled the

---

[1] In 1717 Cadiz replaced Seville as the Spanish port of entry, because the Guadalquivir had become so shallow that it could no longer be navigated by large ships.

king to preserve monopolistic privilege in economic affairs, just as he exercised absolute political sway through the Council of the Indies.

**The Fleets.** In order to facilitate control of commerce and also to guard against privateers and pirates, the fleet system came into operation. Ships, instead of sailing for the colonies as suited the convenience of merchants, had all to go from Seville or from Cadiz at a given time and to a given port in America. Every year two fleets under armed convoy left Spain, one destined for Vera Cruz, with a cargo consigned to various points in Spanish North America, the other destined for Puerto Belo on the Isthmus of Panamá, with a cargo for Spanish South America. Both fleets touched at the island of Dominica on the outward voyage and united at Havana for the return voyage through the Bahama Channel into the Atlantic.

**Fairs.** The arrival of the fleets was the signal for a great fair at each of their destinations. The Puerto Belo fair was the larger, being the emporium of the rich Peruvian trade. It lasted only forty days, but during this period goods to an enormous value changed hands. The fairs in Spanish America recall those of medieval Europe, while the Spanish fleets may be compared with the caravans which once conducted the overland trade of Asia.

**Trade Restrictions.** The Spanish government, true to the principles of mercantilism, made every effort to confine colonial export and import trade to its own merchants. It long forbade any intercourse between colonists and foreigners, on penalty of confiscation of property and sometimes of death. As late as 1776 a royal decree stipulated that no foreigners might reside in Spanish America or trade with its inhabitants without a license, which cost a large sum. Until the middle of the seventeenth century the mere entry of a foreign ship into Spanish American waters was treated as a crime, and stranded shipmasters of foreign nations were frequently executed or sent to the mines for life. Even trade carried on by Spanish merchants themselves encountered hampering restrictions. Commerce with the Philippines was limited to one ship a year sailing from Acapulco. Direct intercourse between Spain and Buenos Aires was either prohibited or else confined to a few licensed vessels; consequently, a settler on the Plata often had to secure his European goods from Lima, to which city they had been

From Thomas Gage's *Voyage*, Amsterdam, 1720

FAIR AT PUERTO BELO

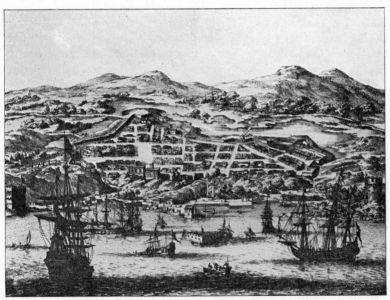

From John Ogilby's *America*, London, 1671

CITY OF SALVADOR

brought from the distant Puerto Belo. It should be noted, further-more, that common European practice led to the formation of trading monopolies in various commodities, such as tobacco, cocoa, and Mexican silver, thus shutting out the competition of other merchants and limiting the scope of business enterprise.

**Smuggling.** After other nations gained a foothold in America, their subjects soon began to smuggle enormous quantities of goods into the Spanish possessions. The English, French, and Dutch islands in the West Indies became the stations for contraband trade. It reached such proportions as to justify the complaint of the Spaniards that foreigners were the ones who really benefited by American commerce, being free in this illicit traffic from the taxes which handicapped their own merchants. The government found it impossible to stop or even check smuggling, which went on with the connivance of corrupt local officials.

**Commercial Concessions.** Another rift in the Spanish exclusion policy resulted from the trade concessions by Spain to her rivals, as the result of success in war. For instance, the so-called Asiento [1] Treaty, made with England in 1713, provided that the English should have the sole right of importing Negro slaves into the Spanish colonies, with the additional privilege of sending annually one ship of five hundred tons burden to the fair at Puerto Belo. English merchants took full advantage of this concession; they secretly enlarged the ship's capacity and accompanied her with transports, which kept out of sight by day, and from which her cargo of European goods was replenished by night. The competi-tion of smugglers and of the English merchants at Puerto Belo sapped the business of the Spanish fleets, until hardly anything remained for them to carry to Europe except the king's share of the produce of the Peruvian and Mexican mines.

**Reform of Commercial Policy.** The government of Spain recognized at last that trade restrictions which were meant to build up a prosperous colonial empire resulted only in stifling Spanish enterprise and in filling the pockets of foreigners with illicit gains. A more liberal commercial policy gradually became effective dur-ing the eighteenth century. Spanish merchants received per-mission to send out ships independent of the fleets, and about 1778 the fleet system was entirely abandoned. Vessels might now

[1] An *asiento* was a contract for slave importation. See page 99.

sail directly to the Plata colonies and to Chile and Perú via Cape
Horn. Then came the opening to all Spaniards of intercourse
between West India ports, and, on the Pacific, between Perú, New
Spain, Guatemala, and New Granada. Even the Seville-Cadiz
monopoly disappeared. All the important Spanish ports secured
the right of trading with the colonies, while across the ocean
Buenos Aires, Montevideo, Valparaíso, Guayaquil, Cartagena, and
other harbors were opened to direct commerce with Spain. Credit
for these liberal measures belongs mainly to one Spanish king,
Charles III (1759–1788). They immensely stimulated colonial
trade, but their beneficial effect, both in Spain and in her dependencies, had not been fully experienced before the Spanish
Americans severed the ties uniting them to the mother country.

**Farming and Stock raising.** After the romantic era of the Conquistadors ended, the majority of the Spanish settlers became
planters and herdsmen. Farming and stock raising were the
principal occupations in colonial times. The Spaniards cultivated
the products already familiar to the Indians [1] and, in addition,
introduced the grains, vegetables, and fruits of southern Europe.
It is said that no less than one hundred and seventy species of
plants and animals, unknown hitherto in the New World, were
brought by the Spaniards from the Old. The climate and soil of
America were very favorable to European domestic animals.
Horses, cattle, sheep, and swine multiplied with great rapidity on
the plains, and stock raising flourished. Beef was so cheap that
cattle were slaughtered simply for their hides and hoofs. The
bulkier agricultural products played no part in export trade, because of costly land transportation and the small size of ships, but
such commodities as sugar, indigo, cacao, vanilla, cochineal,
"Jesuit's-bark" (quinine), and "Paraguay tea" (*maté*), together
with raw hides and raw wool, formed a large proportion of the
cargo of the fleets.

**Manufacturing.** The industrial development of the colonies
was retarded by the lack of capital and credit, scarcity of skilled
labor, high wages, and by the greater profits to be gained from
farming, stock raising, and mining. These conditions account for
the absence of manufacturing on any extensive scale. Spain,
unlike France and England, seems to have placed no serious re-

[1] See pages 13 and 17.

strictions upon the manufactures of the colonies, with the idea of preserving their markets for her own industries. She rather favored, though to little purpose, the colonial development of spinning, weaving, and other mechanic arts, together with sugar refining.

**The Mines.** The most lucrative business, in proportion to the amount of capital invested, was mining. The Spaniards began by plundering the Indians of their stored-up wealth in gold and silver, but the conquest of Mexico and Perú soon opened up for exploitation the great mineral resources of those lands. After the discovery in 1545 of the enormously rich silver mines of Potosí in Bolivia, the output of silver much exceeded that of gold. The total product of the mines probably reached its long-time peak about 1600 and then fell as mines were exhausted. But new mines and new techniques brought a steady increase of production in the eighteenth century. At the opening of the nineteenth century the total annual production may have averaged in value 43,500,000 *pesos* (Spanish dollars), or about ten times the known production of the rest of the world. This is the estimate of Alexander von Humboldt, whose famous figures on earlier production suffered from inadequate data.

**The Royal Revenue.** Most of the treasure produced in America did not stay there. Besides what the colonists paid Spanish merchants and smugglers for manufactured goods, a very large amount went to the Crown. The king enjoyed the "royal fifth" — one fifth of all products of the mines, including gold, silver, and precious stones. He had the proceeds of the Indian tribute, levied on all male Indians of working age. As head of the Church, he received tithes, or a tenth part of the agricultural and pastoral products. The royal revenue was further increased by a sales tax on certain articles bought and sold; by duties on imports from and exports to Spain; by the proceeds of state monopolies, such as those of salt and tobacco; and, finally, by the receipts from the sale of public offices. Even this list by no means exhausts the payments made by the colonists to the Crown. It does not appear, however, that the burden of taxation was more oppressive in Spanish America than in Spain. During the latter part of the eighteenth century the Crown drew about $90,000,000 a year from the colonies, but as much as four fifths of this sum, on an average, went to meet the expenses of colonial administration. A number of the colonies, in fact, did not produce enough revenue to pay for administering them. Until the eighteenth century, or later for some, the Antilles, Venezuela, Florida, Louisiana, and Chile were subsidized by New Spain or Perú. The Spanish government, without the income from the mines, might not have been able to maintain the empire which the Conquistadors had won.

**The Spanish Treasure.** According to mercantilist doctrine the steady stream of treasure to Spain should have made that country very prosperous. The actual result was quite the reverse. The new gold and silver inflated the currency and so led to an extraordinary rise of prices, which, in turn, greatly increased the cost of manufacturing commodities. It cost so much to manufacture in Spain that foreigners could afford to bring their goods there and, after paying the heavy dues demanded of them, could yet undersell the home producers. The influx of treasure, instead of stimulating Spanish industry, had the effect of forcing the people to rely more and more on outsiders to supply their needs. The economic decline of Spain coincided with the very time when the wealth of the New World began to reach her shores. The permanent gain from the treasure went rather to such countries as Holland and England, which were able to employ it productively as capital for industrial, commercial, or agricultural development. Spain thus acted as a huge sieve through which the gold and silver of America entered the other European countries.

**Colonial Wealth.** The Spanish colonists, occupying a region of enormous natural resources, could scarcely fail to prosper. Spaniards formed not more than a fifth of the total population, but they had most of the wealth. New Spain, in particular, became a country of private fortunes not equaled in Anglo-America during colonial times.

**City Life.** Spaniards in the New World, as in the mother country, manifested a great love of city life. While the English colonist expected to live on the land and derive his support from its cultivation with his own hands, the Spanish colonist intended to dwell in the town and to be supported by the labor of Indians, Negroes, or half-castes on the plantations or in the mines. Nearly all the white population of Spanish America was concentrated in the municipalities, which numbered as many as two hundred even before the end of the sixteenth century. The largest places at the close of the colonial era were Mexico City, Quito, Buenos Aires, and Lima. Spanish cities in most cases had an individual founder. He selected the site, marked out the street plan, and indicated the location for the central square (*plaza*), around which arose the church or cathedral, the town hall, the prison, and other public structures. The founder also appointed the members of the *cabildo*, or municipal council, but these in many cases were subsequently elected by the citizens.

**Transportation and Travel.** The Spanish settlements were seldom connected by good carriage roads. Transportation in the mountainous districts was usually on the backs of Indians or of mules, donkeys, llamas, and other pack animals. Heavy carts drawn by oxen served as vehicles in the lowland regions. As far as possible, use was made of water transportation in rafts, canoes, and small boats, and, on the larger rivers, in ships. Travelers journeyed by muleback or horseback, and sometimes in a kind of sedan chair borne by Indians. Stage coaches did not make their appearance until the last decade of the eighteenth century, and then at first only in Mexico.

**Overland Routes.** The two most important overland routes in South America ran from Buenos Aires to Santiago de Chile, and from Buenos Aires to Lima. The latter extended for over twenty-eight hundred miles across the plains and mountains. It was more used during the colonial era than any other long route in the southern continent, because of the Spanish regulations making Buenos Aires a closed port and thus compelling European goods to be imported from Perú. After the middle of the eighteenth century posthouses were established at intervals along the road, at which travelers might obtain horses and carriages. As early as the sixteenth century the Spaniards began to build a great metaled highway across Panamá. Others in Mexico, along the routes already marked by Indian trails, ran from Vera Cruz to the capital, thence to Guadalajara, the second largest city in Mexico, and thence over the mountains to San Blas, once an important seaport. A branch road also extended from Mexico City to Acapulco on the Pacific. These highways tapped the silver mining regions, facilitated the importation of Eastern luxuries from the Philippines, and also served for governmental purposes. The roads in the

Spanish borderlands had necessarily far less importance, but mention should be made of the "King's Road" (*El Camino Real*), which connected the Spanish missions in California between San Diego and San Francisco. It still remains the principal highway of the state.

**The Church.** The sixteenth century in Europe was the age of that revolt against the Roman Church called the Protestant Reformation. What she lost of territory, wealth, and influence in Europe was more than offset by what she gained in the New World. By 1800 the ecclesiastical organization of Spanish America included no less than six archbishoprics and nearly forty bishoprics. So much property accumulated in the hands of the Church that it became customary to estimate the importance of a town or city by the number of its ecclesiastical buildings.

**Church and State.** The close union between the altar and the throne, which existed in the mother country,[1] was extended to the colonies. The king of Spain nominated to the pope all the higher ecclesiastics, and retained for secular purposes one ninth of the tithes. He also added something to his income by the grants of indulgences. No papal bull might circulate in Spanish America without the royal authorization; no church, monastery, or hospital might be built there except in accordance with the royal ordinances; and every priest or monk who proposed to go there had first to obtain the royal license. Members of the religious orders usually went to the colonies at the king's expense and remained under his jurisdiction. The king meant that the clergy should loyally support the government, thus contributing their enormous influence to the maintenance and extension of Spanish rule.

**Ecclesiastical Control.** Except for the Indians, whom it treated with exceptional mildness,[2] the Church displayed as little tolerance in America as in Spain. The Inquisition as an organized body appeared in Perú and Mexico in 1570. It never had anything to do with the Indians, who were regarded as too childlike to be capable of heresy. Owing to the rigid oversight of all immigrants to the colonies, there was small scope for its activities among the Spanish population, so that foreign heretics, Jews, witches, sorcerers, and bigamists principally occupied the attention of the Inquisitors. The punishments were the same as in Spain — fines, confiscations

[1] See page 45.  [2] See page 97.

of property, exile, and in extreme cases death.  The tribunal also administered the censorship of the press and of books.  The aims and methods of the Inquisition are now widely disapproved, but were then common to all nations, to some degree, and in practice the Inquisition in America was milder than in Spain.  Censorship rules were rather laxly enforced.  Books and discussions clearly heretical or dangerous to royal control were suppressed, and scholars were made timid and unoriginal, but they managed to hear of most European ideas.

**Education.**  No system of popular education for all classes of the community existed in the colonies.  The Indians and half-castes as a rule remained illiterate, except for such religious and industrial training as they might receive from village priests or at the mission stations.  There were, however, some schools for native children and those of mestizos.  In fact, two of the earliest separate schools of America were founded in Mexico, 1523 and 1535, expressly for Indians.  Spanish children could attend elementary schools maintained nearly everywhere by the Church or municipalities, and could later pass to colleges, which prepared for the universities.

**Universities.**  Two dozen institutions of higher learning, modelled upon the best Spanish universities, existed in Spanish America in the colonial era.  The university reputedly founded at Santo Domingo in 1538 probably dated in fact only from 1558, but in 1551 Charles I decreed the foundation of universities at Lima and Mexico City.  In 1613 the Jesuits established the University of Córdoba in the Argentine city of that name.  Similar institutions were afterward set up in Santiago de Chile, Caracas, and other provincial capitals.  They offered courses in theology, civil and canon law, medicine, literature, philosophy, and music, chiefly for intending priests, lawyers, and physicians.  As in European universities of the Middle Ages, Latin formed the official language, and the instruction consisted almost entirely of lectures by the professors and disputations by the students.

**Scholarship.**  Colonial scholars made highly important contributions to knowledge in such fields as history, geography, anthropology, and linguistics, where they could work unhampered by the ecclesiastical censorship.  Study of the native languages, customs, traditions, and religions especially interested them, and their books on these subjects remain to this day standard authorities.[1]

**The Printing Press.**  The pioneer printing press in the New World was set up at Mexico City, probably in 1539.  Lima, Manila, Puebla, and Guatemala had one or more by 1700, and other cities later.  The output of printed matter in the colonies reached quite respectable proportions, considering the fact that every local printer had to be licensed and his publications censored.  It was not until the second half of the eighteenth century that periodicals regularly appeared in any of the colonies.

**Belles-Lettres.**  Plays, essays, and poems held a conspicuous place among the lighter forms of literature.  Perhaps the most important literary monument of the colonial era is the epic *La Araucana*, composed by Alonso de Ercilla, and published between 1569 and 1590.  This soldier-poet took for his theme the wars of the Spaniards with the Araucanians of Chile, in which he had fought.  The vivid descriptions and excellent style of the work still secure for it many readers.

**Painting, Sculpture, and Architecture.**  The Spanish colonists brought to the New World the artistic sense which the Church had cultivated in Spain.  Naturally, both painting and sculpture dealt chiefly with religious subjects.  Not only copies, but even the originals, of works by Spanish, Flemish, and Italian masters found their way across the ocean.  Architecture especially flourished.  The rich viceroyalties of New Spain and Perú contained many fine public buildings and monuments, while few important places lacked stately cathedrals or churches.  Private residences, though unpretentious, were often very attractive.  Usually, they consisted of one-storied or two-storied flat-roofed structures, grouped around cool, secluded courtyards (*patios*) and opening on the street through a wide doorway.  Architects of the United States have now begun to appreciate both the charm and the utility of the Spanish American style of architecture, which is so

---

[1] Important ones included: Bernardino de Sahagún, *Historia general de las cosas de Nueva España* (for the Aztecs); Diego de Landa, *Relación de las cosas de Yucatán* (for the Mayas); and José de Acosta, *Historia natural y moral de las Indias* (dealing with both Mexico and Perú).  The mestizo Garcilaso de la Vega, who was educated in Spain, published in 1609 his very valuable *Comentarios reales qui tratan del origen de los Yncas*.

well adapted to the clear atmosphere, brilliant sunshine, and wide vistas of the southwestern states.

**The Old Régime.**  Enough has perhaps been said to afford some idea of the old régime in the Spanish colonies.  Society was here less democratic than in the English colonies.  Spain lacked the popular institutions of England, and the Spanish authorities endeavored to reproduce in America the aristocratic conditions which prevailed in the mother country.  To this end they created a colonial nobility, dispensed orders, decorations, and titles with a lavish hand, and discriminated against the Creoles with respect to all important offices in State and Church.  Economic hindrances to the formation of a democratic spirit appeared in the very extensive land grants to favored individuals, producing a form of feudalism, and in the *encomienda* system, a form of serfdom. And, as already explained, Spanish society, made up of Europeans, Americans of European ancestry, African Negroes, and Indians, combined a great variety of antagonistic elements, whose union in a practical democracy was for the time being impossible.  The task of combining them began with the era of independence in the nineteenth century;  the task is not yet completed.

*     *     *

**Brazilian Institutions.**  The life and institutions of Brazil closely resembled those of Spanish America, but just as there were differences between Portugal and Spain in Europe, so there were in America.  Brazil afforded no basis for the brilliant but costly colonial culture and governmental pomp of Spanish America, and long offered no temptation for Portugal to dissipate her energies on American affairs.  That was especially true in the sixteenth century, when the Portuguese trading empire in Asia absorbed all the men and ships of so small a nation to infinitely greater profit than could be found in sugar and tobacco plantations.  In the early seventeenth century the Dutch and English took over nearly all of Portuguese Asia.  After that, Brazil seemed more valuable and received more attention, but had to wait for the eighteenth century mining era to approximate the life of Spanish America.  Even then conditions remained more like those of the Spanish American outlying provinces than like those of the great metropolitan centers.  The high development of European refine-

THE CATHEDRAL OF MEXICO CITY

The plan is that of a Greek cross, with two naves, three aisles, and twenty side chapels.

*Courtesy F. E. Fanger, Mexico City*

ments of life never appeared in Brazil as in Spanish America, though wealth and luxury vastly increased.  It is, however, worth noting that Brazil, like Argentina, Chile, and Uruguay, may in the long run have benefited from the relative neglect.  Her life had been less distorted by Old World control, and her upper class had a little more self-reliance than in some of the centers of Spanish American culture.

**Portuguese Administration.**  The ideas of Portugal as to how to handle colonies were the same as those of Spain.  It was a matter of course that colonies existed to benefit the mother country.  Rigid regulation of the whole life from the center of the Empire and mercantilism and monopoly were basic principles. They simply were practiced less thoroughly than by Spain — sometimes for good and sometimes for bad, from any given viewpoint.  During the sixteenth century Portugal had no specialized mechanism for controlling Brazil, except an inspectorate of American finances.  Counterparts of Spanish governmental agencies entered Portugal during the Spanish domination.  This resulted in a Treasury Council for the empire absorbing (1591) the work of the Brazilian inspectorate, and a Council of the Indies (1604) taking over supervision of all the Portuguese colonies.  When Portugal regained her independence she changed the name to Overseas Council (*Conselho do ultramar*) in 1641, but continued its use.

**Population.**  The Portuguese mingled freely with the aborigines and also with the Negroes.  The Indian element was relatively smaller, and the African element relatively larger, than in Spanish America.  The Indians were never as numerous as in the favored Spanish areas, and their exploitation was hardly opposed until the seventeenth century.  From that time, Jesuits like Antonio de Vieira sincerely endeavored to protect them, and got aid from royal legislation but could achieve little against universal colonial desires and official venality.  As a result the Indians of the coast had fled to the interior or died before the end of the sixteenth century, and later slaving raids against them failed to satisfy colonial demands.  Negro slaves were brought in increasingly during the first century.  Their importation rose enormously in the eighteenth century as a result of the opening of the mines and after the great Portuguese minister Pombal had issued edicts (1754) freeing the Indians and giving them the same rights as the Portuguese. By 1800 Negroes outnumbered the whites twenty to one in Bahía, but were much less numerous in the south.

**Economic Conditions.** Brazil started as an agricultural colony. Industrious Jews, fleeing from Portugal to escape the Inquisition, introduced the cultivation of the sugar cane. Sugar, together with dyewoods, long formed the major exports of the colony. Tobacco, cotton, and especially coffee became in time important crops. The exploitation of the country's mineral wealth was delayed until the eighteenth century. In spite of the large production of gold and diamonds, mining in Brazil never assumed the importance which it always held in Spanish America. The Portuguese government drew a considerable income from Brazil. Taxes on the output of the mines, the proceeds of the royal monopoly of brazilwood, duties, and excises produced in the eighteenth century an estimated revenue of $10,000,000 a year. Colonial commerce labored under much the same restrictions as in Spanish America, including the use of a fleet system ("caravans") or monopolistic companies from the days of Spanish domination. But these restrictions were applied loosely. Ports and number of ships were more nearly adequate, foreign contraband was less guarded against, and in the seventeenth century England and the Netherlands forced the grant of some legal access to Brazilian trade. Manufacturing, except locally in small wares for lower class use, hardly existed. This may have been due in part to the adequate supplies from overseas, since more rigid trade regulation in the eighteenth century was accompanied by some rise in manufacturing. That in turn was soon crushed by law.

**Religious Life.** The Portuguese Crown had the same general control of Church offices and finances in America as had the Crown of Castile. Into the bargain the Brazilian clergy, finding the tithes insufficient for support in the early days, surrendered them to the Crown in return for salaries. This continued after the growth of colonial wealth, leaving the Church impoverished and lacking influence. In spite of many exceptions, in neither the settlements nor the missions were the clergy of as good type as in Spanish America. Outstanding events were the entry of the Jesuits in 1549, establishment of the first bishopric in 1552, and expulsion of the Jesuits in 1760 as part of the struggle of Church and State in Europe. The Jesuits had formed the great exception to the low type of clergy. Their missions had been conscientiously administered, they conducted most of the colleges, and their departure was a greater blow than it had been in Spanish America.

**Intellectual Life.** Everywhere, in the era under discussion, the Church was the mainstay of intellectual life. Probably as much because of the character of the Brazilian Church as because of the colony's semifrontier conditions, intellectual life remained on a low plane. Even colleges (secondary schools) were few, and no university or printing press existed. Men had to go to the University of Coimbra in Portugal for their higher education, and scholars in Brazil found severe handicaps when they wished to publish. The Crown made sincere and partly successful efforts to improve educational opportunities in Brazil late in the eighteenth century; many men did go to Coimbra; and a fair number of poets and essayists, and some historians, proved ornaments to Portuguese literature. Many of them showed the influence of American environment, but the important anthropologic, linguistic, or scientific work of the Spanish Americans had no counterpart among Brazilians of the colonial era.

**Political Conditions.** Portugal never constructed an administrative machine for Brazil comparable in complexity and rigidity to that which Spain developed for her American colonies. As previously noticed, the Portuguese government introduced the system of feudal principalities, or captaincies, but soon appointed a governor-general to control the captains-donatory. Their power steadily decreased as time went on, and by the end of the eighteenth century royal governors had displaced the feudal proprietors, not only in the twelve original captaincies, but also in the five new ones which had been established as the result of Portuguese expansion along the coast of Brazil and into the interior. The governors, in charge of separate provinces, were to some degree under the oversight of the royal viceroy at Rio de Janeiro. The Portuguese administration seems not to have been very oppressive, and in local matters the colonists always enjoyed a good deal of liberty. Discontent with the rule of the mother country never became so pronounced in Brazil as in Spanish America.

## Words and Phrases You Should Know

asientos
audiencia
cabildo
captain-general
Council of the Indies
Creoles
Destruction of the Indies
encomienda

favorable balance of trade
fiestas
fleet system
hacienda
House of Trade
Laws of the Indies
mercantile theory
mestizos

mita
mulattoes
padre
presidios
romerias
"royal fifth"
viceroy
zambos

## Questions You Should Be Able to Answer

1. How civilized were the natives in America in comparison with Orientals whom the Spaniards expected to find here?
2. Do you think that the *encomienda* system was any better than slavery for the Indians?
3. Why did contact with the white man cause the Indian population to decline?
4. How did the Church seek to better the condition of the Indians?
5. Why was Negro slavery introduced into Latin America? How extensive was it?
6. What intermixtures of races were there in Spanish America?
7. Why did the Spanish government not encourage migration to America?
8. Why was there no middle class in Spanish American society?
9. Explain why the Spanish government did not attempt to lessen the friction between Creoles and peninsular Spaniards.
10. What is meant by the statement that Spanish colonial government was absolutist in character?
11. In what ways was the absolute power of the viceroy checked?
12. What were some of the defects of Spanish colonial government?
13. Why did Spain refuse to allow any but Spaniards to trade with her colonies? How did Spain even restrict trading by her own merchants?
14. "The Spanish government, without the income from the mines, might not have been able to maintain the empire which the Conquistadors had won." Explain.
15. Why did Spain fail to become prosperous even though she received so much gold and silver from her colonies?
16. How would you compare the attitude of a Spanish and an English colonist in regard to farming?
17. In what ways was the Church influential in Spanish America?

18. How would you compare the attitude of the Portuguese government toward Brazil with the Spanish attitude toward Latin American colonies?

## Projects and Activities

1. Write an essay on Spain's treatment of the Indians.
2. Prepare a brief oral report on what the missionaries did for the Indians.
3. Work out a comparison of Spanish and English colonial practice concerning (a) Indians, (b) slavery, (c) racial mixture, (d) immigration.
4. "Spain, as other imperial powers have done, followed the policy of *divide et impera* . . ." Enlarge upon this statement.
5. Construct a chart or diagram illustrating how Spain governed her colonies. Be prepared to explain your work to the class.
6. Using a textbook in American history, compare English and Spanish colonial government.
7. "Politics became entirely a business matter, a private business matter." Explain this statement.
8. Construct a diagram or draw a pictorial map to illustrate how trade with the Spanish colonies was operated.
9. Compose a dialogue between two Spanish merchants who are discussing the difficulties that confront them in trading with Spanish America.
10. By means of a chart compare farming, manufacturing, and mining in Spanish America and in the thirteen English colonies.
11. List the ways in which the king of Spain obtained his royal revenue from the colonies.
12. On a map of Latin America trace some of the overland routes used for trade and travel.
13. On a map of Latin America indicate by brief legends some important developments in education, printing, and literature.

# CHAPTER V

# Latin American Independence

**The Yoke of Spain.** The Spanish colonial system, described in the preceding chapter, had never been designed or operated in the interest of the colonists. Inevitably, they grew restive under laws and regulations which favored the mother country as against her dependencies. The Chinese Wall of commercial restrictions, which Spain had erected around the colonies, began to collapse in the eighteenth century, through the growth of smuggling, the occasional concessions made to foreign traders, and the reforms introduced by the enlightened Charles III. Nevertheless, Spanish Americans were still required to confine most of their export and import trade to Spain, and they were still subjected to other forms of economic exploitation, such as the government monopolies. Politically, the colonists had a great grievance in the preferential treatment accorded to peninsular Spaniards. It was only in the *cabildos* (municipal councils) that the Creoles had a prominent or controlling share in the machinery of local government. Because of some sporadic uprisings on the part of the colonial-born population in the last decades of the eighteenth century, the Crown adhered more strictly than ever to the policy of keeping the higher offices in the hands of natives of Spain. The fact is significant, in this connection, that every important revolutionary leader was a Creole.

**Enlightenment.** The new ideas that grew in Europe from the seventeenth century were by no means barred from the Hispanic empires. They were less prevalent in that of Portugal than in that of Spain, and fright over the French Revolution caused increased restrictions, but generally speaking the so-called "Enlightenment" was welcomed. The ideas of such innovators in philosophy and science as Descartes, Locke, Newton, Leibnitz, and their eighteenth-century followers became commonplaces in the schools and on the printing presses. They taught that man must not blindly accept the authority of Aristotle and the Church, but must seek truth by his own observation and deduction.  Books by men who applied such methods to politics or religion were usually banned, but circulated nevertheless.  Though a long time would be required for liberal doctrines to affect the mass of the people, in both Spanish America and Brazil they became the norm among many upper-class leaders.

**Example of the United States.**  The stirring story of the American Revolution and the foundation of a great republic based on democratic principles reverberated in the Spanish colonies.  French translations of the Declaration of Independence and Spanish translations of the Constitution of the United States soon found their way south into Mexico, New Granada, and Chile, often by contraband traders.  Belgrano, one of the revolutionary leaders in La Plata viceroyalty, exalted Washington as a hero "worthy of the admiration of our age and of the generations to come."  Washington's *Farewell Address*, which Belgrano translated, formed his favorite reading.  The example of the United States also led to the adoption of the federative system of government in the first republican constitutions of Mexico, Central America, Venezuela, Chile, and other countries.

**Influence of France.**  Even before that *annus mirabilis*, 1789, some Spanish Americans of the intellectual class had become acquainted with the writings of Montesquieu, Voltaire, Diderot, Rousseau, and other French philosophers, whose ideas fell like rain upon the parched soil of the old régime.  A Spanish version of Rousseau's *Social Contract* enjoyed a wide circulation, thus spreading abroad the new gospel of popular sovereignty and the rights of man.  The colonists not only read French books, but also watched with growing interest the progress of the Revolution in France, and after their own struggle for independence began they imitated its procedure.  "Liberty, Equality, Fraternity" became watchwords of the Spanish Americans; the liberty cap, their emblem; and the masonic lodges, their Jacobin clubs.  France, as well as the United States, gave them lessons in liberty.

**Foreign Intrigues.**  Ever since the sixteenth century, when the "sea dogs" began to prey on the Spanish treasure fleets, the English and French had sought to destroy Spain's monopoly in the New World.  During the eighteenth century, as a means to the same end, they began to foment revolt, though the French position as an ally of Spain prevented overt acts during most of that era. The Napoleonic Wars brought vigorous British aggressions in the colonies, since Spain made an alliance with Napoleon. In 1797 Britain conquered Trinidad, thus securing a strategic position for trade. In 1805 Nelson destroyed the allied sea power at Trafalgar, permitting a prompt attack on the Plata. Though the Spanish viceroy fled, the inhabitants of Buenos Aires and Montevideo rallied to defend their country, and drove out the invaders.

**Colonial Unrest.** Throughout the century, riots, conspiracies, and revolts had shown widespread colonial dissatisfaction with details of the Spanish régime. Toward the very end, a few men thought also of independence, but they were exceptional. Until 1808 British propaganda from Trinidad or in the Plata, or efforts by the occasional colonial hothead, met no response.

**Napoleon's Intervention in Spain.** Then, in 1808, the event happened which furnished the immediate cause of the Spanish American Revolution. Napoleon Bonaparte, at war with Great Britain, had devised the so-called Continental System for the commercial strangulation of his great rival. Every European country under French control was to exclude from its ports British ships and British goods. The effort to extend the Continental System brought about Napoleon's intervention in Spain, then ruled by Charles IV. This weak and corrupt king and his incompetent son, Ferdinand VII, were speedily persuaded or compelled to renounce their claims to the Spanish throne, upon which Napoleon seated his brother Joseph. The Spaniards, however, would not accept the new sovereign so rudely thrust upon them. They rose in arms and created juntas, or local councils, to govern in the name of Ferdinand VII and carry on the national struggle against the French.

**Colonial Loyalty.** The upheaval in Spain produced an extraordinary situation in the Spanish American colonies. Both peninsular Spaniards and Creoles refused to recognize Joseph Bonaparte, "the intruder king" (*el rey intruso*), and proclaimed their adherence to Ferdinand. But in general the Americans rejected the authority of self-constituted juntas in Spain. Instead, the *cabildos* of the provincial capitals proceeded to set up juntas after the Spanish model. These bodies professed at first to uphold the rights of Ferdinand VII and to govern in his name. But there had always been men of more radical ideas, who now could freely talk, and opposition by the Spanish juntas angered many Americans.  As time went on, and Spanish Americans tasted the sweets of liberty, the juntas became revolutionary governments, with the avowed intention of severing the ties which joined the colonies to Spain.

**The Wars for Independence.**  1809 to 1810 saw risings throughout Spanish America, though only trivial ones in Perú, Central America, and the Antilles.  The wars which now began continued in one part or another of Spanish America for a decade and a half, until in 1826 the Spanish flag was finally lowered on the American continents.  The United States followed the struggle with sympathy and finally sent commissioners to establish commercial relations with the revolutionists.  Great Britain took a more practical interest in them, contributing money, ships, and munitions, and allowing her own subjects to enlist in the patriot armies.  In spite of foreign aid, the contest was long and desperate.  The patriots in the different provinces were too far apart for common action.  They had to overcome the passive resistance of the great body of the people, who saw little importance in a change of masters; their own inexperience and jealousies; and active opposition from royalists, including government officials, large landowners, and the higher clergy — all the people, in fact, who desired the perpetuation of the existing régime.  After the downfall of Napoleon and the return of Ferdinand VII to his throne in 1814, the Spanish king sent as many as twenty-five thousand soldiers to the colonies to put down the revolt.  In 1816 only the Platine areas were still free of Spain.  But the cruelties of the Spanish and loyalist armies, and "Ferdinand's folly" on ascending the throne, raised a desire for independence where it had not existed.  After 1816 one heard no more of loyalty from the American groups.

**Francisco de Miranda.**  The precursor of South American independence was Francisco de Miranda, a native of Venezuela.  His enthusiasm for freedom led him first to North America to serve against the British in the 1780's, and then to France, where he fought in the armies of the French Revolution.  Napoleon once remarked of him, "The man has sacred fire in his soul."  Miranda also lived for some time in London, on terms of intimacy with the younger Pitt and other British statesmen, whom he in-

terested in the cause of the colonials. In 1806 he led two expeditions to the Venezuelan coast. Both failed because of popular
indifference and upper-class hostility, but they made Miranda a
hero of independence.

**Miranda in Venezuela.** Four years later Miranda again re-
turned to Venezuela, after the leading citizens and the *cabildo* of
Caracas had deposed their captain-general and had set up a junta.
Most of the provincial cities followed the example of the capital

city. Largely as a result of Miranda's activity a revolutionary
congress in 1811 proclaimed the
independence of Venezuela. This
was the first formal declaration of
the sort to be made by any of the
Spanish American colonies. The
congress also framed a federal constitution, showing in its clauses
the influence of both the United
States Constitution and the French
Declaration of the Rights of Man.
But genuine popular support of
these measures did not exist, and
dissensions between Miranda and
his associates weakened their cause.
The republic quickly collapsed and
Miranda, left behind when his companions fled, died in a Spanish
dungeon.

FRANCISCO DE MIRANDA

**Simón Bolívar (1783–1830).** The task which Miranda laid down
was taken up by his youthful lieutenant Bolívar. The scion of a
wealthy Creole family of Caracas, educated in Madrid, a student
of the French philosophers, witness in Paris of some of the last
scenes of the Revolution, a traveler in the United States, where
he had an opportunity of observing free institutions in operation,
Bolívar devoted his life and fortune and splendid talents to the
cause of independence. He was both warrior and statesman, able
to organize legions, direct great campaigns, draft laws, and lay
the foundations of republican rule in all the northern part of South
America. Besides winning freedom for Venezuela, Bolívar assured

it for what are now Colombia, Ecuador, and Bolivia, and contributed powerfully to the freedom of Perú. Five nations hold him in grateful remembrance as the Liberator.

**The Revolution in New Granada.** After the overthrow of the first Venezuelan republic Bolívar offered his sword to the revolutionists of New Granada, who in 1813 had declared the independence of the viceroyalty from Spain. Bolívar's campaigns in this region during the next six years revealed his dauntless leadership, which overcame all difficulties — not only the fierce resistance of the royalists, aided by reinforcements from Spain, but also the rivalries and jealousies of the various revolutionary juntas. More than once the patriots were reduced to a few guerrilla bands, while Bolívar himself had to seek refuge in the West Indies. During the later stages of the struggle, he owed much to the services of the "British Legion," veterans of the Napoleonic wars, who were hired by Bolívar's agents in Europe. The battle which liberated New Granada (except the district of Quito) from Spanish domination was fought at Boyacá in 1819. Bolívar followed up his success by overthrowing the royalists of Venezuela in the battle of Carabobo (1821).

SIMÓN BOLÍVAR

A medallion by David d'Angers, 1832.

**"Great Colombia."** These two victories created an independent republic in South America. The former viceroyalty of New Granada and the captaincy-general of Venezuela came together in the republic of Colombia, usually called "Great Colombia" to distinguish it from the smaller state of that name which subsequently emerged. Bolívar served as its first president. The territory of the new republic was soon enlarged by the addition of the Quito district (modern Ecuador). The insurrection there had failed until Bolívar and his lieutenant, José de Sucre, appeared with reinforcements from Colombia. The battle which gave independence to this part of South America was won by Sucre in 1822, on the slopes of the volcano Pichincha, overlooking the capital city of Quito.

**The Revolution in La Plata.** Meanwhile, an active revolutionary movement had been in progress since 1810 in the viceroyalty of La Plata. It began when the Creoles of Buenos Aires deposed their Spanish viceroy and established a central junta to carry on the government, in the name of Ferdinand VII. The pretence of affiliation with Spain was slowly abandoned. A patriotic congress met at Tucumán in 1816 and adopted a declaration of independence for the "United Provinces in South America." Comprehensive though the expression was, it applied in fact mostly to the area of present-day Argentina. The congress contained no representatives from the intendancy of Paraguay or from the *Banda Oriental*, the region lying between the Uruguay River and the Atlantic Ocean. These two districts finally established themselves as independent republics, that of Paraguay under Dr. José Gaspar Rodríguez Francia. For the time being, the efforts of José de Artigas in Uruguay resulted only in the area being taken over by Brazil, after an involved struggle with Argentina and Artigas.

JOSÉ DE SAN MARTÍN

**José de San Martín (1778–1850).** San Martín was the hero of the south. Of aristocratic lineage, the son of a Spanish captain in the viceroyalty of La Plata, San Martín received a military education in Spain and served there with distinction in the national struggle against Napoleon. News of the uprising in Buenos Aires caused him to return to his native land, where he soon became prominent. A great general, though personally less brilliant than Bolívar, San Martín showed himself equally devoted to the cause of independence. He liberated Chile from Spanish rule and began the liberation of Perú.

**Liberation of Chile.** A revolt had started in Santiago de Chile, as in other South American capitals, upon the deposition of Ferdinand VII. It was soon crushed by the Spanish authorities, who sent down an army from Lima. The Chilean patriots, in-

cluding the valiant Bernardo O'Higgins, son of a former Irish governor of Chile, were obliged to flee across the Andes to Mendoza. Here they joined San Martín, who had conceived the bold plan of first ousting the royalists from Chile and then of proceeding against the stronghold of Spanish power in Perú. Aided by O'Higgins, San Martín collected, drilled, and equipped the mixed force of Argentines and Chileans which formed the "Army of the Andes." When all was ready,

BERNARDO O'HIGGINS

San Martín led his soldiers over the mountain passes, 13,000 feet above sea level — a feat equal to Hannibal's or Napoleon's crossing of the Alps — and fell like a thunderbolt upon the enemy. The victory of Chacabuco (1817) placed the nationalists once more in control at Santiago de Chile. The royalists, who still held the region south of the capital, were subsequently defeated in the great battle of Maipú (1818). These successes not only gave independence to Chile, but also put new life into the patriotic cause throughout Spanish South America.

**Liberation of Perú.** The viceroyalty of Perú, rich, populous, and strongly garrisoned with Spanish troops under great viceroys, formed the heart of the Spanish resistance to the revolution. It lay like a huge wedge thrust between the two independent areas in the north and in the south. The attack on the viceroyalty was launched in 1820 by the patriots of the south. San Martín embarked his brave troops on ships supplied by the British admiral, Lord Cochrane, and landed unopposed near Lima. The Spaniards evacuated the capital without a blow, preferring to make a stand in the mountainous region of the interior. Entering Lima, San Martín proclaimed Peruvian independence and took over the reins of government. His cautious military preparations and known monarchist theories aroused suspicions. Deciding that he could do no more, he advised his men to join Bolívar, who was advancing from the north, and resigned. A united army of Colombians, Peruvians, Chileans, and Argentines won the battles of Junín and Ayacucho (1824), one under Bolívar and the other under Sucre, sealing the fate of the Spanish régime.

MIGUEL HIDALGO

**Upper Perú.** Bolívar and Sucre, after these victories, marched into the region of Charcas, or Upper Perú. This part of South America declared itself in 1825 an independent state, independent alike of Spain, Perú, and the United Provinces of La Plata. The new republic, in honor of the Liberator, took the name of "Bolívar" — afterward Latinized into Bolivia — and its capital, Chuquisaca, was rechristened Sucre.

**The Revolution in New Spain.** The revolution in Mexico, which began like those of other regions, soon took another character. Its leader, Miguel Hidalgo, an able but somewhat visionary priest, had long been interested in improving the Indian status. At first the revolt showed promise of success, but it was joined by so many Indians that it soon became virtually a war of Indians against whites. White supporters abandoned the cause. The numerous but ill-equipped and worse disciplined rebels were defeated. Hidalgo and later his successor Morelos were captured and shot. Guerrilla warfare in the outlying provinces under men like Guerrero smoldered on, and six years later furnished a basis for success. The second phase began after a revolution had broken out in Spain against the despotic Ferdinand VII. This time rebellion in Mexico enjoyed the support of the whites, especially of the peninsular Spaniards, who feared that the Spanish liberals, now supreme in the mother country, would curtail their privileges. Matters came to a head when Augustín de Iturbide, a Creole officer in the vice-roy's army, conceived the idea of uniting both whites and Indians in a common resistance to Spain. The idea found expression in the so-called "Plan of Iguala" (1821), which proclaimed Mexican independence and drew out a sketch of a provisional government.

**The Mexican Nation.** The intention was to set up in Mexico a constitutional monarchy separate from the Spanish Crown and ruled by Ferdinand VII himself, or, if he declined the honor, by some other Bourbon prince. The Cortes of Spain refused to sanction the arrangement. Thereupon Iturbide "allowed" his soldiers to choose him as Emperor, and the Congress had to ratify their choice. In 1822 he assumed the title of Augustín I. This first Mexican Empire had lasted less than a year before a republi-can insurrection forced Iturbide to abdicate and seek refuge in Europe. He ventured to return a few months later, but upon landing was seized and executed. The Mexican Congress now took steps to reorganize the government. A federal form of republic, with a written constitution, was adopted. Guadalupe Victoria, one of the leaders in the revolt against Iturbide, became in 1824 the first president of the United Mexican States.

**The United Provinces of Central America.** The five districts composing the captaincy-general of Guatemala achieved a blood-less revolution. Spain had no troops in this part of the New World, and the captains-general had retained office since 1810 by accept-ing colonial advice. When the Americans decided to declare their independence (1821), the captain-general peacefully left. The Central American states formed a part of Mexico during the brief reign of Iturbide, but regained their autonomy upon the downfall of that emperor. In 1823 Guatemala, Honduras, Salvador, Nica-ragua, and Costa Rica combined to form the United Provinces of Central America.

**Foreign Recognition.** The wars for independence were not over before both the United States and Great Britain decided to recog-nize the new Spanish American republics. This was done by the United States as respects Mexico, Colombia, Chile, and La Plata in 1822–1823, and at a later date as respects the other countries that had won freedom. Great Britain took similar action in 1825–1826. Meanwhile, the Monroe Doctrine had been promulgated by the United States. Support by Great Britain, for her own interests, removed the danger believed imminent that the reactionary European powers might intervene in Latin America and aid Spain to reconquer her colonies.

**Spain and Spanish America.** The surrender, in January, 1826, of the garrison occupying the Peruvian fortress of Callao left no more Spanish troops on the American continents. The revolution was a *fait accompli*. Nevertheless, many years passed before the government of Spain consented to acknowledge the independent status of its former colonies. Mexico, the first Spanish possession on the mainland, was the first to receive recognition by the mother country (1836). Others sometimes waited half a century. The bloody, protracted struggle had made deep scars, which only time could heal.

**The Spanish American Republics.** By 1826 Spanish America included eight republics. Their boundaries roughly coincided with those of the political divisions on the eve of the revolution. The United Mexican States and the United Provinces of Central America corresponded to the viceroyalty of New Spain. "Great Colombia" coincided with the viceroyalty of New Granada. Perú and Chile once formed the viceroyalty of Perú. Bolivia, the Argentine, Uruguay, and Paraguay once composed the viceroyalty of La Plata. The fact that both Guatemala and Chile had formerly been captaincies-general, and the existence of colonial *audiencias*, also had influence in forming the boundaries of the several states.

**Napoleon's Intervention in Portugal.** The revolution in Brazil, like that in Spanish America, was linked with European events. The little kingdom of Portugal had been a commercial ally of Great Britain for over a century. When Napoleon, pursuing the will-o'-the-wisp of his Continental System, demanded that all Portuguese harbors should be closed to British ships, Dom John, the Prince Regent,[1] refused to obey. The French emperor thereupon signed a secret treaty with the Spanish government providing for the partition of Portugal. A large army of French soldiers

---

[1] Son of the demented Queen Maria I.

and Spanish auxiliaries entered the country in 1807. They moved so rapidly that the Portuguese had no time to organize an effective resistance.

**The Flight to Brazil.** The government sought safety in flight to its great transatlantic possession. Just as the invaders were about to enter Lisbon, a Portuguese fleet, bearing the Prince Regent and other members of the royal family, together with many nobles and officials, sailed from the Tagus and proceeded to Rio de Janeiro. The seat of the Portuguese government was thus transferred to the capital of the viceroyalty of Brazil.

**Reorganization of the Brazilian Viceroyalty.** The inversion of the political relationship between Brazil and Portugal, whereby the former became the dominant state and the latter the dependency, had important results. The Prince Regent immediately abolished the old commercial policy and threw open the Brazilian ports to the trade of all friendly nations. He issued a decree which removed the restrictions upon industrial undertakings, established a national bank and royal mint, built roads, fostered schools, libraries, and scientific institutions, and encouraged foreigners to settle in the country. Such beneficial reforms infused new energy into what had been a stagnant land.

**The Movement toward Independence.** The spectacle of the Spanish American struggle for liberty could not but awaken a desire for independence among patriotic Brazilians. The Prince Regent realized this fact, and in 1815 he went so far as to proclaim the colony of Brazil a kingdom, with the same political status as the mother country. The next year, upon the death of Queen Maria, he himself became king of Portugal and Brazil, with the title of John VI. The Brazilians, nevertheless, remained dissatisfied. They had no more offices than before, taxes rose to pay for the better institutions and the Portuguese court, and merchants were ruined by the foreign competition. Republican propaganda became active, and there occurred a serious revolt in 1817. Discontent increased as a result of the events of 1820 in Portugal. Here a revolution had overthrown the regency governing the country after the removal of the royal family to Brazil. The Portuguese liberals demanded the establishment of a limited monarchy and the return of John VI to reign over them as a constitutional sovereign. As for Brazil, the Lisbon Cortes proposed

LATIN AMERICA
AFTER THE WARS FOR
INDEPENDENCE (1826)

to reduce it once more to the level of a colonial dependency.  The movement in favor of autonomy consequently became almost universal in Brazil, as even thoroughly loyal men saw the loss of the better position that Brazil had achieved.

**Brazilian Independence.**  King John decided to accept the invitation of the revolutionists and nominated his son Pedro to be Regent of Brazil.  Just before sailing for Portugal the king said to him, "Pedro, if Brazil is to separate itself from Portugal, as seems likely, you take the crown yourself before anyone else gets it." Pedro, a popular figure among the Brazilians, followed the paternal advice.  In 1822 he proclaimed Brazil an independent state and assumed the title of constitutional emperor.  It was impossible for Portugal, with a smaller population and perhaps less wealth than Brazil, long to oppose this action.  The Portuguese government accepted the inevitable, and three years later recognized Brazilian independence.

### Words and Phrases You Should Know

| | |
|---|---|
| "Army of the Andes" | liberal doctrines |
| "British Legion" | "Liberty, Equality, Fraternity" |
| "enlightenment" | popular sovereignty |
| "Great Colombia" | "United Provinces of South America" |
| junta | "United Provinces of Central America" |

### Questions You Should Be Able to Answer

1. What economic and political grievances caused many Spanish Americans to become restless under Spanish rule?
2. What events in the United States and in France in the eighteenth century influenced Spanish American leaders?
3. What ideas from France were popular in the Spanish colonies?
4. How do we know that Spanish American leaders were familiar with our Constitution?
5. In what way were Spanish Americans influenced by the career of George Washington?
6. How did the Napoleonic wars in Europe contribute to the overthrow of Spanish rule in America?
7. How long did the wars for independence in Spanish America last?
8. In what ways did the United States and England show their sympathy for the revolutionists?

9. What were some of the difficulties that confronted revolutionary leaders in Spanish America?
10. What experiences of Miranda and Bolívar made them both fighters for independence?
11. In what way did Miranda pave the way for Bolívar?
12. How would you compare the work of Bolívar and San Martín?
13. Which Latin American patriot or patriots would you compare with George Washington?
14. What evidence can you give to show that not all Mexican revolutionists were republicans? Which group was successful, monarchist or republican?
15. Why were the United States and Great Britain so much interested in the Spanish American republics?
16. What was the attitude of Spain toward her former colonies after they became independent?
17. What action did the Portuguese government take when Napoleon invaded Portugal?
18. What is your opinion of King John's attitude toward Brazilian independence?

## Projects and Activities

1. Construct a time line on which you show the outstanding events in the Spanish American wars for independence.
2. Prepare imaginary newspaper headlines for several of the events in the Spanish American struggle for independence.
3. On a map show the activities and successes of several of the revolutionary leaders.
4. Prepare a chart showing the work of the Spanish American revolutionary leaders. Use these headings: Leader; Places Where He Fought; Results of His Work.
5. Outline the steps by which Brazil became independent of Portugal.

# CHAPTER VI

# South America

**The New States.** South America, at the close of the wars for independence in 1826, contained six Spanish-speaking states. They were "Great Colombia," Perú, Chile, Bolivia, the Argentine Confederation, and Paraguay. The year 1828 saw the secession of Uruguay from Argentina and Brazil, and the year 1830, the break-up of "Great Colombia" into Colombia, Ecuador, and Venezuela. The nine states thus formed have continued in existence until the present day.

**Republics, not Monarchies.** Many Creole leaders of the revolution, realizing that only a strong government could save the new states from internal dissensions and military despotism, were monarchists. They regarded constitutional monarchy as the best strong government for people of political inexperience. Belgrano, San Martín, Sucre, and others wished to see "tempered monarchy" established in various countries. But republics and not monarchies were created. The people did not distinguish between the absolutism of a Ferdinand VII in Spain and the liberal rule of an English sovereign. Monarchy seemed to them slavery, republicanism seemed to them freedom. It is probable, indeed, that no lasting dynasties could have been founded in South America. The objections to monarchy were summed up by Bolívar in the following cogent sentences: "No foreign prince would accept as his patrimony a principality which was anarchical and without guarantees; the national debts and the poverty of the people leave no means to entertain a prince and a court, even miserably; the lower classes would take alarm, fearing the effects of aristocracy and inequality; the generals and the ambitious of every stamp could never support the idea of seeing themselves deprived of the supreme command; the new nobility, indispensable to a monarchy, would issue from the mass of the people with every species of jealousy on the one hand and of pride on the other. No one could patiently endure such a miserable aristocracy, steeped in ignorance and poverty and full of ridiculous pretensions."

**The Constitutions.** As the United States was virtually the only important republic, the states naturally adopted many features of the United States Constitution. But French ideology was also highly popular and better known, and British influence may also be seen. Other provisions bore the impress of colonial customs and the old Spanish régime. All the constitutions were liberal documents. They had much to say, in the language of the first ten Amendments to the Constitution of the United States and the French Declaration of the Rights of Man, about liberty, justice, and the indefeasible privileges of citizenship.

**Parties.** There were usually two basic parties under various names. Conservatives and Clericals would set up limited suffrage, reserve the offices for the aristocracy, maintain Roman Catholicism as the established religion, and exclude other faiths. Liberals and Radicals demanded universal suffrage, disestablishment of the Church, and other reforms in the modern spirit. Those who advocated giving the provinces much local autonomy were called Federalists, whereas Centralists favored a unitary or centralized system, subordinating the provinces to the national authority. Centralists were commonly, but not always, liberals as to social policy.

**Political Inexperience.** Too often party struggles degenerated into the quarrels of factions. The people, indeed, were not ready for democracy. The Creoles, who carried through the revolution, lacked political experience. Spain had not given to them, as England had given to her North American colonists, provincial legislatures, town meetings, county courts, and religious assemblies in which the laity bore a part. Under the rigid sway of the Council of the Indies, the South American colonists learned to obey their superiors, both civil and ecclesiastical, but not to govern themselves. As for the ignorant Indians and half-breeds, who composed the mass of the population, they were citizens only in name and without any ambition to take part in public life.

**Militarism.** Fifteen years or more of almost constant warfare had developed among the people military habits, a contempt for the arts of peace, and a willing resort to the sword for settlement of disputes. There was, after all, no tradition of the more peaceful technique of "counting heads" to see which side had the more adherents. Obviously, therefore, the machinery of popular government could not operate with any real success.

**Revolutions and Civil Wars.** These things being so, the inevitable happened. One state after another lapsed into a condition of chronic disorder. The insurrections against the government received the dignified name of "revolutions," as if some great political principle had been at stake; they were rather squabbles between the "outs" and the "ins" for office and the rewards of office. Nor were they usually protracted, sanguinary struggles involving the entire population of a country. Only small armies followed a revolutionary leader, and a very little bloodletting generally sufficed to decide whether he would become the new president or face a firing squad.

**Dictatorships.** The military chieftain (*caudillo*), who reached the presidential chair, posed as the "regenerator," "restorer," or "liberator" of his afflicted country. In truth, he was a dictator, the real successor of the Spanish viceroy or captain-general, but without the sense of responsibility and legal restraint of either. He ruled by force. If he ruled badly or made himself otherwise unpopular, by force he was overthrown. The dictator usually preserved constitutional forms. The citizens went through the farce of electing a president, but his soldiers controlled the elections. Legislators continued in session, but they passed only such laws as pleased him. Judges still sat on the bench, but they did his bidding. Not all these presidential despots were selfish, wicked men, intent only on enjoying ill-gotten gains. Some of them accomplished a great deal for the material prosperity of the countries over which they held sway. Their strong hands preserved internal order and prevented aggression from without. It may be plausibly argued that, until the people were ready for democracy, a wise and kindly, but firm, dictatorship formed the only practical method of government. A few men like Bolívar had foreseen this and argued for a "lifelong presidency." Most had to learn by dearly bought experience.

**Tropical Handicaps.** Revolutions, civil wars, and dictatorships characterized the history of nearly all the states for a half century after independence, and these conditions have lasted till the present in certain tropical countries. The population in those areas is largely of Indians, mestizos, and Negroes, untrained for the responsibilities of citizenship and ill-adapted to life by the standards of the small, white, ruling class. European immigrants and

European capital alike avoid these countries, where the climate (except as modified by altitude and coastal currents) is enervating and political conditions are so unsettled. The temperate-zone states — Chile, Argentina, Uruguay — with an invigorating climate, a population more white than colored, and a constant influx of foreign capital and foreign immigrants, have made by far the greatest advance in democratic government during the past fifty years.

**Greater Colombia.** The republic which Bolívar founded and over which he ruled as president lasted little more than a decade. Dissensions began almost at once. The highly liberal constitution (1821) and later laws, especially those tolerating Protestantism and restricting the place of the Church, aggravated the troubles, but their immediate causes were regional and personal jealousies. Venezuela and Quito disliked location of the capital in distant Bogotá. Men like Páez of Venezuela disliked the fact that a Colombian, Francisco de Paula Santander, was vice-president and therefore ruler during Bolívar's absence. Santander, though able and well meaning, added to their irritation by dictatorial conduct. When Bolívar hurriedly returned from Perú and attempted to patch up the rifts, he was himself suspected of planning tyranny and perhaps monarchy. The Liberator died, brokenhearted, in December, 1830. Before then Venezuela and Quito, or Ecuador, had set up as independent states.

**Colombia.** The remaining area was reorganized as the republic of New Granada, a name later changed to Colombia. The nation started with good resources and a truly cultured upper class, but in addition to the handicap of tropical population conditions, it suffered a serious geographic split. It is still hard for men living on its seacoasts to see eye-to-eye with men hundreds of miles away on a plateau a mile and a half above sea level. It was nearly impossible with the primitive communications of a century ago. Civil wars and dictatorships long marked the nation's history, but it is noteworthy that revolts were not usually successful in changing officeholders, and frequently had a basis of principle.

**First Half Century.** The first constitution (1832) called for a centralized government. It was operated at first by men like Santander (1832–1836) and Tomás Cipriano Mosquera (1845–1849) who came to be called Conservatives, but would properly be called Moderates.  In spite of some trouble over arbitrary rule and the anticlerical aspects of policy, fair order was maintained. Steamships were introduced, the Panamá railroad was started, antislavery laws were passed, and education and the National Library received attention.  Religious toleration was established and some restrictions were laid on the clergy.  In 1849, partly as a repercussion of the European reform movements of 1848, the Conservatives split and control passed to the Liberals.  Their great program of legislation emphasized anticlerical laws that ended clerical privileges in 1851.  Scholarly work, road building, cattle breeding, and crop improvements were not forgotten.  A new constitution and its amendments (1853–1858) established freedom of the press and manhood suffrage, and disestablished the Church. It also made the States nearly independent of each other.  Grave disorders and civil wars followed.  Decentralization had gone too far, and much of the liberal program went too fast.  The clerical question especially created bitterness not previously felt.  Economic and intellectual retrogression set in, and even many Liberals finally deserted the party.

**Conservative Régime.**  In 1884 the Conservatives regained control, and kept it for nearly a half century.  Though the change resulted in general from the difficulties of the preceding years, it centered about the work of Rafael Núñez, a former Liberal and near Socialist.  Service as president during the turbulent years of 1880 to 1882, and travel thereafter in Europe, convinced Núñez that Colombia needed strong government, and that a strong Church must be the backbone of such a government.  Reëlected president in 1884, he succeeded in having a new constitution adopted in 1886.  This provided for a completely centralized government, with a president for six years whose large powers included even some legislation.  Religious toleration was provided, but the Roman Church was established and education was required to be in harmony with its teachings.  Núñez ruled firmly until his death (1894), and he and other Conservative presidents gave Colombia more peace than had the Liberals.  But the peace was marred by constant Liberal revolts, and by the terribly destructive civil war of 1899 to 1903.

**Territorial Problems.**  Practically from 1830, Colombia had disputes with Central America, Venezuela, Perú, Ecuador, and

Brazil as to her proper boundaries. These disputes had become serious enough to unsettle domestic politics by the later nineteenth century, and were not finally settled until well into the present century. In spite of some unfortunate violence, most of them were decided by arbitration, and Colombia fared well enough in the decisions. Her dispute with Central America centered about the boundary of Costa Rica. This was eliminated by the loss of Panamá. The old province of Panamá had resented the loss of its autonomy, and it suffered more severely than other parts of the nation during the civil war of 1899–1903. Its hopes of restored prosperity through the digging of a canal were dashed when the Congress refused to ratify a treaty leasing the Canal Zone to the United States. On November 3, 1903, local leaders proclaimed an independent republic. On November 6 the United States recognized the republic, and on the eighteenth it signed a canal treaty with the agent of the new government. There is doubt as to United States responsibility for starting the revolt, but the local leaders unquestionably expected the United States to preserve them from harm, and United States forces did forbid the passage of Colombian troops to attack the rebels.

**Peace and Reconstruction.** Exhaustion from the war, and the shock of losing Panamá, developed a desire for peace that overcame some of the former political bitterness. A minority representation law (1906) and later amendments to the constitution provided a basis for peaceful rule. Under the excellent presidents Rafael Reyes (1904–1910) and Carlos Restrepo (1910–1914) and their successors the country settled down. Economic consolidation was aided by the $25,000,000 paid by the United States (1922–1926) as compensation for Panamá, and by the development of banana and oil industries. Prosperity and peace were accompanied by a program of public improvements, with emphasis on education.

**Venezuela.** The early history of Venezuela centers about the dominating personality of General Páez, who had been a lieutenant of Bolívar. Páez became the first president of Venezuela and furnished strong but not dictatorial guidance for many years. As in Colombia, the early government was Conservative in name but moderate in policy. Páez and his contemporaries gradually restricted the power of the Church, aided economic development, established the national library, and extended civil rights, though they were less interested in education than were their Colombian contemporaries. But partisanship increased, and from about 1850 what had been merely occasional revolts became nearly constant turbulence. The troubles centered about the rise of a tendency to complete dictatorship, and efforts by a new group of rulers to establish a federal form of government. The latter was achieved in the constitution of 1864.

The Dictators. Real dictatorship arrived with Antonio Guzmán Blanco, who held the supreme power from 1870 to 1889. Guzmán Blanco evaded the constitutional prohibition against reëlection by putting a henchman in office between his two-year terms, and ruling through him. He was a "benevolent despot." In spite of many faults, to him Venezuela owed orderly government, completion of the anticlerical campaign, free primary education, reformed law codes, an excellent monetary system, roads, railways, and telegraph lines, and other improvements. By 1889 he realized that his day had ended, and he settled in Paris. Except for four good years under Joaquín Crespo (1894–1898), it was nearly a half century before Venezuela again had a government satisfactory to her men of good ideals. One of the worst type of dictators, General Cipriano Castro (1899–1908), involved the country in serious international difficulties. He refused to pay debts owed by Venezuela abroad or to make compensation for losses suffered by foreign investors in its industries. Warships of Great Britain, Germany, and Italy blockaded the Venezuelan coast in 1902–1903. Castro took shelter behind the Monroe Doctrine and appealed to the United States to intervene. President Roosevelt advised the allied powers that no permanent seizure or occupation of territory in Venezuela would be permitted. At his suggestion the dispute was referred by mutual consent to mixed tribunals for arbitration. A few years later Castro picked a set of fresh quarrels with foreign countries. Both France and the United States broke off diplomatic relations with Venezuela, and the gunboats of Holland instituted another blockade of its ports. Juan Vicente Gómez, who overthrew Castro, governed Venezuela in person or through puppets until his death in December, 1935. He repressed bandits, built roads, and otherwise fostered the material improvement of the country. He paid the whole foreign debt, had oil produced without surrender to foreign capital, and distributed some land.  But corruption was appalling, political opposition was brutally crushed, and intellectual and other freedoms became nonexistent.

**Ecuador.**  The "Republic of the Equator," with numerous paper constitutions (eleven between 1830 and 1906), insurrections and counterinsurrections, and dictatorships, has been a particularly unfortunate state.  It is not easily accessible, and its people are nearly all Indians or half-castes.  Its history has been complicated by its weakness compared to its neighbors, but most of the events of its early history were focused about a contest for control between General Juan José Flores and Vicente Rocafuerte. Though liberalism and especially anticlericalism were involved, principles seem to have mattered less than personal ambitions. So far as anyone had control from 1845 to 1860, the Liberals were in power and — perhaps unjustly — they and liberalism were discredited by the complete collapse of Ecuadorean prosperity and government.  In 1860 Gabriel García Moreno, disgusted with years of anarchy, tried to remedy conditions by establishing a conservative régime and subjecting the State entirely to the Church.  García Moreno was able, energetic, and fanatically honest, and achieved much temporarily.  But his clerical devotion and his general methods aroused bitter resentment, and he was assassinated in 1875.

**Last Half Century.**  Anarchy followed the death of García Moreno, but the Conservatives retained most of what control existed until 1895.  In that year the Liberals acceded to the power, and have retained it since.  Eloy Alfaro and Leónidas Plaza between them ruled from 1895 to 1916, and have been succeeded by other men, such as Isidro Ayora (1926–1931), of a distinctly better type than those of the earlier days.  The new constitution of 1897 and later legislation again deprived the Church of its favored position.  Considerable interest has been shown in railroads, education, public health, and even the abolition of some parts of the evils of Indian status.  But dictatorship has remained the only form of government that permits continued peace and action in reforms, however mild it has become under the better presidents. A large part of the territory originally claimed by the republic has been acquired by its neighbors, in a long series of boundary settlements.  An agreement on the dispute with Perú was reached by delegates of the two countries at Rio de Janeiro, January, 1942, and the agreement was ratified later by both sides.

**Perú.** Perú faced somewhat the same difficult conditions of national life, at the start of independence, as did Ecuador. The results were equally unfor-

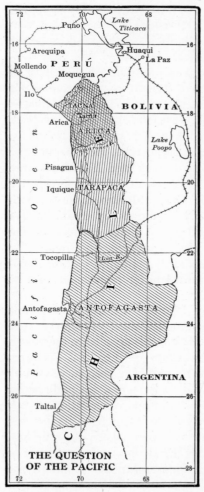

THE QUESTION OF THE PACIFIC

tunate. Personal rivalries, impractical constitutions, boundary disputes and the seizure of Perú by Santa Cruz of Bolivia (1836–1839) kept the country in turmoil until 1844. From then until 1862 Ramón Castilla, as virtual dictator, restored order and aided the prosperity of the country. Later men, though often personally of good quality, were less able to maintain order, but made some further advances in economic development. The greatest setback to the progress of Perú resulted from her participation in the "War of the Pacific" (1879–1884), as an ally of Bolivia against all-powerful Chile. The Peruvians were defeated on sea and land, and Lima was occupied by the victorious Chileans. By the Treaty of Ancón, Perú ceded to Chile the province of Tarapacá outright, and further allowed the victor to occupy the provinces of Tacna and Arica for ten years, when their final ownership should be decided by a majority vote (plebiscite) of the inhabitants. This plebiscite was never taken, but after years of wrangling the two countries, with the good offices of the United States, settled the question by treaty in 1929. Since then, Chile has owned Arica, and Tacna belongs to Perú. At the opening of the twentieth century Perú seemed to have passed beyond the stage of military dictatorships, but as late as 1919 a *coup d'état* installed Augusto B. Leguía, a business man and former president.

**Bolivia.** Upper Perú, freed from Spanish rule by Bolívar and Sucre, began in 1825 its career as an independent republic. Bolívar prepared the first constitution and Sucre served as the first president. Repeated revolutions and dictatorships have characterized Bolivian history. Except for the strong rule (1829–1839) of the able and not unenlightened Andrés Santa Cruz, little of permanent importance occurred. José Ballivian (1841–1847) did about all that could be hoped for in such troubled times, but the work of these earlier men was more than offset by the type of man who mostly succeeded in gaining office. One of the worst dictators of all American history, Mariano Melgarejo (1864–1871) was probably insane. His bloodthirsty revenges occupied five years of his rule, and he thought to perpetuate himself to posterity by coining *melgarejos* in his own honor. In fact he perpetuated himself in his country's history by selling at public auction many of the Indian communal lands, increasing what had already been appallingly wretched living conditions. By 1898 a real Liberal party had emerged and took control. Under such men as Ismael Montes (1904–1909) some advances have been made between the more troubled eras.

**The Bolivian Boundaries.** Bolivia's foreign relations have resulted nearly as unhappily as have her domestic struggles. Her position among more powerful neighbors, when coupled to lack of peace and unity at home, has been disastrous. The War of the Pacific was even more injurious to her than to her Peruvian ally. She relinquished to Chile the entire department of Atacama, a territory rich in nitrate deposits and containing her only seaports. Bolivia thus became a landbound state, without an outlet through her own territory to the ocean.[1] Boundary disputes with Brazil over the rubber-producing districts of Acre were finally settled in 1903 by their cession to the Brazilian government, in consideration of a cash indemnity of $10,000,000. More recently she lost

[1] Chile, however, has completed a railway from the port of Arica to La Paz, over which Bolivia enjoys the perpetual right of commercial transit.

most of her serious claims to lands at the headwaters of the Plata River, in the Chaco War with Paraguay and the consequent treaty of 1938. Despite these losses, Bolivia remains a large state, including a large area in the rich but undeveloped region east of the Andes.

**Paraguay.** The district between the Pilcomayo River on the west and the Paraná on the east formed in colonial times a separate intendancy of the viceroyalty of La Plata. As the republic of Paraguay it became independent of Spain in 1811. Dr. José Francia, an able, cruel, and capricious dictator, ruled Paraguay from 1811 until 1840. Chief executive, chief legislator, chief judge, and head of the Church, Francia deserved the title of *El Supremo* which his terrorized subjects conferred upon him. During his dictatorship — the longest in South American history — Paraguay remained entirely aloof from the rest of the world. No one might enter the country and no one might leave it. This policy kept Paraguay quiet and led to somewhat improved economic conditions, but was disastrous as a whole. Francia was followed as dictator by his nephew Carlos López and the latter by his son Francisco. The younger López, a despot without a single redeeming feature, aspired to be the Napoleon of southern South America. In 1865 he precipitated the Paraguayan War, in which Paraguay fought singlehanded against Brazil, Argentina, and Uruguay. It lasted until the death of López in 1870. In the course of this frightful struggle Paraguay lost at least half of its total population — almost all the men and boys capable of bearing arms, besides thousands of women, who fought in the ranks. No country in modern times has come nearer to annihilation than Paraguay. The war ended the rule of the Francia-López dynasty and prepared the way for constitutional government. Paraguay necessarily took so long to recover from the effects of the López régime, and has suffered so many difficulties from its landlocked situation, that conditions are still unsettled. But the investment of foreign capital in meat packing and other industries, together with the completion of a railroad between Asunción and Buenos Aires, has done much to break down the traditional seclusion of the country, and advances are being made toward better conditions for the common man in spite of much political instability.

**Chile.** The history of Chile affords a striking contrast to that of the backward states. Chile almost from the start has been a constitutional republic, rarely disturbed by revolutions and civil warfare. Its orderly development may be due in part to many natural advantages: a temperate, healthy climate; a remarkably long coast, which puts every part of the country in touch by sea with every other part and with the outside world; and (in the south) an extensive, fertile, well-watered area admirably adapted for agriculture and stock raising. Chile has also been favored in its population. A good deal of pure Spanish blood survives from earlier days, and the mestizos, the most numerous class, are unusually sturdy, industrious, and intelligent. Furthermore, the long struggle with the Indians and the necessity for hard, continuous work, because of the absence of precious metals, no doubt helped to produce in the Chileans the hardy character that distinguishes them among South Americans.

**The Chilean Constitution.** The captaincy-general of Chile, freed from Spain by the victories of San Martín and O'Higgins, started out as an independent republic in 1818. O'Higgins ruled it, virtually as a dictator, for the next five years. His administration aroused much hostility, which culminated in an uprising and his enforced resignation. The Liberals, who now came into power, could not keep order; one weak government followed another; and Chile promised to relapse into the chaotic condition of the neighboring states. From this the country was rescued by the Conservatives — clergy, businessmen, and great landowners — under the leadership of Diego Portales. The Conservatives in 1833 promulgated a new constitution, which, with some modifications, remained the organic law of Chile until 1925. It set up a strong but aristocratic government, concentrating authority in the hands of a few leading families.

**Internal Development of Chile.** Peace and order once assured, Chile began to be a prosperous country. The consolidation of the foreign debt, regular payment of interest, and foundation of several banks improved its financial condition. The working of coal mines, building of railways, erection of telegraphs, and establishment of steamer lines along the coast and to Europe fostered its industries. Schools, libraries, and other agencies of popular education were also promoted by the government, which, if not democratic, was animated by a progressive spirit.

**Civil War in Chile.** Political conditions in Chile remained generally tranquil for nearly sixty years after the Conservatives came to power. The Liberals, as time went on, recovered much of their influence, and dominated national politics from 1861. They were distinctly of the aristocratic class, but advocated many social reforms, such as a widening of the suffrage, the separation of Church and State, attention to popular education, and extensive public improvements. Rapid progress was made in all these matters, though temporarily halted by the Balmacedist War. The Chilean Congress, since the time of Portales, had practically controlled the president by the requirement that his cabinet should be supported by a congressional majority. José Manuel Balmaceda, an honest, able, but inflexible president, wanted to make the members of his official family independent of the legislative branch, as in the United States; the Congress believed that he wanted to set up a dictatorship. The parliamentary contest finally became a civil war (1891), with the two chief cities, Santiago and Valparaíso, backing Balmaceda and the country districts upholding Congress. Bloody conflicts took place by sea and land for six months. The Balmacedists at length capitulated, and their leader committed suicide.

**Chilean Politics.** The failure of Balmaceda and his followers meant that the Chilean president continued to be dependent upon a Congress which represented not the whole people, but an oligarchy of leading families. The country gentry, who held large estates, thus managed to keep the government in their own hands. The peasants were usually content to be guided by their landlords in political matters and, if allowed to vote at all, voted as directed by them. This system doubtless helped to make Chile the most stable of Spanish American states, but stability was purchased at the cost of democracy.

**Expansion of Chile.** The republic added largely to its territory during the latter part of the nineteenth century. The northern boundary, which originally was drawn at the parallel of 24° south latitude, was pushed up to 18° south latitude by the "War of the Pacific." By the treaties of 1884 Chile acquired title to Atacama,[1] at the expense of Bolivia, and to Taracapá, at the expense of Perú, together with control of the Peruvian provinces of Arica

[1] Now included in the Chilean province of Antofagasta.

and Tacna. The former province, as was explained above, she kept by the final settlement of 1929. Not less notable has been the southern expansion of the republic beyond the River Bio-bio, into the forested region once held by the Araucanian Indians. The boundary in this direction was finally carried to Cape Horn by a treaty in 1881 with Argentina, providing for the partition of Patagonia. The two countries agreed to divide the island of Tierra del Fuego between them and to declare the Strait of Magellan a neutral, unfortified waterway, open to the ships of all nations.[1] Chile retained both shores of the strait, control of which seems hardly less essential to her national security than is the control of the Isthmus of Panamá to the United States.

**Argentina.** First in size, first in population, and first in wealth among the Spanish republics of South America, Argentina possesses both the natural resources and the population necessary for the development of a great democratic state. Her pampas, a vast area of pastoral and arable land, her many navigable streams, her long coast line, and her climate, temperate and equable except in the tropical north and the frigid south, provide the basis of material prosperity. She has the further advantage of being inhabited by white men, chiefly the descendants of Spanish and Italian immigrants. Indians and mestizos are far fewer than in any other Latin American state. The proportion of non-Caucasian blood probably does not exceed five per cent for the nation as a whole. Racially, no people in the New World, except the Canadians, are so European as the Argentines.

**The Argentine Constitution.** Argentina arose in 1816 out of a union of the interior provinces of La Plata viceroyalty.[2] Two political parties, or factions, soon appeared in the republic. The Centralists favored a centralized form of government; the Federalists stood for the idea of a loose confederation of self-governing provinces. Their antagonisms often gave rise to armed struggles. The usual dictators came to the front, the most remarkable being Juan de Rosas (1829-1852), whose tyrannical nationalistic rule led to his being styled the "Robespierre of South America." After the expulsion of Rosas the Argentines adopted a federal constitution in 1853 modeled upon that of the United States, and designed to harmonize the conflicting political tendencies in the republic.

[1] See the map on page 64.   [2] See page 131.

This constitution has continued to be the fundamental law of Argentina.

**Argentine Politics.** The people of Argentina since 1853 have accustomed themselves more and more to constitutional methods of government. They slowly realized that economic prosperity depended on political stability, for only settled conditions would attract the foreign capital and foreign laborers needed for the development of the country. There were still parties in Argentina,

DOMINGO FAUSTINO SARMIENTO

but their leaders tended more and more to be lawyers instead of soldiers. At first, the province of Buenos Aires refused to join the Confederation of 1853, but was forced to do so in 1860. The first two presidents thereafter, Bartolomé Mitre (1862–1868) and Domingo Faustino Sarmiento (1868–1874), rank among the greatest statesmen of Latin America. Their successors, though less notable, were mostly good men, and Argentine politics became relatively free from the turmoils of civil war. Arms yielded to the gown, rhetorical *pronunciamientos* of would-be dictators gave way to calm discussion of public questions in newspapers and on the platform.

**Prosperity and Learning.** Internal peace was accompanied by notable economic developments. Transportation facilities expanded in all directions, the rich land of the southern Pampas was cleared of Indians and opened to agriculture, and Argentine wheat and beef rose to a major place in the world market. Great numbers of immigrants, chiefly from Italy and Spain, added desirable elements to the population. General education was much fostered by the "Schoolmaster President" Sarmiento, though the later and more aristocratic administrations did little to aid it as to schools for the masses. Nevertheless, literacy became more common than in most Latin American countries, and a brilliant *intelligentsia* developed among the upper class, with excellent universities, museums, and libraries, and notable scholars in many fields.

**Expansion of Argentina.** The Argentina of today contains, besides the federal district of Buenos Aires, fourteen provinces and ten territories. These last are the extensive but thinly settled areas in the northern and southern parts of the country. As the outcome of the Paraguayan War, Argentina acquired additional territory on the left bank of the Paraná River and on the right bank of the Paraguay River. The treaty of 1881 with Chile confirmed Argentina in the possession of most of Patagonia, a region whose climate is less severe than used to be believed and whose resources in forests and minerals, as well as in fertile land, are by no means inconsiderable. The Falkland Islands, which at one time had been included within the viceroyalty of La Plata, are naturally claimed by Argentina, but since 1833 they have been occupied by Great Britain.

**Uruguay.** A war between Argentina and Brazil for control of the old *Banda Oriental* ended in 1828, through the mediation of Great Britain. The republic of Uruguay, the smallest in South America, arose as a buffer state. It was formally constituted in 1830. Control was contested by the *Colorados* or liberals and the *Blancos* or conservatives. Partisanship was bitter to an unprecedented degree, and Uruguay lapsed at once into chronic disorder, for the conflicts of parties at the polls were generally transferred to the field of battle. This situation lasted all through the nineteenth century, though 1868 marked the start of slightly better things. On the whole the Colorados won, being far the more numerous. In 1904 the opposing factions made peace, discontinued their feuds, and began to take an interest in good government rather than in revolution. The history of Uruguay since then has been marked by economic prosperity, the beginnings of really democratic government under a unique constitution, extension of education, and a program of social welfare that has caused Uruguay to be regarded as an outstanding example of experimentation in that field. So far as one man can have the credit, these things were the work of President José Battlé y Ordóñez (1904–1908, 1912–1916). Under his influence, the state entered upon ownership of public utilities, banks, factories, and even pleasure resorts, and adopted a new constitution in 1918. This was especially notable for its division of power between the president and an elected National Council of Administration.

**Brazil.** The Spanish countries of South America, having secured independence, passed abruptly from the status of colonies to that of republics, though not yet fitted for self-government. No wonder, therefore, that revolutions, civil wars, and dictatorships marked their history during the greater part of the last century. Brazil, on the other hand, has been more nearly exempt from such disorders, not because the country was better fitted than its neighbors for self-government, but because historical accident was fortunate enough, and its leaders were wise enough, to set up an hereditary, constitutional monarchy, which steered the middle course between anarchy and absolutism.

PEDRO II

**Pedro I, Emperor of Brazil.** The youthful Pedro I mounted the throne in 1822, as "Constitutional Emperor and Perpetual Defender" of Brazil. He did not long remain popular. His subjects expected republican realities under the forms of monarchy; they found, instead, that their new ruler wanted to be a real king. "I will do everything for the people, but nothing through the people," he said. Dissatisfaction grew steadily. Abdicating in 1831, Pedro went to rule Portugal, leaving a five-year-old son to succeed him in Brazil.

**Pedro II, Emperor of Brazil.** A regency carried on the government until 1840, when Pedro II became emperor. He reigned until 1889, the last monarch in America. A kindly, unostentatious, enlightened gentleman, Pedro II was that rare phenomenon, a philosopher on the throne. He always acted in a constitutional manner, choosing his ministers alternately from Liberals and Conservatives, as one party or the other commanded a majority in the popular branch of the legislature. The emperor, however, took less interest in politics than in the welfare of his people. Brazil at this time moved rapidly forward. The extension of railroads and telegraphs, the growth of commerce, the increase of the imperial revenues, the influx of European immigrants, the multiplication of public schools, and, finally (in 1888), the complete abolition of slavery showed that the country was beginning to assume its rightful place among the great nations of the world.

**Revolution in Brazil.** Pedro II sometimes called himself the best republican in his dominions. At any rate he never really combated the movement in favor of a republic, which gathered strength as the years went by. Opposition to the monarchy was directed less toward the emperor himself than toward his daughter, heiress to the throne, whom the people suspected of absolutist tendencies. The emancipation of the slaves, without any compensation to their owners, also provoked great discontent among the powerful class of planters. Minor quarrels had meanwhile alienated the Church. In 1889 the agitators at Rio de Janeiro, having won over the garrison there, proclaimed Brazil a republic, placed the emperor and his family on shipboard, and sent them to Portugal.

**Republican Brazil.** The change from monarchy to republic did not mean much in substance, for the emperor had exercised very little power. Brazil received in 1891 a new constitution setting up a federal union of the former provinces, which now became states. The constitution closely followed that of the United States, except that the powers of the federal government were more narrowly limited. Illiterates — the great majority of the inhabitants — might not vote. Their exclusion from the suffrage seemed particularly necessary in Brazil, where by an estimate of 1885 about one third of the population were whites or "passed for whites," the rest being Indians, Negroes, and half-breeds, who knew nothing of politics. The republic, therefore, could not be called a democracy. It was governed by the intelligent minority, not only landlords, as in Chile, but also business and professional men. Compared with most South American republics it was governed well, by civilians and by constitutional methods.

**Territorial Growth of Brazil.** The boundaries of Brazil in 1822 were those which had been laid down by the Treaty of San Ildefonso between Portugal and Spain.[1] Brazil also occupied the

[1] See page 91.

*Banda Oriental* as far south as the Plata River, but soon had to consent to the creation of the free and independent state of Uruguay.[1] The boundary between Brazil and her new neighbor remained undefined until 1851, when by treaty she gained title to an extensive region lying east of the Uruguay River. The Paraguayan War gave her a slice of Paraguay, and treaties with Bolivia, Ecuador, Colombia, and Venezuela considerably extended her frontiers on the west and the north. Brazil also acquired additional territory in the Guianas, as the outcome of disputes with Great Britain, Holland, and France over the limits of their colonies in this part of the New World. The United States of Brazil, as the republic is officially named, consists of twenty states, one national territory (Acre), and a federal district containing the capital city, Rio de Janeiro. With an area of about 3,275,000 square miles Brazil is exceeded in size only by the combined area of all the Spanish American countries in South America.

**Unitary and Federal Republics.** The republics which now exist throughout South America are either unitary or federal in type. Under the first come Colombia, Ecuador, Perú, Bolivia, Chile, Paraguay, and Uruguay; under the second come (to use the official designations) the United States of Venezuela, the Argentine Republic, and the United States of Brazil. In the unitary republics the political divisions are mere administrative departments, as in France, and their chief executive is ordinarily appointed by the national president. In the federal republics the political divisions are self-governing states,[2] comparable to the commonwealths of the American Union. Each elects its own governor and other officials, has its own judiciary, and makes its own laws in all matters not expressly reserved by the constitution to the nation as a whole. In Brazil, Venezuela, and Argentina there has been a decided trend toward the unitary type through presidential action, whereas Chile and Colombia have recently moved toward decentralization in their legal makeup. On the whole, it may be said that the French ideals have prevailed in the South American constitutions, rather than those of the United States or Great Britain.

[1] See page 155.
[2] Though in Argentina called provinces, and everywhere much interfered with by the central authority.

EXPANSION OF
BRAZIL

- - - - Line drawn between Brazil and Spanish-
America by Treaty of 1777, approximately.
— · — Present boundaries of Latin-American States.

**A** Territory secured by Brazil from Venezuela,
Treaties of 1859, 1905.

**B** Territory from Colombia, Treaty of 1907.

**C** Territory from Ecuador, Treaty of 1904.

**D** Territory from Bolivia, Treaties of 1867, 1903.

**E** Territory from Paraguay, Treaty of 1872.

**F** Territory from Argentina, arbitral award
of 1895.

**G** Territory from Uruguay, Treaty of 1851.

**Presidential and Parliamentary Systems.** All the constitutions establish executive, legislative, and judicial departments. The president holds office for varying terms: often four years, but five in Ecuador and Venezuela and six in Argentina, Brazil, and Chile. He is usually elected by popular vote, directly or through electors. Many constitutions forbid his reëlection or else declare him ineligible until the term of his successor has expired. The example of the United States has been followed in sharply separating the executive department from the legislature, thus providing for the presidential system of government. Only in Chile, and there in a modified form, did the parliamentary or cabinet system appear, until Uruguay in 1934 and Cuba in its constitution of 1940 approved it. In fact here, as in regard to the question of federal or unitary form, local conditions were stronger than any political theory. With rare exceptions, the only hope of obtaining good government lay in finding a good governor, and leaving him large power in the hope that the benefits would be greater than the abuses.

**The Suffrage.** The illustrious San Martín, who like Bolívar recognized the fact that the South Americans were not ready for democracy, favored a limited suffrage giving the vote only to the upper classes. This is what actually prevails in all the republics, except in Argentina, Chile, and Uruguay, which are so European in population. Indians and mestizos take little or no part in politics. They are most commonly excluded by an educational qualification for voting, as in Brazil, Ecuador, Paraguay, Perú, and Bolivia. Colombia has a combined educational and property qualification. Venezuela nominally provides for universal manhood suffrage, but the Indians never think of voting, and the mestizos, except in the few towns, seldom exercise their political privileges. The result is that in most of the South American countries the electoral body forms a small, sometimes a very small, proportion of the population. Where a virtual dictator has not established himself, there is class rule by a comparatively few persons who have enough intelligence to take an interest in public questions and enough property to feel a stake in the government. These countries, then, are either autocracies or oligarchies. They are not democracies. But a widespread aspiration for democracy and increased facilities for education have improved conditions, and the future is by no means unpromising.

**Party Organization and Practice.** Parties in South America, as in France, Italy, and other European lands, tend to break up into numerous groups, rather loosely organized, without very definite programs, and subject to constant fluctuation. Their struggles are often concerned rather with personalities or the spoils of office than with abstract political principles. The secret, or Australian, ballot is the exception and not the rule. Elections, therefore, are often conducted unfairly, and when fraud proves ineffective to elect a candidate, a resort to force may be looked for. On the whole, however, political corruption has declined and the general tone of public life has sensibly risen during recent decades, especially in the more progressive states.

**South American Nations.** The Spanish-speaking inhabitants of South America, under the rule of Spain, had one language, one king, one Church, and a common culture. They were essentially a single people. The revolt from Spain, with the political changes which almost immediately followed the era of independence, produced nine republics, and these are now so many distinct communities. Each has its separate government, its peculiar historical traditions, its own ambitions, aspirations, and ideals. Each has acquired an individuality, a distinctive character which marks it off, more or less sharply, from its neighbors. The same process went on in Brazil. There is nothing in history comparable to the creation of so many new nations over so enormous a region and in so short a time. The territorial limits of the (Spanish) republics were determined by the existence, during colonial days, of the various viceroyalties, captaincies-general, and intendancies; their boundaries naturally became those of the new states as well. Having secured freedom and definite frontiers, each people started to differentiate from its neighbors. Geographical isolation contributed largely to this result. Chile, for instance, is separated from Perú by a desert and from Argentina by a lofty mountain range. Paraguay dwells secluded in almost inaccessible forests. Colombia, Venezuela, and Ecuador are similarly cut off, one from the other, by physical barriers. Climatic differences, as seen in the contrasts between the tropical and the temperate countries, played an important part. Differences in occupations — compare the importance of mining in Perú and of pastoral pursuits in Argentina — have had their effect. Much stress should be laid on the presence or absence of a large aboriginal or Negro population, leading to greater or less racial mixture, and thus modifying, in different degrees, the white population of each country. How unlike, as respects their inhabitants, are Ecuador, with two thirds Indians and most of the rest half-castes, or Colombia, with over one third Negro or mulatto and most of the rest Indian or mestizo, from Argentina or Uruguay, over 85 per cent white. Differentiation has likewise been brought about as the result of revolutions and civil and foreign wars, which, whatever their other consequences, certainly fostered patriotic sentiments and thus strengthened the feeling of nationality. Lastly, increasing political stability, together with growing population, wealth, and power, has done much to induce a strong national self-consciousness. Several states now rank as nations in the fullest sense of the word. The others seem also destined to attain complete nationhood.

## Words and Phrases You Should Know

| | | |
|---|---|---|
| Balamacedist War | Declaration of the | limited suffrage |
| benevolent despot | Rights of Man | local autonomy |
| cabinet system | established religion | oligarchy |
| *caudillo* | federal republic | republic |
| Clericals | insurrection | universal suffrage |
| constitutional monarchy | Liberals | "War of the Pacific" |

## Questions You Should Be Able to Answer

1. Can you name the countries of South America?
2. How did San Martín and Bolívar differ in their ideas as to the best form of government for the South American states?
3. What did South American constitutions borrow from our Constitution?
4. Name the several political parties usually found in South American countries and tell what each believed in.
5. Why were the people in South American republics not ready for democracy, whereas the people in the English colonies in North America were?
6. What is the difference between an insurrection and a revolution? Why were there so many insurrections in South America?
7. Why were dictatorships so common in South America?
8. What did the Liberals in Colombia accomplish in the years before 1884?

9. Why did Panamá want to become independent of Colombia? How did the United States contribute to the establishment of Panamanian independence?

10. Why did Venezuela become involved in disputes with European nations on several occasions?

11. What conditions in Ecuador and Perú have made orderly government very difficult?

12. "No country in modern times has come nearer to annihilation than Paraguay," page 150. Explain why this was so.

13. In Chile, stability was purchased at the cost of democracy. Explain.

14. What advantages did Argentina have that enabled her to make great progress?

15. How would you compare the government of Brazil with that of the other South American republics?

16. In what way are South American constitutions more French than English or American?

17. Why do so few people vote in South American countries?

18. How do you explain the fact that there are twenty republics south of the Rio Grande and only the United States and Canada north of it?

## PROJECTS AND ACTIVITIES

1. List the objections to monarchy given by Bolívar. Be prepared to explain what each means.

2. The constitutions of the South American republics borrowed from the first ten Amendments to our own Constitution. Look up these Amendments in an American history book and plan to discuss their importance with the class.

3. "It may be plausibly argued that, until the people were ready for democracy, a wise and kindly, but firm, dictatorship formed the only practical method of government," page 142. Be prepared to uphold or object to this statement.

4. Work out a comparison of political parties and their beliefs in South America and the United States.

5. Compose newspaper headlines for the outstanding events in the history of one or more of the South American republics.

6. Prepare a biographical chart of leaders in the South American republics. Use these headings: Name; Country; Political Party; Method of Governing; Accomplishments.

7. Make a chart of boundary disputes in South America, showing how each was settled.

8. "The history of Chile affords striking contrast to that of the backward

states." List the backward states, and then list the ways in which Chile was a striking contrast to them.

9. Draw a diagram illustrating the system of government common in South American republics.

10. Let a committee construct a multiple time line illustrating the outstanding events in the history of the South American countries. Each member of the committee might be responsible for the events of one country.

# CHAPTER VII

# Mexico and Central America

**Character of Mexican History.**[1]  Mexico, like the other Spanish American states, secured independence from Spain only to enter upon a long period of disorder.  Counting regencies, emperors, presidents, triumvirates, dictators, and other rulers, the country had as many administrators during the first half century of its existence as the colony had viceroys throughout the whole era of Spanish rule.  Then came the long autocracy of Díaz, to be followed by fresh revolutions, the setting up of new governments, and almost continuous civil warfare.  The fundamental cause of the repeated upheavals must be sought in the economic and social conditions of Mexico, where privileged classes were opposed to the great mass of the population.  Ambitious military leaders exploited this opposition in their own interest.  The general instability of affairs was intensified by the extreme poverty of the peasantry, making the soldiers reluctant to return to civil life, and by the concentration of wealth in a few hands.  A revolutionary chief could usually be sure of obtaining not only the men but also the money required for his enterprises.  It needs also to be pointed out that Mexico, in common with the rest of Latin America, suffered from the absence of any large middle class, which might at least have served as a buffer between discordant factions, even if unable to weld them together into a society with common desires and aspirations.

**Political Turmoil.**  The downfall in 1823 of the first Mexican Empire of Iturbide (Augustín I) led in 1824 to the formation of the United Mexican States,[2] a federation of nineteen states and four territories.  Those Mexicans who hoped that a federal system would operate just as smoothly in their country as in the United States were soon undeceived.  Discord quickly arose between

---

[1] Most of the generalized comments at the beginning and end of the preceding chapter apply also to this one.

[2] See page 134.

Centralists and Federalists, the former representing higher ecclesiastics, great landowners, army officers, and other persons with monarchical leanings, while the latter stood for republicanism. According as one faction or the other triumphed at the polls or on the battlefield, the form of government shifted violently from federal to centralized and back again to federal. At the same time, the chief magistracy became the sport of rival generals or of politicians, with their hordes of hungry followers.

**Antonio López de Santa Anna.** The dominant personality in Mexican politics for three decades after independence was that of Santa Anna, who had first become prominent as the instigator of the rebellion against Iturbide. Without marked talent either as general or as statesman, nevertheless Santa Anna's energy, personal courage, and consuming ambition soon brought him to the front. His contemporaries likened him to the chameleon for shiftiness and to the tiger for cruelty. Elected president in 1833, as the candidate of the Federalists, he promptly switched over to the Centralists and put through a series of laws suppressing the state legislatures and converting the states themselves into mere departments of the national government. The federal system was thus reduced almost to a nullity.

**Independence of Texas.** The overthrow of the constitution by Santa Anna led in 1835 to the revolt of Texas.[1] The white population of this Mexican state consisted largely of colonists from the cotton-growing and slaveholding area of the American Union. They introduced Negro slavery into the country, even though it had been prohibited by Mexican law. Fearing the end of their political freedom and of slavery under the centralized government, the Texans soon rebelled. At first unsuccessful, they were nerved to desperate resistance by Santa Anna's massacre of his prisoners after capturing the Alamo Mission fort at San Antonio. "Remember the Alamo" became their battlecry. General Sam Houston in 1836 brought the struggle to an end by totally defeating the Mexicans at San Jacinto. Meanwhile, the insurgents organized a separate republic, whose independence was soon recognized by the United States and by several European powers. The Mexican government, however, refused to renounce its sovereignty over Texas.

[1] See page 85.

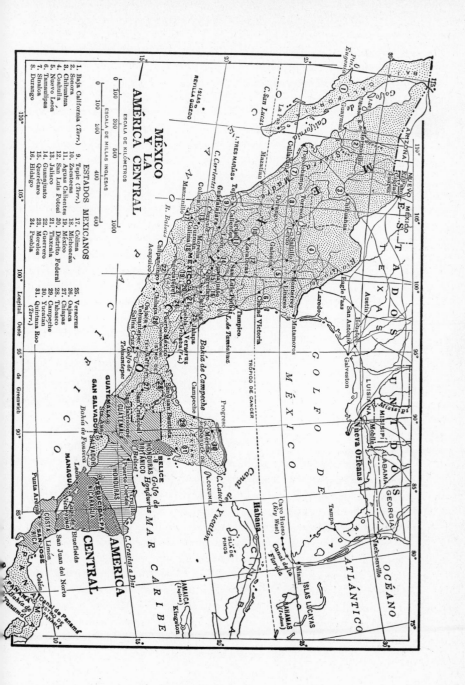

# MÉXICO Y LA AMÉRICA CENTRAL

ESCALA DE KILÓMETROS

0 — 100 — 200 — 300 — 400 — 500 — 600 — 1000

ESCALA DE MILLAS INGLESAS

0 — 100 — 200 — 300 — 400 — 500 — 600

### ESTADOS MEXICANOS

1. Baja California (Terr.)
2. Sonora
3. Chihuahua
4. Coahuila
5. Nuevo León
6. Tamaulipas
7. Sinaloa
8. Durango
9. Tepic (Terr.)
10. Zacatecas
11. Aguas Calientes
12. San Luis Potosí
13. Jalisco
14. Guanajuato
15. Querétaro
16. Hidalgo
17. Colima
18. Michoacán
19. México
20. Distrito Federal
21. Tlaxcala
22. Guerrero
23. Morelos
24. Puebla
25. Veracruz
26. Oaxaca
27. Chiapas
28. Tabasco
29. Campeche
30. Yucatán
31. Quintana Roo (Terr.)

**Origin of the Mexican War.** The citizens of the "Lone Star Republic" hoped for immediate annexation to their homeland, but antislavery agitation delayed this step for nearly a decade. Texas did not enter the American Union until 1845. According to the extreme boundary claims of the Texans, the new state reached southward and westward to the Rio Grande to its source and thence northward to the forty-second parallel; thus delimited, it even included a considerable slice of New Mexico. As a member

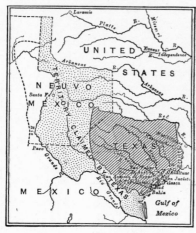

MAP OF THE REPUBLIC
OF TEXAS

Showing territory claimed by Texas.

of the Mexican federation, however, Texas had never reached farther south than the River Nueces. President James K. Polk determined to support the Texans and ordered United States troops to cross the Nueces and take up a position on the left bank of the Rio Grande. When these were attacked by the Mexicans, Polk sent a message to Congress stating that Mexico had shed American blood upon American soil. "War exists, and, notwithstanding all our efforts to avoid it, exists by the act of Mexico herself." Congress accepted the issue thus raised, and the conflict began in 1846.

**Campaigns of the Mexican War.** The United States at once took the aggressive. General Zachary Taylor drove the Mexicans across the Rio Grande, captured Monterey, and defeated Santa Anna decisively at Buena Vista. Meanwhile, Colonel (afterward General) S. W. Kearny started from Fort Leavenworth, occupied Santa Fe, the capital of New Mexico, and proceeded across the desert and mountains to San Diego. He found much of Upper California already in the possession of United States naval forces. The final blow was delivered by General Winfield S. Scott, who seized Vera Cruz and then, following closely the route of Cortés, fought his way inland and stormed the defenses of Mexico City. By the end of 1847 the conflict was over.

**Treaty of Guadalupe Hidalgo.**   Mexico, prostrate before the northern invader, made peace on humiliating terms.   By the Treaty of Guadalupe Hidalgo (1848) she ceded to the United States Texas, New Mexico, and Upper California — in all about

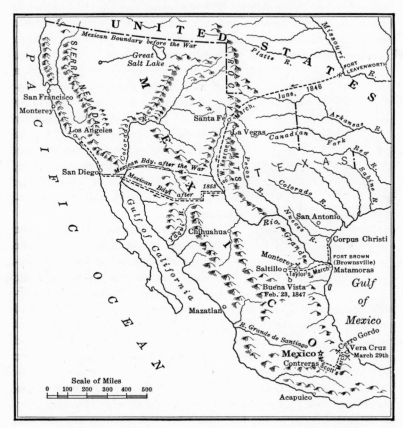

MAP ILLUSTRATING THE MEXICAN WAR, 1846–1848

two thirds of her territory.   The United States, in return, agreed to pay the defeated nation $15,000,000 and to assume liability for certain claims of its citizens against the Mexican government.

**The Gadsden Purchase.**   The location of the boundary between the Rio Grande and the Colorado River gave rise to renewed controversy between the two countries.   It was settled in 1853 by the purchase, on the part of the United States, of a strip of Mexican territory south of the Gila River. James Gadsden, the United States minister to Mexico, who conducted the transaction, paid the Mexican government $10,000,000 for this part of the Southwest.

**Downfall of Santa Anna.** The war with the United States left Mexico in chaos. Santa Anna, who had become president for the ninth time, took advantage of the situation to proclaim himself dictator, with the title of "Most Serene Highness." His royal or

imperial designs soon provoked a revolution on the part of the Mexican liberals. Unable to quell it by force of arms, Santa Anna hastily quitted the country in 1854, as Iturbide had done thirty-one years previously. He afterward returned, not to meet the fate of Iturbide, but to end his days in well-merited obscurity.

**The Constitution of 1857.** The Mexican liberals proceeded to frame a new constitution, which reëstablished the federal system in its original form. There were also articles guaranteeing the liberty of the press, granting the right of petition, prohibiting arbitrary punishments and confiscation of property, and abolishing special privileges, both ecclesiastical and military. This constitution remained the organic law of Mexico for the next sixty years.

BENITO JUÁREZ

**Benito Juárez.** One of the leaders of the revolutionary movement was Benito Juárez, a full-blooded Indian. His employer, noticing his intelligence, had him educated. Juárez studied law, entered politics, rose to be governor of his native state of Oaxaca, and later became president of Mexico. Juárez stood for liberal, anticlerical government. In 1859 he promulgated the famous Reform Laws, which suppressed the religious orders, nationalized ecclesiastical property, and granted freedom of worship, thus disestablishing the Roman Catholic Church. The new president executed these laws throughout Mexico, in spite of armed opposition on the part of clericals, conservatives, and militarists.

**Foreign Intervention.** Juárez triumphed over domestic foes, only to find himself confronted by enemies from abroad. The disturbed conditions prevailing in Mexico for many years had left its finances extremely embarrassed, so that the government could neither pay interest on the debt owed foreign countries nor satisfy the claims against it for outrages committed on the persons and property of Europeans. Under these circumstances Great Britain, France, and Spain reached an agreement to occupy Mexican seaports and collect the customs duties until their pecuniary demands should be satisfied. Troops of all three countries accordingly landed at Vera Cruz. Great Britain and Spain soon withdrew their contingents after it became plain that France, then ruled by the ambitious and unscrupulous Napoleon III, was intent upon the conquest of Mexico. This undertaking was less preposterous than it seems, for Napoleon III expected to receive, and did receive, the support of Mexican reactionaries, who preferred a foreign master to the radical Juárez.

**Second Mexican Empire.** A French army, thirty thousand strong, entered Mexico City in 1863 and set up a provisional government representing clericals and conservatives. Mexico was declared a hereditary, constitutional monarchy, under a Catholic emperor. Archduke Maximilian of Austria, brother of the Austrian ruler, Francis Joseph I, accepted the imperial crown. For a time he held sway over about two thirds of the country, while the Juarists, as the Mexican patriots were styled, maintained themselves by guerrilla warfare in the provinces of the extreme north and south. Maximilian's power rested on the bayonets of his foreign soldiery. The United States, at this time in the throes of the Civil War, refused to recognize him. After the close of the war the United States protested vigorously to Napoleon III against the presence of the French in Mexico and backed up its words by sending troops to the Rio Grande. Partly because of this action and also because of his growing fear of Prussia, Napoleon III in 1867 withdrew his forces from Mexico. Maximilian remained, only to be captured by the Juarists, and after a hurried court-martial to be shot as a rebel against the lawful government. Thus failed the second attempt to set up an empire in Mexico.

**Porfirio Díaz.** Ten years later, Porfirio Díaz, who had been the ablest lieutenant of Juárez in the struggle against the French,

became president of Mexico.  Except for one interval (1880–1884),
he governed the country with an iron hand until 1911.  The title
of president only veiled the real dictatorship which Díaz exercised.
Half or three fourths an Indian, his descent inspired confidence in
the mestizos, while his practical gifts as a soldier, ruler, and
diplomat won for him the support of the upper classes.  Díaz, in
truth, stood forth as the strong, stern man who alone could lift

PORFIRIO DÍAZ

Mexico out of the welter of
turmoil and revolution.

**Pacification of Mexico.**
Díaz soon gave peace to
Mexico.  His methods, if
harsh, had at least the merit
of effectiveness.   Bandits
and professional trouble-
makers were promptly ap-
prehended and shot — to
the number of eleven thousand altogether, it is said.
Order was maintained partly
by a well-disciplined army
and partly by the *rurales*, a
mounted police made up of the
class which in former days had drifted into brigandage and revolution.

**Economic Progress.**  Peace once secured, Díaz began his work
of transforming Mexico into a prosperous, modern state.  The size
of the country, its lack of navigable rivers, and its sparse population emphasized the need of railroads.  The presidencies of
Díaz saw the construction of many important lines, notably those
which run northward from the capital city to the frontier and link
up there with the trunk systems of the United States.  The rapid
extension of telegraphs accompanied the work of railroad building.
Internal improvements, such as harbors at Tampico and Vera
Cruz and a great drainage canal in the Valley of Mexico, were
completed.  Native manufactures were fostered by means of
protective tariffs.  Colonization was encouraged, and every effort
was made to attract the investment of foreign capital in Mexico.
Above all, Díaz labored to place the finances on a sound basis by
adjusting the claims of European bondholders, founding banks,

and establishing the gold standard as the basis of the monetary system. The Mexican treasury now began to exhibit a surplus, instead of the usual deficit, and the government found it possible to borrow abroad the sums required for its undertakings, on the sole security of the national credit. The economic progress of Mexico under Díaz thus abundantly justified his ideal of government — "Not much politics, but plenty of administration."

**Foreign Relations.** Díaz kept Mexico on good terms with other nations. Diplomatic intercourse was resumed with various European countries, even including France. The relations between Mexico and the great republic on the north were particularly friendly. When difficulties arose between the United States and Great Britain over the Venezuelan boundary, Mexico expressed adherence to the Monroe Doctrine, but suggested that it should be upheld by all American powers, instead of by one power. The second Pan-American Congress met in Mexico City. The Mexican government also took part in setting up a permanent Court of Arbitration to keep the peace between the turbulent states of Central America.

**Mexico in Revolution.** The year 1911 found Díaz filling his eighth term as president. His long dictatorship had given to Mexico peace and order, financial stability, and an amazing industrial development, the benefits of which were appropriated by the upper classes. It had done little or nothing for the lower classes — the proletariat in the towns and the peasants in the country. Díaz would not tolerate trade unions, nor did he attempt by labor legislation and other remedial measures to improve the lot of the workers. At the same time he permitted wealthy proprietors to secure the lands which had been held by Indian pueblos or tribes in common ownership, and often, also, to evict the peasants from their own tiny holdings. The condition of the common people thus became more and more intolerable. The revolution which occurred in 1911 was, in large measure, an economic movement on the part of the downtrodden and poverty-stricken masses. Nor did it lack political aspects. Educated, patriotic Mexicans resented more and more what they sometimes called *diazpotism;* they wanted a free press, liberty of suffrage, honest elections, the resignation of Díaz, and, in general, a return to constitutional government.

**Downfall of Díaz.** These demands found their most eloquent advocate in Francisco L. Madero, a member of a wealthy and distinguished family in northern Mexico. Here he raised the standard of revolt. Díaz, no longer so masterful as of yore, seems to have underestimated the strength of the revolutionists. He tried to compromise with them, but Madero insisted upon his retirement from office. The aged dictator finally resigned and sailed for Europe, quitting forever the country over which he had held sway for thirty years.

**Madero President.** Madero, a few months later, was elected to the presidency. He held it less than two years. A reformer and an idealist, one who in quieter times might have won the esteem of the people, Madero lacked the resolute character so necessary for a Mexican chief magistrate. The revolution soon passed beyond his control, when his followers discovered that the program of reforms could not be put immediately into effect and an economic and political millennium inaugurated. Insurrections against the new president broke out in every part of the country. Finally, in 1913, his enemies made him prisoner, forced him to resign, and then killed him.

**Huerta President.** Madero's successor — and his reputed murderer — was a revolutionary general of Aztec descent, Victoriano Huerta. He restored, or tried to restore, the Díaz régime. Though many Latin American and European nations recognized Huerta, the United States, under President Wilson, would not enter into diplomatic relations with his government. President Wilson even went so far as to send troops to Mexico, in return for an affront offered by Mexicans to United States sailors at Tampico. Vera Cruz was occupied by forces of the United States for several months during 1914. Meanwhile, the followers of Madero and other Mexicans dissatisfied with Huerta's rule started another uprising in northern Mexico. The two leaders were Venustiano Carranza, governor of Coahuila, and a bandit chieftain, Pancho Villa. Together they forced Huerta's resignation.

**Presidency of Carranza.** First as a provisional president and subsequently as a regularly elected executive, Carranza held the chief magistracy of Mexico for nearly six years (1914–1920). They were troubled years. Villa, that redoubtable bandit, soon took up arms against his former leader. In a vain effort to capture him and end his depredations across the border, the United States sent an expedition, led by General Pershing, into northern Mexico. Carranza considered this action a violation of Mexican sovereignty, and clashes occurred between his soldiers and those of the United States. Such incidents, fortunately, did not lead to further hostilities between the two countries. During the World War Carranza observed what he described as a "rigorous neutrality." It scarcely disguised his pro-German sympathies. Public opinion, however, increasingly favored the cause of the Allies. Early in 1917, when Germany was about to proclaim unrestricted submarine warfare and believed that intervention of the United States would follow, she invited Mexico to enter into alliance with her, promising aid in helping that country recover the American Southwest. The Mexican government took no notice of this proposal.

**Constitution of 1917.** The most important development in the internal affairs of Mexico during this period was the adoption of a new constitution, replacing that which had been in effect since the time of Juárez. Some of its provisions were intended to prevent future revolutions and dictatorships, by reducing the length of the presidential term and prohibiting reëlection. Other provisions were aimed at foreign capitalists, who might not, henceforth, acquire title to valuable oil and mineral lands in the republic. The new constitution also forbade religious organizations to own real property or to conduct any primary school or charitable institution. Mexico, under Carranza, thus showed the same pronounced anticlericalism as under Juárez.

**Presidency of Obregón.** Popular dissatisfaction with the Carranza régime produced another revolution in 1920. The movement spread with surprising rapidity throughout the country and soon forced Carranza to abandon the capital city. While attempting to escape, he was assassinated by one of his former followers. General Alvaro Obregón, most prominent of the revolutionaries, was elected to the presidency.

**Central America.** The former captaincy-general of Guatemala started its independence with a misleading tradition of governmental unity. Such unity had depended upon control from Spain, and would be hard to perpetuate if it depended on local conditions. The colonial division into provinces had bases of a permanent character. Geographical barriers separated the provinces from each other. All except Salvador had both Pacific and Atlantic interests, and interior handicaps to communications. In all except Costa Rica the Hispanic population was concentrated in plateaus and mountain valleys near the Pacific. Fertility and the exploitable character of the Indians were at their height in Salvador and Guatemala. In Honduras and Nicaragua there were broad slopes on the Atlantic side of the divide, which suffered from excessive heat and rainfall. These had been virtually abandoned by white men. Unlike Honduras, Nicaragua possessed a valuable river route to the Atlantic coast, but the advantages from this were offset by greater foreign aggressions. Costa Rica, short on exploitable Indians but long on fertile lands and good mines, had built up a strongly white population, many of whom owned and worked small farms. Elsewhere appeared the typical life of Spanish America: a population predominantly Indian and landless except for communal property in villages, ruled by a very few landed whites. In Salvador, however, racial amalgamation had produced a fairly homogeneous mestizo people. A few Negroes already lived along the Atlantic, and in later years they became numerous throughout Nicaragua and even more so in Honduras. Obviously it would be hard to handle such diverse cultural groups under one government.

**Political Conditions.** The typical Latin American party divisions promptly appeared. Conservatives (often called Serviles or Aristocrats) were led by the great landowners and higher clergy, and had their major center in Guatemala. Liberals (often called Anarchists or "Hotheads" — *fiebres*) were headed by the professional men of the cities and by leaders of the newly important *ladinos* (Hispanicized mestizos and Indians). They were well represented everywhere, but were especially strong in Salvador, Honduras, and Costa Rica. Leaders of either party theoretically desired unity, but probably few of them really favored it unless they and their regions could head the union. Whoever headed it faced not only the jealousy of the others, but interference of Powers greedy for the mines, such produce as bananas or coffee, and especially the interoceanic routes of the struggling little nations.

**The United Provinces, 1823–1839.** The federal republic known as the United Provinces of Central America started with a constitution modeled upon that of the United States. There was a president, a bicameral legislature, a supreme court, and a federal capital at Guatemala City. Each province enjoyed local self-government. Location of the capital at Guatemala City was natural, but roused old jealousies, which were increased by the fact that though each state had two senators, Guatemala's large population gave it seventeen out of thirty-nine deputies. Liberals started with control, and kept it except for a civil war from late 1826 to early 1829. From then until the end, the Union was ruled by the great Honduran Liberal, Francisco Morazán. An anti-slavery decree (1824) and aid for popular education marked the early years. The clerical question soon rose, resulting in a complete anticlerical victory during 1829 to 1832. Plans for a Nicaragua canal were made by treaty with the Netherlands (1826) and legislative encouragement was given to agriculture and colonization by foreigners. The reforms were costly; they increased taxes, and they angered the clergy and pious masses. Conservative resentment grew, and even the Liberals split. Rebellion broke out in Guatemala in 1837 under Rafael Carrera, an illiterate Indian leader. Though Morazán defeated him, the spirit of secession increased. In 1838 the federal congress suggested dissolution, and when in 1839 Morazán's presidential term ended, all the states had seceded or were about to do so. Morazán resisted, but was ejected from the country. He was shot when, in 1842, he attempted to return.

**The Separate States.** Though the states of Central America have been separated since 1839, their history has shown three common threads. One has been interest in renewed federation. Another has been the struggle against interference from abroad. The third has concerned social reform in politics, involving especially the privileged position of the Church and of the landed aristocracy. Renewal of federation, several times tried, has never found all the states ready at the same time. The struggle against foreign control has included interferences by one Central American state against another, as well as by the great Powers. Part of the Central American interferences sprang from boundary disputes. But especially among the neighbors of Guatemala, a Conservative or Liberal group commonly aided its fellows battling in near-by states, with disastrous results for order and good feeling.

The major interference from the Powers came from Great Britain until 1859, due to British canal aspirations and claims to the coast from Yucatán to the mouth of the San Juan River. Thereafter the United States largely protected Central America from Old World aggressions, but increasingly interposed its own influence.

The course of reform in politics has been most interesting. Generally speaking, from the overthrow of the Liberal federation until 1870, though Liberals held office briefly, the Conservatives had control. Since this was partly due to the activity of the Conservative Guatemalan dictator Carrera, it is less true of distant Costa Rica than of the others. Nicaragua was also a partial exception, owing to foreign complications. About 1870 the Liberals returned to power everywhere except in Nicaragua, where the change was delayed until 1893. Too much importance should not be ascribed to shifts in party control, since personal and regional ambitions outweighed principles for most of the members. Except in Guatemala, for instance, the Conservative "Thirty Years" had made little change in national policies. But the Liberals did tend to represent a group which had achieved its ruling status since independence, and was therefore hostile to the inherited status of the Conservative leaders. Their return to power proved to be the end of the old régime socially as well as politically in Costa Rica and Guatemala, and to a large degree elsewhere.

**Constitutions.** Constitutions, it may be noted, have been very numerous in Central America. From an early date each state had at least a "Fundamental Charter," which usually provided for the machinery of democratic government, and frequently for manhood suffrage. Education and civil and religious liberties were commonly demanded from the later nineteenth century. But such constitutions have meant very little. The seemingly large number of new ones that stud the pages of Central American history were little more than a substitute for minor amendment, and a sort of celebration for a change of control. Most presidents had won the title of "General" before they rose to office, and continued to rule in the spirit of martial law. Some of the increasingly numerous exceptions will be noted below.

**Guatemala.** The republic of Guatemala started with a tradition of strong government centered in Guatemala City. That metropolis has always been the only large city in the republic, and has had nearly the whole of the small white ruling caste. No regional jealousies could develop, and one who could control the capital controlled everything. As a result of the whole situation, Guatemala has had less revolutionary disturbance but more long-term dictatorship than the others. From 1839 to his death in 1865, the well-meaning but bullheaded and ignorant Carrera ruled. He actively suppressed Liberals at home and abroad and replaced the Church in much of its old status, though he refused to restore the tithe and some of the privileges. The Liberal victory (1871) led to the dictatorship of Justo Rufino Barrios, 1873–1885.

**Barrios.** Barrios was a well-educated *ladino*, in most things tolerant and farsighted, though he acted harshly against political opponents and marred his chances of domestic reform by unceasing efforts to force Central American reunion. On the other hand, he freed his nation of a long and hopeless boundary dispute by admitting the essential justice of Mexican claims to Chiapas, which had voluntarily joined Mexico during the days of independence. Under him the liberal constitution of 1879 was promulgated, and he did so thorough a job of exiling and imprisoning Conservatives that they have never since had the character of a strong semihereditary ruling class. He restored the anticlerical laws of the earlier days, confiscated clerical property, encouraged popular education, and transformed clerical colleges and the university into secular institutions. A program of public improvements in the capital included reorganization of the police force under an inspector from New York City. He was equally desirous of fostering agriculture, trade, and communications. Low finances handicapped execution of the last part of the program, but he reorganized the post office, introduced the telegraph, built bridges, connected the capital by rail with San José on the Pacific (1884), and started other railways before his death. Manuel Estrada Cabrera, who ruled from 1898 to 1920, contrasted painfully. He rose to office from the vice-presidency by assassinating his superior, and held office by one of the harshest tyrannies that Central America has known. He toadied to foreign capital without gaining much benefit for the nation, engaged in wars with his neighbors, and practically killed the still tender intellectual and economic life that started under Barrios. In 1920 a group calling itself Unionist, and probably more nearly representative of national unanimity than anything previously known in Guatemala, overthrew him.

**Salvador.** The smallest American mainland republic has benefited from its racial homogeneity, its lack of geographic diversity, and its fertility as an aid to prosperity. Lack of an Atlantic seaboard has made it relatively free of interference from the Powers. But its leaders caused it trouble by an interest in reunion and in its neighbors' politics, and its presidential successions were long achieved by violence and revolt. It is still completely a country of dictatorship, and its ancient upper class seems to have been less shaken by Liberal rule than elsewhere, but it reached fair tranquility before any of its neighbors except Costa Rica. The Liberals were so strong that even during the Conservative era they held office from 1845–1852, and 1860–1863. In 1871 they came permanently to control. Under Santiago González (1871–1876) a new Constitution was adopted. Though it retained the Established Church, it had advanced provisions for civil rights, the suffrage, religious toleration, and free primary education. The Conservatives revolted, but González managed to finish his term and pass the office to an elected successor. That successor was promptly overthrown by Rafael Zaldívar. The latter perverted the constitution to reëlect himself until 1885, when widespread revolt replaced him with Francisco Meléndez. Meléndez restored the national finances and built a railroad, but neither he nor his two successors could quite complete their terms before impatient office seekers ejected them. By 1898 even Salvadorean political fervor was somewhat quenched, and presidents learned to maintain strong armies. Starting with Tomás Regalado (1898–1902) no president was overthrown until depression caused a world cycle of revolutions. In 1931 General Maximiliano H. Martínez seized control, and he still had it ten years later. The present constitution dates from 1924. There has been no more popular government since 1898 than earlier, but the long era of peace has led to prosperity, the dictators have been enlightened men, and economic, educational, and social advances promise well for the future.

**Honduras.** The republic of Honduras has suffered from the political ineptitude of its population, but any nation located among more powerful neighbors, as it is, would have had trouble. Besides neighboring invasions, Great Britain's efforts to expand her sway though her vague protectorate over the coastal Mosquito Indians caused Honduras a long controversy and some warfare. In 1841 Britain assumed formal control over the Bay Islands. The United States ended these episodes only after they had disrupted what chance Honduras might otherwise have had for domestic quiet. Honduras, in truth, has no domestic history that interests foreign readers. Man after man climbed to office by violence; most of them left by the same route. A recurrently determining factor in their rise and fall was involvement in the quarrels of Salvador, Guatemala, and sometimes Nicaragua. The long dominance of Francisco Ferrera as president or minister of war (1840–1852) and the tyranny of Santos Guardiola (1856–1862) marked, if they hardly ornamented, the Conservative era. That era ended in 1872 only because the new Liberal rulers of Guatemala and Salvador felt it necessary to have a politically sympathetic neighbor. Of the later men, only Dr. Marco Aurelio Soto (1876–1883) did much to cause historians to celebrate him. He founded the National Library and several hospitals, began building roads and improving the post office, and tried to encourage mining. But falling out with Barrios of Guatemala, he removed hastily to the United States. The political merry-go-round continued far into the present century, though United States influence largely eliminated the meddling of Honduras's neighbors. Tranquility improved after 1925, and General Tiburcio Carias Andino (1932–   ) has shown a real interest in various types of progress.

**Nicaragua.** Nicaragua, possessing domestic conditions similar to those of Honduras, has rivaled that state in turbulence and in the lack of importance to foreign readers of any one administration. Being stronger than its immediate neighbors, it has suffered less than Honduras from Central American interference. But possession of a natural crossing between two oceans has given its history a distinctive character. Most of the population has always been concentrated at an altitude under one hundred and fifty feet, in the broad valley of lakes Managua and Nicaragua. These are separated from the Pacific by a narrow and easily crossed mountain range. From Lake Nicaragua the great San

Juan River flows to the Atlantic.  The river is always navigable, though dangerous, for small craft, and plans for its canalization go back to colonial days.  It invited constant encroachment by foreign nations.  Into the bargain, it built up a rivalry between two cities.  During colonial days León was, for historic reasons, the capital.  Granada on the lake, better situated for trade to the sea, became the stronghold of the wealthier merchants and the landed aristocracy.  Rivalry was bitter.  After independence it became an article of faith that León was Liberal and Granada was Conservative, and never the twain should meet except in battle. Managua, between the two, became the capital in 1845 to remove part of the dissension.  The parties differed little as to activities. After 1838 they alternated in violent control of the country, until foreign influences became dominant.

**Foreign Influences.**  Nicaragua suffered as much as did Honduras from British imperialism.  As early as 1841 Britain laid claim to San Juan de Nicaragua (Greytown) at the mouth of the river.  She moved in forcibly in 1848, as she saw the United States about to become a Pacific power through the acquisition of California.  The United States finally succeeded in protecting the country against Great Britain, but itself soon became the major influence in Nicaraguan political life.  The California gold rush caused the United States owned Transit Company to acquire concessions.  United States filibusters, seeking room for expansion of slave territory, also pushed themselves into Nicaraguan history. During a fiercer domestic struggle than usual, the Liberals foolishly invited aid from the adventurer William Walker.  The latter, with help from the Transit Company and other interests in the United States, took control of Nicaragua for himself.  Finally he fell out with the Transit Company, and was attacked by all the other Central American states.  England, France, and Spain encouraged or aided the latter as they could.  Walker was permanently eliminated only in 1860.  The outcome was a reaction against Liberalism that prolonged the Conservative régime for twenty years after it ended elsewhere.  The presidential succession was usually peaceful.  Tomás Martínez (1857–1867) laid a legal basis for economic recovery, paid attention to primary and higher education, and negotiated a new Concordat that abolished the tithes and certain other clerical privileges.  Pedro Joaquín Chamorro (1875–1879) established free primary education in 1877, expelled the Jesuits, introduced the telegraph, and began railroads. Others carried on fairly well. But by 1893 governmental finances were in ruins, and President Roberto Sacasa had alienated leaders of both parties by his favoritism for, and dependence on, a small group of close friends. Granada and León revolted — separately. The outcome was the return of a Liberal era. Thus began the dictatorship of José Santos Zelaya (1893–1909). Zelaya made some economic changes through extravagant foreign loans, and treated Conservative leaders so harshly as virtually to end them as an aristocracy of inheritance. Otherwise he was an unmitigated nuisance; a master of graft, and a confirmed meddler in his neighbors' affairs.

**The United States and Nicaragua.** Officially termed "a blot on the history of Nicaragua" by the United States Department of State, Zelaya was eliminated in 1909. This proved the start of twenty years during which the United States meddled instead of Zelaya. In 1907 the Central American states had agreed by treaty not to recognize presidents who rose to office by force. Chiefly for reasons of "Dollar Diplomacy," though partly through a muddled belief in constitutional government and complete ignorance of Central American realities, the United States assumed a "moral mandate" to foster self-government in Central America by pre-venting revolutions. It maintained a Legation Guard or other marines in the country most of the time from 1912 to 1932, and fought several small but bloody wars. It thereby maintained in office Conservatives friendly to United States capital. Consider-ing everything, United States domination was decently used. The Bryan-Chamorro treaty (1916) gave the United States the exclusive right to a canal, but at a price satisfactory to Nicaragua. A United States appointed collector-general of customs, payment for the canal rights, and a financial commission dominated by United States experts restored Nicaraguan financial solvency by 1924. New election laws (1923 and 1927) were used, under United States supervision, for elections generally regarded as the only honest ones ever known in the country. Roads were built, schools and ports were improved, and other material benefits were clear. The National Guard, under training by Marine officers, became a highly disciplined body. But any foreign control was obnoxious to the Nicaraguans, and the United States slowly learned that an imposed peace was no answer to Central American political turbulence. Election of the Liberal, José Moncada (1928), proved the end of meddling as an avowed policy, though hopes of benefits from a canal make Nicaraguan statesmen amenable to suggestions from the United States. Politics are now less violent but no less dictatorial. President Anastasio Somoza, elected in 1936 for four years, extended his term to 1947 by constitutional amendment.

**Costa Rica.** Costa Rica's strongly homogeneous and white population, its compact ruling class, its large percentage of small farms, and its isolation from the interventionists of the northern states, enabled the nation to achieve relative political success before the others. Plenty of revolutions, due to quarrels over location of the capital and the usual vigorous partisanship, marred the first half century. Even so, they caused less violence than elsewhere. Once in office, either party usually followed a fairly progressive program. During the predominantly Conservative era, major figures were Braulio Carrillo (1838–1842) and Juan Rafael Mora (1837–1838, 1849–1859). Both seem to have been Liberals before dissolution of the Federation. Carrillo became a Conservative, but acted no more arbitrarily than Mora. Both men tried to improve economic life and showed some interest in education. Carrillo is notable for spreading coffee cultivation, which had much to do with later prosperity.

**Rise of the Middle Class.** In 1870 General Tomás Guardia seized power, and held it until his death in 1882. Theoretically under the constitution of 1871, he ruled very arbitrarily. He pursued an aggressive policy toward Nicaragua, and he left a heavy debt as a result of starting an interoceanic railway against expert advice. But he got the road started and it was later finished; he introduced the telegraph, he aided agriculture, and he fostered schools. And since he was not of the old ruling class which had furnished leaders to Liberals as well as to Conservatives, at the slightest excuse he vigorously persecuted its members with fines, confiscations, and exile. The clique was never so important thereafter, and new men had a better chance to rise. From Guardia's day to the present, elections have been the means of changing administrations, and Costa Rica has continued on the road to middle-class economic and social welfare. José Joaquín

Rodríguez (1890–1894) and Ascención Esquivel (1902–1906) were outstanding figures in laying the foundations of the free and compulsory education, generally sound finances, and orderly self-government that have long characterized the country. Rodríguez's election gave the first clear example of the popular will in politics. When as a Conservative he was elected in 1889, adherents of his excellent predecessor, Dr. Bernardo Soto, were much inclined to discover Soto indispensable for the nation's welfare. The small farmers prepared to march on the capital, Soto supported them, and Rodríguez peacefully took his seat.

**Panamá.** The leaders of Panamá received none too good training in peaceful politics while citizens of Colombia, but they faced a relatively easy task on becoming independent. Settlement of the hundreds of miles of useful Pacific coastlands may eventually create regionalism, but so far only the cities of Panamá and Colón, at opposite ends of the Canal, have played any part in national politics. And the Canal insures a considerable revenue to the republic. United States influence has been so overwhelming that one cannot estimate the probable success of Panamanian life without it, but apparently rather good political health has been built up. The Constitution of 1904 established a centralized government, required popular education, and gave the United States the right to control sanitation of the two terminal cities and to intervene to preserve order. The latter was necessary only two or three times. Other aspects of the national life have developed satisfactorily, and the presidents have all proved good leaders. Politics has centered about relations with the United States. Genuine bases for disputes have existed over use of the Canal Zone for residence and business beyond control or taxation by the republic. In addition, existence of the protectorate offended pride, and charges of acquiescence in United States control have commonly been used by politicians of the opposition. The United States long ago ended the worst abuses of the Zone by domestic regulation. A treaty on the whole matter was delayed by the question of security for the canal, since that waterway cannot be defended solely from the Zone. In 1936 the countries signed a treaty abolishing the protectorate and the sanitary control, and correcting the other abuses. The United States Senate delayed ratification until 1939, since under its terms defense of the

Canal might be handicapped.   Arnulfo Arias, elected president in
1940, was replaced in 1941 by Ricardo Adolfo de la Guardia.
Arias opposed coöperation in hemisphere defense and forced
adoption of a doubtfully democratic constitution (January, 1941).

**Central American Reunion.**   Repeated efforts to bring the
republics together in federal union have failed.   The last federation, established in 1921, could not secure adhesion by Costa Rica
and Nicaragua, and collapsed in 1922.   The next year saw a more
promising approach to the subject.   In 1923 Guatemala, Honduras, Salvador, and Costa Rica signed a convention which limits
each republic to a few armed men, forbids acquisition of warships,
and prohibits trade in arms and munitions among themselves.
Accompanying conventions provided for a customs union, and for
establishment of a Central American court, or international
tribunal.   A three-power agreement in 1927 pledged Salvador,
Guatemala, and Honduras to common policy in matters of general
concern to Central America.   The importance of such treaties
remains to be seen, but interstate relations have been fairly
peaceful in recent years, and benefits to domestic peace if not to
the movement for reunion are certain.

### WORDS AND PHRASES YOU SHOULD KNOW

| | | |
|---|---|---|
| Alamo | Gadsden Purchase | proletariat |
| anticlericalism | *ladinos* | Reform Laws |
| Centralists | "Lone Star Republic" | *rurales* |
| *diazpotism* | "moral mandate" | Treaty of Guadalupe |
| "Dollar Diplomacy" | "Most Serene High- | Hidalgo |
| Federalists | ness" | |

### QUESTIONS YOU SHOULD BE ABLE TO ANSWER

1. What economic and social conditions in Mexico invited revolution?
2. What groups of people in Mexico were generally opposed to republican
   ideas?  Why?
3. How was Texas colonized?   What led Texas to revolt against Mexico?
4. How did war between Mexico and the United States break out?
5. Do you think the peace terms after the Mexican War were severe?
   Give your reasons.
6. What groups opposed the reforms of Juárez?  Why?
7. How did the French obtain control in Mexico?   What caused the
   collapse of their power there?
8. What did Díaz do to make Mexico prosperous and modern?

9. What is meant by the statement that the revolution of 1911 was largely an economic movement?
10. How did the United States become involved in Mexico's troubles?
11. What were some of the provisions of the Mexican constitution of 1917?
12. Why were the peoples of Central America unable to maintain a united country?
13. Were political conditions in Central America similar to those in Mexico?
14. Why was Britain interested in Honduras and Nicaragua?
15. Why did some Americans become interested in Nicaragua in 1848? What was the effect of this foreign interest?
16. Why did the United States government become especially interested in Nicaragua in the twentieth century?
17. How do you account for the comparatively orderly progress of Costa Rica?
18. What has been the result of United States activity in Panamá?

## PROJECTS AND ACTIVITIES

1. Construct a time line showing the outstanding events in Mexican history since 1821.
2. Make a chart showing United States interest in Mexico and Central America. Use these headings: Country; Nature of United States Interest; Results of United States Interest.
3. Prepare a debate on the subject: "Resolved, that the policy of the United States toward Central American countries has been wise."
4. List the five men in the history of Mexico and Central America that you think did the most for their country. Beside each name indicate the accomplishments of the man.
5. Make a chart showing European interest in Mexico and Central America. Use the headings suggested in Project 2.
6. In two columns list the things that Liberals and Conservatives in Mexican and Central American politics usually stood for.
7. Draw or trace a map of Mexico and Central America. Indicate thereon ten outstanding events which showed progress toward a better society.
8. Compose brief newspaper items for five significant events in Central American history in which foreign nations were involved.
9. Write a political speech as you imagine it might have been written by a *fiebre* or a Conservative.
10. Imagine that you are a journalist sent to interview a Central American dictator. Write a dispatch in which you give an account of your interview.

# CHAPTER VIII

# The West Indies

**The West Indies under Spain.** Something has been said in a previous chapter concerning the discovery of the West Indies by Columbus. Accounts of their fabulous wealth stirred the imagination of the Spaniards and soon led to the exploration and conquest of the archipelago. For over a century Spain's possession of the islands was not seriously disputed by other powers, but her actual occupation was confined to the Greater Antilles. The Spaniards had all the New World before them; nothing tempted them to settle on the Lesser Antilles, which were mostly too insignificant and too far away from the mainland to receive attention.

**Smugglers and Privateers.** The young, seagoing peoples of Europe — English, French, Dutch, and others — ere long sought out the West Indies. Unable to trade there legitimately because of Spain's exclusion policy, they became smugglers. Bases were needed for their illicit operations, and these were found in the smaller islands of the archipelago, which the Spaniards had neglected. The islands also made convenient jumping-off places for raids by privateers in time of war. The "seadogs" of England, France, and Holland liked nothing better than to capture Spanish treasure ships, laden with ducats and doubloons. Sometimes they even attacked the settlements in Haiti and Cuba and along the "Spanish Main," as the Caribbean shore of South America was formerly called. One of these intruders, Sir Francis Drake, penetrated to the Isthmus of Panamá, where he obtained his first view of the Pacific and vowed some day "to sail an English ship" in the South Seas. Drake's celebrated voyage around the world (1577–1580) was the result of this experience.

**Buccaneers and Pirates.** Smuggling and privateering easily degenerated into the semilegal piracy of the buccaneers. These desperadoes belonged to different nationalities, but all were united by the desire for adventure and gain and by a consuming hatred

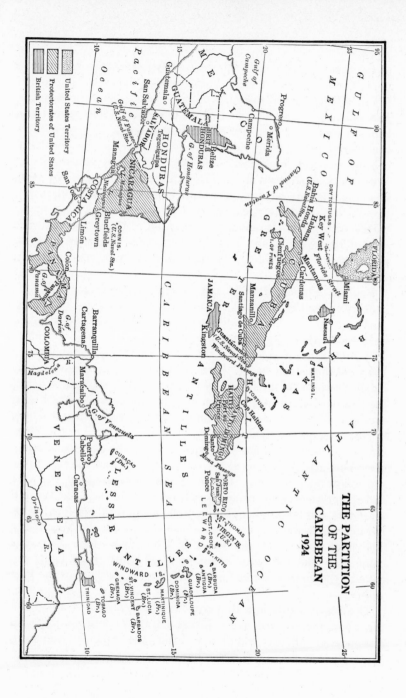

THE PARTITION OF THE CARIBBEAN 1924

British Territory

Protectorates of United States

United States Territory

of the Spaniard, which in their eyes justified any attack upon his person or property. Their headquarters at first were on the little island of Tortuga (off the northwestern coast of Haiti) and later on Jamaica, after it became an English possession. The seventeenth century was the golden age of the buccaneers. They swept over the Caribbean, seizing Spanish vessels, cutting the throats of captain and crew, and making off with their bloodstained plunder. Wealthy Spanish cities on the mainland were also sacked by them. Buccaneering, as an organized and more or less legitimate profession, began to disappear after 1670, when Spain, by a formal treaty with England, renounced her claim to the exclusive ownership of the West Indies. Nevertheless, piracy lingered here and there in the Caribbean until the early years of the nineteenth century.

**English, French, Dutch, and Danish Colonizers.** The buccaneers opened the eyes of the world to the weakness of Spanish dominion in the West Indies and so led to the acquisition of possessions there by England, France, Holland, and Denmark. The first English colony in the archipelago was established in 1623 on the island of St. Kitts. Barbados was settled by the English two years later. A fleet sent out by Cromwell to attack the Spaniards captured Jamaica in 1655. Meanwhile, the French established themselves in Martinique and Guadeloupe, the Dutch in Curaçao, off the Venezuelan coast, and the Danes in the Virgin Group. These and other islands, secured at the expense of Spain, often changed ownership as the result of European warfare during the following centuries. The geographical position of the West Indies between two continents naturally made them the scene of sea fights and land fights innumerable, a "natural cockpit" of the nations which were trying to establish colonies in the New World. The final division of the spoils of Columbus's first discoveries came after the war with Spain in 1898, which freed Cuba and gave to the United States for the first time a foothold in the West Indies.

**The Slave Trade and Slavery.** We have already learned that the aborigines of the West Indies (Arawaks and Caribs) soon disappeared almost completely after the Spanish conquest.[1] Their place as slaves was taken by African Negroes.[2] Hardly any-

---

[1] See page 96.        [2] See page 99.

one thought it wrong to kidnap or purchase the black men, pack them on shipboard, where many died in the stifling holds, and carry them across the ocean to labor on the plantations. It is estimated that before the slave trade ended more than three million Negroes were thus transported to the New World, chiefly to the West Indies, and that at least a quarter of a million more perished on the way thither. This shameful traffic reached its greatest proportions after the English had begun to encroach upon the West Indies and to develop, far more thoroughly than the Spaniards had done, the cultivation of cotton, tobacco, and, above all, of sugar cane. During the eighteenth century the West Indies supplied the world with sugar. The millionaires of those days were Europeans who had invested in large plantations there and worked them with cheap slave labor.

**Abolition of the Slave Trade and Slavery.** Agitation for the prohibition of the African slave trade began toward the close of the eighteenth century. The philanthropists naturally encountered much opposition from those who profited so richly from the business. Denmark was the first country to declare the traffic in slaves unlawful. Great Britain and the United States took the same step in 1807–1808, and in subsequent years France, Holland, Spain, and other nations agreed that it should no longer enjoy the protection of their flags. The suppression of slavery in the West Indies came next. Great Britain in 1833 passed an act to free the slaves in her possessions there, paying one hundred million dollars to their former masters as compensation. This measure is a monument to the humanitarian labors of William Wilberforce, who devoted his wealth, his energies, and his powerful oratory to the cause of the oppressed blacks. Within the next half century slavery disappeared by law in the Danish, French, Dutch, and Spanish possessions in the West Indies.

**Population.** Slavery is responsible for the great preponderance of Negroes and mulattoes throughout the West Indies. In Cuba colored peoples form a quarter, in Puerto Rico between a third and a fourth, and in Jamaica about nine tenths of the population. The inhabitants of Haiti are almost entirely either full-blooded Negroes or the mulatto descendants of Spanish and French settlers. There is also a large African element in Santo Domingo. The abolition of slavery has led to a considerable importation of

East Indian coolies and Chinese into a number of the islands, chiefly those belonging to Great Britain.

**Cuba.**  Spain retained Cuba, after her colonies on the mainland fell away during the first quarter of the nineteenth century. The "Pearl of the Antilles" was a valuable possession. Spaniards went there in large numbers, acquired extensive estates and many slaves, and drew riches from the cultivation of sugar, tobacco, and

JOSÉ MARTÍ

coffee. Commerce also became more profitable, now that piracy had ceased and Havana and other ports had been opened to the shipping of all nations. But material prosperity did not reconcile the inhabitants to Spanish rule. Much unrest existed among all classes of the population. The Negroes wanted to be free, but Spain would not give them freedom. The Creoles, excluded from all important public offices, demanded the right to take part in their own government. Even the peninsular Spaniards resented more and more the arbitrary sway of the captains-general, the corrupt exactions of Spanish officials, and the heavy burden of taxation. Cuba was a "milch cow" that Spain seemed willing to drain dry.

**Cuban Insurrections.**  The unrest came to a head in 1868. This year saw in Spain a liberal revolution, which dethroned Queen Isabella, the daughter of Ferdinand VII, and, like her father, a thorough reactionary. The Cubans seized the opportunity thus presented to start an insurrection. It lasted ten years, cost Spain 100,000 men and $200,000,000, and ended only when she promised various reforms, including abolition of slavery and representation of Cuba in the Cortes. These promises were kept, but Spanish misgovernment of the island continued. Discontent grew apace, and in 1895 another bloody insurrection began. It was organized and promoted by José Martí, a Cuban man of letters, who had been educated in Spain and had lived long in the United States. With him were associated General Máximo Gómez and the other leaders of the earlier rebellion. The insurgents conducted a guerrilla warfare, avoiding the armies sent against them, but doing as much damage as possible in the rural districts. The Spaniards under General Weyler built barbed-wired fences and lines of block-houses across the narrow parts of the island, in order to isolate their foe. They also adopted the policy of concentrating in the towns, under military guard, great numbers of noncombatants, who were suspected of aiding the insurgent cause. These *recon-centrados* endured extreme suffering; many died from starvation. The sight of the wholesale devastation and slaughter going on in Cuba made a very painful impression upon the people of the United States.

**The Cuban Question.** Cuba lies close to the mainland and commands the entrance to the Gulf of Mexico. Its possession by any strong foreign power might be highly dangerous to the safety of the United States. The economic relations of the island with the American Union are also very intimate. Cuban sugar and tobacco find their chief market in the United States, and Cuban imports of foodstuffs, manufactures, and machinery come mostly from the United States. No wonder, therefore, that Cuba's destinies seemed to be bound up with those of the great republic to the north. As early as 1823 President Monroe declared that Cuba would be "the most interesting addition" to the United States. Twenty-five years later the American government offered $100,000,000 for the island, but Spain replied that rather than sell Cuba she would prefer to see it "sunk in the ocean." President Grant, while the first Cuban insurrection was in progress, declared that the United States might have to intervene in Cuba to protect her own interests. President Cleveland, after the second insur-rection began, likewise hinted at the possibility of action by the United States to save "a rich and fertile country, intimately related to us," from ruin.

**Intervention of the United States.** Intervention became a fact in 1898, under President McKinley. The immediate cause was the destruction of the United States battleship *Maine*, by an explosion which sent her to the bottom of Havana harbor and caused the loss of most of her crew. A court of inquiry decided

that the vessel had been blown up from the outside.  The facts
are still obscure, but opinion already inflamed by reports of
atrocities rose to the fighting point.  Congress passed resolutions
declaring that the Cubans were henceforth free, demanding that
Spain relinquish her authority over them and withdraw from the
island, and authorizing the president to use the land and naval
forces of the government "to carry these resolutions into effect."
McKinley signed them, though Spain frantically offered to meet
the demands of the United States, and hostilities began.

**The Spanish-American War.**  The war was short and decisive.
It could not be otherwise, considering how unmatched in strength
were the contestants.  The United States navy blockaded Cuban
ports and utterly destroyed in a few hours a Spanish squadron
trying to escape from Santiago de Cuba.  That city, which in the
meantime had been invested by United States soldiers, among
them Roosevelt's "Rough Riders," soon surrendered.  An American army then made what can only be described as a military
promenade of Puerto Rico; the Spanish forces there made no
effective resistance, and the inhabitants welcomed the invaders.
Spain now sued for peace.  By the Treaty of Paris, signed at Paris
in 1898, she renounced her sovereignty over Cuba and ceded
Puerto Rico and other smaller islands to the United States.  Thus
disappeared the last vestige of the Spanish colonial empire in the
New World.

**The United States in Cuba.**  The United States disclaimed any
intention to annex Cuba, but kept the island under military rule
for three years, until the machinery of a new government could be
installed.  Much was now done, by United States officials and at
the expense of the United States, to "clean up" Cuba.  School
systems were organized, the civil service and judiciary reformed,
burdensome taxes abolished, and unsanitary conditions in Havana
and other cities eliminated.  The eradication of yellow fever,
which had been the scourge of Cuba for centuries, dates from this
period.  These things accomplished, the United States in 1902
handed over the island to its inhabitants.

**Republic of Cuba.**  The new republic was not to be wholly
independent.  By the Platt Amendment [1] Cuba had to insert in
her constitution several clauses which in effect made the new

---

[1] So called after its author, Senator O. H. Platt, of Connecticut.

Underwood and Underwood

HAVANA, CUBA

James Sawders

THE CAREENAGE, BRIDGETOWN, BARBADOS

republic a ward of the United States. Cuba was bound not to allow any foreign power to acquire or control any territory in the island, not to incur debts in excess of her current revenues, to lease naval stations (since located at Bahía Honda and Guantánamo) to the United States, and finally, to permit the latter country to intervene in Cuban affairs for the purpose of maintaining public order. An occasion for such intervention arose in 1906, and again in 1912, when a revolt started against the lawful president. The first time the United States set up a military occupation lasting over two years. In spite of some external troubles after the United States troops were withdrawn, for some years the Cuban Republic continued to progress in both material prosperity and stable government.

TOUSSAINT L'OUVERTURE

**Haiti.** The island called by its natives Haiti (mountainous country) and by Columbus Española (anglicized as Hispaniola) was the first Spanish colony in the West Indies. During the seventeenth century some French and English buccaneers, who had previously seized Tortuga, obtained a footing on the western end of Haiti. There they established plantations, bought Negro slaves, and prospered exceedingly. The part which they occupied was ceded by Spain to France in 1697. The French called their colony Saint-Domingue, a name which applied to all Haiti for a few years after 1795, when France, by treaty with Spain, acquired title to the entire island.

**Haitian Independence.** The Negroes and mulattoes of Saint-Domingue greatly outnumbered its white population. The disturbed conditions in France, following the outbreak of revolution there, offered the Haitian blacks a favorable opportunity to win their own freedom. This they started to do under the leadership of Toussaint L'Ouverture, one of the most remarkable men the Negro race has ever produced. He made himself virtual dictator, drew up a constitution, abolished slavery, and declared the inde-

pendence of the island. Napoleon Bonaparte, then supreme in
France, sent thirty thousand troops to subdue the Haitians. A
bloody, barbarous struggle followed. Toussaint, induced by the
most solemn guarantees on the part of the French, finally laid
down his arms. He was sent as a prisoner to France, to die there
of neglect and starvation. The infuriated blacks now renewed
the struggle. Yellow fever came to their aid, and at length the
remnant of the French expedition evacuated the island. In 1804
the Haitians proclaimed their independence anew and set up a
republic from which they barred whites.

**Republic of Haiti.** No country in the New World led a more
troubled existence during the past century than Haiti. The
Hispanic colonies had an upper class accustomed to minor self-
government, well educated, somewhat experienced in business,
and accepted as natural rulers by the lower class. The Haitians
eliminated their whole ruling class, and the new, self-established
ruling groups had to lift themselves by their bootstraps while
trying to run the country. It is easy to see, looking back on conditions of a century ago, that they have accomplished wonders, but
Haitian history was long a record of little except revolution, civil
warfare, and military despotism. Dusky "emperors," "kings,"
and "presidents" followed one another in rapid succession, all of
them despots and nearly all of them notoriously inefficient and
corrupt. The constitution, though republican in form, was not
observed. The legal code, based on that of France, was not
enforced. The state religion of Roman Catholicism remained
only a veneer for inherited African beliefs. The finances fell into
disorder, public improvements lapsed, and both agriculture and
commerce declined. The Haitians possessed in their fertile,
beautiful island almost everything that a civilized nation could
desire, but for a hundred years they made limited progress.

**The United States and Haiti.** Both the United States and
European powers from time to time have interfered in the affairs
of Haiti, theoretically on behalf of the foreign residents. In 1915,
United States troops occupied the island, disarmed the inhabitants,
and restored order. Military intervention soon passed into a close
political and fiscal protectorate. A treaty between Haiti and the
United States, ratified in 1916, put the finances of the Black
Republic under American control, created a native constabulary

under American officers and provided for American engineers to supervise public works and sanitation. The United States also undertook to intervene, when necessary, for the preservation of Haitian independence and the maintenance of a stable and effective government. The treaty was to remain in force for twenty years. The last marines were withdrawn in 1934. Stenio Vincent, president from 1930 to 1941, continues to dominate Haitian affairs. Minor disorders only have occurred since 1934.

**Dominican Republic.** Santo Domingo, or, more properly, the Dominican Republic, in area is almost twice as large as Haiti. Its population, however, is less than one half that of the neighboring state. The inhabitants form a mixed race of European and African blood, speaking the Spanish language, and preserving to a considerable extent Spanish culture. As previously noticed, the Spaniards kept control of the eastern part of the island until the end of the eighteenth century. Spanish rule was reëstablished after French rule from 1795 to 1808, by a successful revolt of the people. These, in 1821, gained independence from Spain, only to be coerced into uniting with Haiti. This ill-sorted union lasted until 1844, when the Dominican Republic came into being. In 1861 the nation tried reincorporation with Spain, but soon became discontented, and regained its freedom in 1865. Since then it has remained independent, though much interfered with by other states.

**The United States and the Dominican Republic.** The usual revolutions have occurred in the Dominican Republic, with the usual results. Its financial condition became desperate, and the prospect opened of intervention by European countries to collect debts due their citizens. In 1907 the United States became fiscal adviser to the bankrupt republic. This arrangement was followed in 1916 by military occupation and the setting up of a protectorate by the United States. The United States hoped to show the Dominican people what honest, efficient administration could accomplish, as well as the futility of "government by revolution." The finances were put on a sound basis, roads and bridges built, schools established, sanitary conditions much improved, and many other reforms introduced. The Dominicans, however, protested strongly against such an attack on their independence, and against certain features of the policies, and in 1924 the marines were withdrawn. On the whole, the reforms started before 1924 have been well continued since, and the worst days of Dominican national life are far in the past. A United States-appointed Customs Collector remained under new agreements of 1924 and 1934, but these were abrogated in 1941. A new constitution, adopted in 1929, was modified in 1934. European refugees have been welcomed as a means of colonizing some of the areas along the Haitian frontier, or elsewhere. The first group arrived in May, 1940. President Rafael L. Trujillo (1930–1938; 1942–    ) dominates the national life.

**British West Indies.** The possessions of Great Britain in the West Indies comprise the Bahamas, Jamaica, Trinidad, Tobago, Barbados, and various islands in the Windward and Leeward groups. All these rank as Crown colonies, with governors sent out from Great Britain. The larger islands possess a considerable measure of self-government by elective legislatures. The white population is small, but the colored peoples, both Negro and mulatto, have been quick to assimilate British culture. The abolition of slavery, by cutting down the supply of cheap labor, produced a long period of depression in the sugar industry, which was also adversely affected by the competition of European beet sugar. The principal staple is still sugar, but in recent years fruits, cacao, rice, and (in Trinidad) oil have been increasingly exported. The World War brought about a remarkable revival of prosperity in the British West Indies, and their economic future appears brighter than at any time within the past century.

**French West Indies.** France possesses two important colonies in the West Indies — Guadeloupe and Martinique. Their inhabitants, most of whom are Negroes and half-breeds, number about half a million. Economically, the colonies are in a flourishing condition. Martinique, a very beautiful island, embowered in trees and flowers which grow with all the luxuriance of the tropics, was the birthplace of the Empress Josephine. As all the world remembers, an appalling eruption of Mont Pelée in 1902 destroyed the chief city, St. Pierre, with a loss of forty thousand lives. Here, as elsewhere in the Lesser Antilles, frequent eruptions and earthquakes show that these islands are of volcanic origin and, geologically speaking, of recent date.

**Dutch West Indies.** Three small islands,[1] strung along the Venezuelan coast, belong to Holland. Though reckoned in the West Indies, they really are part of the continental system of South America. Curaçao, the largest of the group, is the seat of government. The Dutch West Indies also include several islands [2] in the Lesser Antilles, east of Puerto Rico.

**Puerto Rico.** The island of Puerto Rico, though the smallest of the Greater Antilles, has an area of 3,435 square miles and a population of about 1,800,000. The whites, now regarded as three fourths of the inhabitants, are rapidly increasing in number, while both Negroes and mulattoes are decreasing. As a Spanish colony Puerto Rico enjoyed remarkable prosperity. Under the rule of the United States productiveness of the island as a whole grew by leaps and bounds, though the effect on the individual peasant has been far from happy as large-scale sugar growing was emphasized. The great bulk of the trade, both import and export, is with the United States. Sugar, tobacco, coffee, fruits, and other Puerto Rican products enter the United States duty free. Many public improvements, such as roads and bridges, schoolhouses, waterworks, and electric-lighting plants, have been made within the last four decades. Much is being done, also, to spread elementary education and to better living conditions. By the Jones Act of 1917, and later amendments, the people elect their own legislature, but their governor holds office through appointment by the president of the United States. The governor may veto acts of the legislature; if he is overridden by a two-thirds vote, the president may interpose a final veto. The president and Senate of the United States, rather than the Puerto Rican legislature, also control appointment of Supreme Court Judges, and the heads of certain executive departments. Citizens of Puerto Rico are citizens of the United States. Probably most are content to be so, but distress among the peasants and ambitions of some of the leaders have led to a movement for independence which is more vociferous than sincere. The generation born and educated under the American flag gained control of the legislature in the elections of 1940 and began to work on a program of social reform. The Land Law of April 13, 1941, limits corporate holdings to five hundred acres.

---

[1] Aruba, Curaçao, and Buen Ayre.

[2] Saba, St. Eustatius, and part of St. Martin.

## Words and Phrases You Should Know

| | | |
|---|---|---|
| buccaneers | "Pearl of the Antilles" | "sea dogs" |
| Greater Antilles | Platt Amendment | "Spanish Main" |
| guerrilla warfare | protectorate | Tortuga |
| Lesser Antilles | *reconcentrados* | Treaty of Paris |

## Questions You Should Be Able to Answer

1. Why was there so much smuggling in the West Indies?
2. "The seventeenth century was the golden age of the buccaneers." Explain.
3. Why were the West Indies a "natural cockpit" for conflicts between rival nations?
4. For what purpose were the millions of Negro slaves brought to the West Indies?
5. How would you compare the British method of freeing slaves with the method used in this country?
6. What West Indies islands now contain large numbers of Negroes?
7. Why was there so much dissatisfaction with Spanish rule in Cuba?
8. What methods used by General Weyler aroused protests in the United States?
9. What strategic and economic interests did the United States have in Cuba?
10. What were the circumstances that led the United States to intervene in Cuba?
11. To what extent did the United States control Cuba after the Spanish-American War?
12. How did Haiti secure its independence?
13. Why was there so little progress in Haiti? Why has the United States interfered in Haiti and in the Dominican Republic?
14. How do you account for the fact that the British West Indies have, in recent years, become relatively prosperous?
15. When did the United States acquire Puerto Rico?
16. Although there has been some prosperity in Puerto Rico, there has been much discontent among the lower classes. Why?

## Projects and Activities

1. Draw or trace a map of the West Indies. Indicate thereon the independent islands and those that are under the control or protection of the United States and European nations.

2. Write a short essay on the effect of slavery on the West Indies.
3. Using this chapter and the *World Almanac*, make a chart of the economic activity (products and trade) of several of the islands of the West Indies.
4. List the islands which contain large numbers of Negroes. If possible, indicate the ratio of Negroes to other peoples in each island.
5. Prepare a chart showing American interest and intervention in West Indian islands.
6. Look up additional information on Toussaint L'Ouverture and prepare an oral report on his life.
7. Construct a diagram of the government of Puerto Rico.

# CHAPTER IX

# Nationalism and Democracy
# since the World War

**A New Type of Life.** In the last twenty years, the history of Latin America has taken on a conspicuously different character from that of earlier days. In general, economic and cultural conditions have improved, and disorders and revolutions have become less frequent. On the other hand, all but a few nations, including several which had long enjoyed stable government, have experienced revolutions since 1930. Casual observers have interpreted these facts as a result of the World War and of the world-wide economic crisis that began in 1929. Yet even casual observers sometimes sense, what is entirely true, that the events in Latin America represented more than the old familiar struggle for the spoils of office. "The War and the Depression" account for much, but they were influences secondary to other, and internal, developments.

**A Century of Evolution.** It has been shown in earlier chapters that the Latin American people started their independent history under many handicaps. The type of life which they inherited from colonial days differed from that of the foreign nations which they desired to emulate. The liberty from close Spanish tutelage which they gained by independence was so sudden as usually to turn to license, the people knew nothing of compromise as the basis of self-rule, and the only leaders whose qualities they had tested were leaders for warfare — men who at best knew little except the theory of democratic self-government, and frequently were out of sympathy with its practice. The resulting era of revolution and dictatorship has been described. As years passed, the old leaders and the old traditions died, and leaders and people learned that to lose something by peaceful compromise was better than to lose all by revolt. The result was, as related above, improved conditions everywhere and, in such countries as Argentina,

Brazil, Chile, Colombia, Mexico, and Uruguay, stable though non-democratic upper-class governments. By the second decade of the twentieth century, a further stage in human development had appeared — the final flowering of democratic government among a people grown nationally self-conscious — and it was directed to the betterment of masses rather than classes. Though the stable aristocratic governments had done little or nothing for the common man as such, they had fostered transportation, industrialization, immigration, and upper-class education. This brought upper-class thinkers into greater contact with the modern world, and many of them, becoming conscious that their nations had antiquated modes of life, were also genuinely distressed by the misery of their humbler fellows. Meantime the rise of a class of skilled workers, concentrated in the towns, furnished the common man some chance at education, and gave rise to organized labor movements with a program of social reform similar to that in all industrialized countries. Finally the immigrants, understanding nothing of the inherited family and regional feuds in politics, and often accustomed to better conditions in the countries they had left, demanded peace, prosperity, and a modernized social system.

**World War and Depression.** The temporary prosperity of the World War quickened many of the above changes. Also, the Latin Americans as a whole, sitting as spectators of the struggle, had thought upon world affairs forced upon them. Their favor was courted by all, during the war and after it, and they participated in the League of Nations on equal terms. From all these sources they gained new ideas, new self-esteem, and increased determination to modernize their life. As will be seen below, many of them had already made important changes in their institutions and their political habits, when the economic crisis that started in 1929 began to affect them. So much of their economic and political welfare was based on foreign loans and the export of one or two basic crops or minerals that they suffered as severely as any other part of the world, and perhaps more than most. As in other countries, the subsequent distress was blamed on the institutions and groups in power, and a wave of revolution followed. Omitting consideration of the Central American states, in some of which disorder was endemic, and in most of which United States influence and Central American treaty arrangements created a special situation,[1] only three Latin-American countries escaped a revolutionary change of government. Those three were Colombia, Venezuela, and Mexico. Even in those, a severe crisis had some effect on politics. In Colombia, for instance, following serious disorders, the Liberal party won its first national election in over forty years. The Conservatives proved that Colombia had learned good constitutional habits, by a friendly and peaceful transfer of the control, in the spirit of the best democratic government. In Venezuela, tension became so great as to force the old dictator Gómez to emerge once more from his preferred lair as Commander in Chief of the Army, and assume open control (1931) as president, following the convenient resignation of the legal holder of that office. In Mexico the civilian president Ortiz Rubio was quietly replaced by the soldier Rodríguez (1932), technically because of Ortiz Rubio's ill health, but actually because of some political crisis not yet understood outside party councils. Santo Domingo, Bolivia, and Perú suffered revolts in 1930, and Panamá, Ecuador, and Paraguay followed the example in 1931. Perú, Bolivia, Ecuador, and Paraguay have also had later violent changes of government. Upheavals in Argentina, Brazil, Chile, Cuba, and Uruguay will be discussed with more detail in succeeding sections of this chapter. Whether these commotions and revolts speeded or retarded the underlying process of social readjustment remains to be seen, but there is no question that many of the revolts reflected that process quite as much as they reflected the world-wide economic crisis.

**The New Social Ideals of Latin America.** That all parts of Latin America are aiming at the same type of national reform can be seen by studying recent constitutions and laws. Since 1917, Mexico, Uruguay, Honduras (1924), Chile, the Dominican Republic, Ecuador (1929), Perú, Brazil, Venezuela, Nicaragua (1939), Paraguay (1940), Panamá, and Cuba have new constitutions. In these, and in the laws of states which have retained their older constitutions, one notes significant similarities. First, one finds an effort to adapt governmental forms to fit Latin American conditions to a greater extent than has generally been true before. The outstanding case is that of Uruguay, but many

[1] But note that Salvador, which had not changed a president by violence in two generations, did so in 1931.

others have attempted to limit the presidential power and achieve a more direct election of officials. Second, one finds detailed provisions for social justice for the masses. This usually involves an effort to abolish peonage, to furnish universal education, and to protect labor. It also includes at times a start toward various other reforms such as a more modern status for women, and a temperance movement. Third, one finds a tendency to adopt ideas that are usually called "socialistic," especially as to public ownership and regulation of large industries and public utilities. Fourth, the evils that are believed to be the result of exploitation and control by foreign residents and foreign capital are attacked through special limitations on foreign industry and foreign landholding, and sometimes on foreign clergymen. Finally, in countries where the Church had retained all or a part of its privileged status, one finds provision for the disestablishment of the Church, or action of a definitely hostile character. Argentina, Perú, and other nations do retain an established Church, and other exceptions to the above can be found, but none of the established Churches enjoy their ancient enormous privileges, and there is no doubt of the general trend. It can be traced in more detail in the history of the nations which for one reason or another need special treatment.

**Argentina.** The aristocratic régime in Argentina ended in 1916. Dissatisfaction with the rule of the oligarchy had long existed. Elections became so farcical under the domination of the conservatives and the provincial bosses — commonly called the "Córdoba Clique," after the center of their operations — that opposition groups practically ceased to vote after 1892. By the early twentieth century, however, the old opposition, or so-called Radical party, had been greatly reinforced. The working classes and the immigrant groups composed an increasingly large body of potential voters clamorous for a voice in the government. They were joined by many intellectuals and young men from the old aristocracy, and by the bulk of the many persons newly arisen to wealth and education. Into the bargain, years of freedom from serious competition at the polls had caused the oligarchs to divide among themselves. An unsuccessful revolt in 1905, and evidences of increased public unrest thereafter, finally forced the electoral reform laws of 1911 from the government. These provided for a secret ballot, compulsory voting, and minority representation in national politics. In spite of widespread but, as it proved, un-justified skepticism about the manner in which the laws would be enforced, the Radicals went to the polls in 1912 and captured about one third of the seats in the national Congress. In the next few years they also won control of several important provinces, and in 1916 elected their candidate Hipólito Irigoyen president. He took office without incidents of violence.

**Popular Rule under Irigoyen.** From 1916 to 1930, the "Radi-cals" — a party name with no more significance in Latin countries than that of "Democrat" or "Republican" in the United States — managed Argentine affairs. Irigoyen (1916–1922) was suc-ceeded by Marcelo T. Alvear (1922–1928) and then reëlected (1928) for another term. As Alvear, though more or less repre-sentative of another wing of the Radical party, and an excellent president, was completely overshadowed by Irigoyen and carried out his policies, the fourteen years are normally regarded as the work of Irigoyen alone. Irigoyen, a well-educated rancher sprung from a humble Basque family, had been prominent in the Radical party since 1880. He was distinctly a "man of the people," en-joyed tremendous popularity with them, and intended to help them in all things. On the other hand, he was an autocrat by nature, was defiantly independent of public opinion or even the advice of his friends, and was rather advanced in years when he first took office. As a result he rode roughshod over opposition, and interfered with provincial politics to an extent unusual even in the past. He also pursued a policy of national self-assertion in foreign affairs. His refusal, probably against the popular will, to let Argentina enter the World War is one illustration of this, how-ever beneficial it may have been in itself. Others appear in a quarrel with the Papacy over appointments (1923–1926), in his vigorous protests against the United States Tariff Acts of 1922 and later, and in his efforts to make Argentina assume the leader-ship of the Latin American countries in the League of Nations and the Pan-American congresses. This aggressive foreign policy, however, is typical of the acts of all nations as they first become nationally self-conscious, and it must be said of Irigoyen's other political activities that he did not follow the dictatorial policy of attacking the persons of the opposition, and that his interferences in the provinces were partly excusable in view of the methods of the Conservative politicians who controlled those entities.

**Social Reforms.** The program of social reform placed on the statute books between 1912 and 1930 is so lengthy as almost to defy summary. Much of it provided protection for laborers as to minimum wages, maximum hours, employers' liability, the right to strike, the use of arbitration, and a Pension Act (1923) based on equal contributions from laborers and employers. The status of the privileged was shaken by an inheritance tax, and during the quarrel with the Papacy mentioned above there was talk of disestablishment of the Church. A homestead law and an agreement with the railroads offered the poor man a chance at land. Public health was cared for through provisions for controlling the purity of drugs, the manufacture of poisonous types of matches, and the care of lepers, and through encouragement of water and sewerage systems for all towns. Education of the masses was a primary care, some thousand lower schools being opened in Irigoyen's first term alone. Realization of the Radical ideals except on paper was hampered by a strong Conservative opposition, and by the lack of moderation of Irigoyen and his followers. Apparently the land laws had no effect, and the Pension Act of 1923 proved so unworkable in the face of employers' opposition that it had to be repealed in 1926. Labor freed from its bonds often proved as unreasonable as its employers had been, and educational opportunities, especially for girls, were still below modern requirements. Nevertheless, a tremendous advance had been made by 1930 in most fields, with no evidence of the bad effect on Argentine prosperity which had been predicted by opponents.

**Return of the Oligarchy.** In September, 1930, Irigoyen was overthrown by a barracks uprising under General José Uriburú. Beyond question the world depression plus the example of other revolutions in Latin America was the immediate occasion of his fall. But Irigoyen had interpreted an overwhelming majority of votes in 1928 as a vote of complete power; he had reached, if not his dotage, at least too great an age to retain all his powers of judgment and action; he trusted no one to administer any detail of government and yet he could not possibly govern everything himself. His acts were more arbitrary than before, and governmental efficiency had not in years been so low. The army acted only after large numbers of students and civilians had demonstrated against him, and his overthrow was plainly popular. Once in power Uriburú, though personally of good character, proved himself a representative of the old Conservatives and aristocracy, acting in an arbitrary and dictatorial manner. Public opinion increased against his unconstitutional rule, and finally forced him to allow an election (November, 1931). This was probably conducted fairly so far as concerns intimidation of voters or counting of ballots, but the Radicals were forbidden to offer a candidate or otherwise function as a party, and General Agustín P. Justo, the Conservative candidate, won. He was succeeded in 1938 by Roberto Órtiz, a former Radical. Justo's acts showed respect for the Radical predominance among the populace, and Órtiz leaned strongly toward restoration of fully representative rule. The social program continued, somewhat modified. The depression was met with measures of State control reminiscent of those of the United States. The Radicals soon returned to the provincial polls, and in 1940 captured control of the Federal House. Their prospects of regaining complete control were injured by the retirement of Órtiz (1940) due to illness, and his death in July, 1942, since Vice President Ramón S. Cantillo was a strong Conservative.

**Brazil.** Recent events in Brazil differ from those in Argentina and other countries discussed below in that no important movement of popular or genuinely democratic government has yet come to the surface in the great Portuguese American nation. But recent events do show an awakened social conscience at work, and Brazil is for other reasons too important a state to neglect. As has been remarked, since the late nineteenth century government had proceeded on constitutional lines but had remained exclusively in the hands of the aristocracy. Its relatively orderly political life was based, apparently, on a compromise among the politicians by which no one of the individual states — more important and more diverse in Brazil than in most Latin American countries — expected two of its leaders to succeed each other in the presidency. In practice, with only two exceptions, the office was held by men from the southern and rather advanced states of São Paulo or Minas Geraes from 1894 to 1930. There was healthy political activity in some states, but once the "official" candidate had somehow been decided upon, the outcome of the national election was a foregone conclusion. The election of 1910 was a partial exception and is regarded by many as the beginning of Brazil's awakening to real democratic self-government. But at best it was an awakening within the ranks of the aristocracy, and not a popular movement. In 1930 President Washington Luiz Pereira de Souza, of São Paulo, who had been an excellent president, tried to bring about the election as his successor of the then governor of his native state. He probably felt justified in his action by the desirability of ensuring continuance of the ideals of his government, but he nevertheless broke the compromise tradition. How far other factors were involved in the subsequent revolt is uncertain. But Brazil was sharply affected by the world depression, which cut off the foreign loans that enabled her to conduct her scheme for controlling coffee production and prices, as well as decreasing the market. An ever larger surplus piled up in the government warehouses, and prices fell abruptly. Many planters were ruined, and distress was widespread. Washington Luiz was defeated and exiled in the only successful revolution in the history of the Brazilian republic, by a so-called Liberal Alliance, and Getulio Vargas of Rio Grande do Sul became provisional president.

**The Vargas Régime.** Vargas, as a dictator, ruled Brazil ably for three years. He promulgated many liberal decrees dealing with labor, child welfare, public health, and similar subjects. He much improved public finances. He made a bold attempt to solve the coffee problem by destroying at national cost over thirty million bags of surplus low-grade coffee — about fifteen months' supply for the whole world — and by limiting the planting of new trees and encouraging the growth of other crops. The program, however, increased taxes, especially in the wealthy states of the South, and the denial of constitutional rule was widely resented. São Paulo revolted in 1932. Although the movement was suppressed after a bitter struggle, it probably did much to hasten return to constitutional government. Vargas treated the defeated rebels and areas with conspicuous mercy, and called an assembly in 1933 to consider a new constitution. This having been promulgated on July 16, 1934, the Assembly elected Vargas as first president under the new régime.

**New Type Constitutions.** The new constitution had many economic and social clauses typical of the new ideals of Latin America, but was chiefly remarkable for its new political provisions. The president was to be elected by secret and direct ballot, and his power to intervene in the states was strictly defined. Other interesting features provided for equal suffrage, for deputies in the Congress to be chosen partly on a population basis and partly on one of occupation, and for technical councils (*conselhos technicos*) of "experts" attached to each executive department. For three years Vargas ruled under this Constitution, still dictatorially but with encouraging results in the social and political fields. A healthy election campaign for the next president got under way in 1937. But in November of that year Vargas overthrew the Constitutional régime and set himself up as dictator. He promulgated a new constitution by decree. It was conspicuous for the nearly unlimited powers of the president, for its near destruction of state autonomy, and for "corporative" economic provisions patterned after those of European fascism. Vargas has ruled as a military dictator since that time, though on the whole with moderation. He has repressed political dissent along with such extremist groups as the Communists and the *Integralistas*. (The latter, an authentic but largely native fascist party, came into existence in 1932.) The middle-class worker group, increasingly evident before 1937, is no longer politically active, but its sentiments are to some degree reflected in the decrees of the dictator. The latter has vigorously dealt with the problem of the coffee surplus and has fostered public improvements and diversified industries and agriculture.

**Chile.** Chile, the most stable of all Latin American nations in the first century of its independence, has been the most disturbed of the major countries in recent years. As already suggested, its years of peace, prosperity, and cultural progress occurred under the control of an aristocracy which divided within itself but allowed the populace no votes or voice in the handling of their own affairs. In 1920 this rule ended, under the impact of a genuinely popular middle-class and lower-class movement. Much as in Argentina, industrialization and immigration gave rise to an articulate and organized workers' group, with leaders from the younger men or the newer families of the aristocracy. Moreover, the parliamentary system of government that Chile used after the failure of Balmaceda's revolt (1891) was unsuited to Chilean conditions, so that the efficient if autocratic government of the nineteenth century was a thing of the past by 1920. In that year, an alliance of liberal groups elected Arturo Alessandri to be president, by a very close vote. Alessandri, a lawyer of humble ancestry, is something of a puzzle to this day. He is emotional rather than intellectual, he seems often to believe that the end justifies the means, and he exercises all the arts of the demagogue in his very successful swaying of the crowd. Yet his honesty and sincerity have not seriously been questioned even by his opponents. In any case, he has been the major personal influence on Chilean affairs now for twenty years. His first term was handicapped by the hostility of the conservatives, who used all their wealth and political experience to block his program. He suffered also from a crisis in the market for nitrates, caused partly by a post-war depression, and partly by the increased production of synthetic nitrates in Germany and other countries. He probably was handicapped as much also by his own unwisdom and that of his followers. Alessandri interfered in the congressional elections against a thirty years' tradition, after assuming office. The resulting body of deputies showed its quality by neglecting the budget and the program of social legislation, while playing politics and voting themselves salaries for the first time in Chilean history. The salaries may, in themselves, have been necessary if the new popular party representatives were to live, but they did much to hasten the swing of feeling against Alessandri and the movement which he typified. In September, 1924, a Junta of officers from the unpaid army and navy demanded action. Alessandri offered his resignation. The Junta granted him, instead, six months' leave, and he sailed for Europe.

**The Constitution of 1925.** The Junta started well, even to promulgating some of the program of liberal legislation. But it drifted toward a more conservative policy, and its unconstitutional character was offensive. In January, 1925, a group of civilians and discontented younger officers overthrew the Junta and invited Alessandri to return. He did so, having been promised the chance to form a new constitution. As his popularity was now higher than ever, his views were adopted in the new instrument, practically without debate. The resulting constitution presented many social reform features, such as suffrage for all literate adult males, disestablishment of the Church, and provision for an income tax. The Church was granted a subsidy for five years, thereby removing much of the hardship of the transition period. The new basic law also provided for some decentralization in government by creating provincial assemblies. Its major political reform, however, was its definite provision for a strong, independent executive. Since 1925 the president has been elected for a six-year term, with immediate reëlection forbidden. His granted powers are large. They include especially the right, based on hard-won experience in the past, to pass a budget if Congress does not act on it within four months of its presentation. After adoption of the constitution, Alessandri resigned, in a successful effort to force certain members of his cabinet also to resign, and thereby prevent official manipulation of the next election. Emilio Figueroa-Larrain was chosen president for the next five years in the election of 1925.

**Rule of Ibáñez.** Figueroa-Larrain, though elected as a "national" or compromise candidate, and a man of unquestioned patriotism and general ability, was a member of the old aristocracy, and too antiquated and inflexible in his ideas to adapt himself to the new conditions. He was compelled to execute the laws of the previous administration, although he was probably unsympathetic toward them. They were, besides, costly and sometimes out of touch with reality, and he got the blame for events really beyond his control. In April, 1927, after months of futile effort, he resigned. Carlos Ibáñez, the Minister of War and "strong man" of the Cabinet, who had been virtually running the government for several months, was chosen president in May. Ibáñez showed himself somewhat interested in education, better living conditions for labor, and better public finance. Finding the nitrate industry bankrupt, he tried to revive it by giving the United States Guggenheim interests control. In 1930 the earlier arrangement was replaced by the so-called Cosach (*Compañia Salitre de Chile*), a monopolistic combine in which the Guggenheims and the government had each a half interest. He showed himself also a terror against governmental corruption and overstaffed government services. On the other hand, he acted with typical dictatorial violence and use of exile against all opponents from Alessandri and the labor leaders to the chief justice of the Supreme Court, the brother of Figueroa-Larrain. Public displeasure grew rapidly, and the world depression proved the last straw. Chile was perhaps hurt worse by the depression than any other Latin American country. Her exports of copper and nitrates, almost her only source of wealth, dropped during the period from 1929 to 1933 from a value of $278,000,000 to one of $44,000,000. Also, much of Ibáñez's success depended on large expenditures for public works, which in turn depended upon large revenues and foreign loans. When efforts of Cosach to maintain nitrate prices by agreement with foreign synthetic producers broke down in July, 1931, the student and professional classes began a demonstration which was aided by a general strike of the labor unions, and after relatively little violence Ibáñez fled.

**Political Chaos.** Briefly, Chile enjoyed an orderly and fairly moderate government, but public opinion had, during years of suppression, violence, and dislike of Cosach as a foreign exploiter, tended toward extremes. A troubled and confused period ensued. Carlos Dávila, a former ambassador to the United States, in the summer of 1932 attempted to set up a socialistic but otherwise moderate state. Even his three months were interrupted by a revolt under Ibáñez and an effort by Colonel Marmaduque Grove to force a much more radical régime upon the country. Finally a provisional government held an election (October, 1932). In this a Chile tired of radicalism and unrest, but unwilling also to return to the old Conservative rulers, chose Alessandri as its leader.

**Recent Years.** Alessandri, securely in office with more votes than all the other candidates together, promptly began the restoration of civilian rule and the liberal program. He was compelled to suppress Grove's radicalism by exile and force, and to put down an agrarian revolt in the South as late as July, 1934. Some unrest still exists, but on the whole Chile had a stable political life under him. He dissolved Cosach in January, 1933, and reorganized the combine under a plan giving the State a larger share of the profits. He combated unemployment by fostering "emergency" gold mining, and by an edict of 1933 which encouraged building by giving a ten-year tax exemption to edifices

completed before 1936. A gradual improvement of world conditions helped him, and unemployment dropped from 125,000 in
1932 to 13,000 in 1935. In spite of that, there was, and has been,
enough distress to favor the rise of truly radical parties. In 1938
Alessandri was succeeded by Pedro Aguirre Cerda, elected by a
coalition of all the parties from the Radicals (*i.e.*, Moderates) to
the Communists. Accession of this "Popular Front" to power
nearly led to revolt by the old line Liberal and Conservative
parties, but Chilean political health proved good, and Aguirre
Cerda took office. In practice the Popular Front has been dominated by its moderates, and has given Chile a liberal rather than
a radical régime. No Communist has ever sat in the Cabinet.
Internal dissensions have several times threatened its control,
but a split was recently averted by ejecting the Communists from
the group. Aguirre's death led to election (February 1, 1942) of
the Front's candidate, Juan Antionio Rios, a "Rightist" Radical.

**Uruguay.** Uruguay, which apparently had survived the depression and the wave of revolutions, ended its constitution by
violent means in 1933, and adopted a new constitution in 1934.
The reasons are not yet clearly understood abroad. However,
opponents of the socialistic ideals and of the diminution of presidential power favored by Battlé had always been numerous, and
they probably took advantage of disturbed economic conditions
to achieve their aims. Perhaps it is also significant that a president
who could not legally have succeeded himself under either the
old or the new constitution was in fact reëlected as first president
under the new régime. Accepting the face value of events, President Gabriel Terra (1931–1938) was a minority choice for the
office, and as his opponents controlled the National Council of
Administration, he lacked patronage power and lost control of
the government. After a year's effort to rule under the constitution, he overthrew it. The new instrument promulgated in 1934
abolished the dyarchy, substituting for it a modified form of
parliamentary government. Under it the Cabinet, and the
president through a more complicated procedure, can be forced
out by the Congress. Voting is compulsory. The social welfare
clauses and laws of the preceding years were largely incorporated.
In 1938 Alfredo Baldomir became president, campaigning on a
platform of democratic government.

**Colombia.** In 1930 the Liberals in Colombia elected their first president in two generations. A financial crisis began in 1927, due to a faulty currency law passed many years earlier. It was added to by the world depression. The Conservatives split, and Enrique Olaya Herrera, the Liberal candidate, won. Alfonso López (1934–1938), Eduardo Santos (1938–1942), and again López (1942–    ) continued the Liberal régime. The Liberals have themselves faced dissensions, especially over the more radical aims of López, but have pushed steadily ahead on a clean-cut program of constructive social changes. Education, restriction of the power of the Church, and modernization of transportation have received the care to be expected. Laws intended to limit the influence of foreign capital included a new Petroleum Code (1931) and bans upon withdrawing large profits from the country. López was exceptionally active in extending protection to organized labor, and endeavored to benefit the peons by distributing land. The constitution of 1936 incorporated most of the laws, and declared that the rights of society were above those of private property, giving the government the right to expropriate property for national uses. Political quarrels have been warm, the Clerical question continues, and the old-time Conservatives remain unreconciled. But on the whole, campaigns have been free from governmental interference, the high percentage of illiteracy is dropping, and economic and social welfare has improved. The Liberal régime appears to be established for years to come.

**Perú.** Leguía, who seized power in Perú in 1919, had been a Conservative while he served as Minister of Finance or as President from 1903 to 1912. In 1919 he posed as a champion of the workers and peons, and claimed to be acting to avert election frauds. He quickly replaced the constitution of 1860 with that of 1919. This substituted a council for the vice-presidency, and began decentralization by erecting three provincial legislatures to enact local laws. It broadened the suffrage, called for an improved status for labor, the Indians, and mass education, and established legal toleration for all religions for the first time in Perú's history. Though Leguía ruled arbitrarily from the start, for a time he brought about material advances. Foreign loans enabled him to build roads and railroads, to improve sanitation in the cities, and to build fine public buildings and some schools. But he handled opposition with increasing harshness, he mortgaged the country's best resources to the foreign bankers, and he failed to push schools, or labor, land, and other reforms. Distress caused by the depression aided in his overthrow in 1930 by Colonel Luís Sánchez Cerro. The latter was assassinated in 1933. General Oscar Benavides, who was elected for the unexpired term, increasingly suppressed the opposition. His constitution of 1933 was similar to that of 1919, but banned officeholding by members of international parties. This was aimed even more at the native *Apristas* than at the Socialists and Communists. In 1936, to prevent an electoral victory by the leftist candidate, Benavides forced Congress, again through a "new" constitution, to extend his term for three years with dictatorial powers.

**The Apra.** Though Perú lacks popular government, it is the home of a strong movement in that direction. The movement includes the usual liberal objectives such as anticlericalism and labor legislation, but centers about Indian status. Indians make about sixty per cent of the population, and mestizos are another third. In 1919 about thirty-five per cent of the total population still dwelt in exclusively Indian villages. They were organized in their ancient communal *ayllus*, and lived almost as in the pre-Conquest days. In spite of some extra-legal encroachment by white neighbors, the *ayllus* had retained most of their lands. But landed or landless, the Indians were miserably oppressed as to taxes and external government, and many were held in debt peonage. A notable group of intellectuals has studied and agitated for reforms throughout the twentieth century. Though these men do not necessarily belong to or approve of the *Apra (Alianza Popular Revolucionaria Americana)*, that party has become the leader of the political campaign for reforms. The Apra program called for the usual liberal changes but emphasized division of the great estates and aid for the Indian. Since it arose among radical students as a protest against Leguía's ties with foreign capital, it long featured anti-imperialism and an attack on foreign or other capital through nationalization of land and major industries. It is headed by Victor Raúl Haya de la Torre, has members outside Perú, and carries on effective verbal and printed propaganda. It also maintains some coöperative enterprises. Benavides drove it underground in 1933 as an international organization. But even he was moved to promote education, social insurance, roads, and irrigation and diversified industries, in an effort to decrease its chances of success. A well-run Bureau of Indian Affairs was long ago added to the government for much the same reason.

**Recent Events.**  Manuel Prado Ugarteche was put into office by Benavides in the elections of 1939, but Benavides shortly left for a European embassy and Prado has followed an independent policy of civilian and reasonable government.  Haya de la Torre lives openly in Perú, to the knowledge of everyone except the police. Maturity, years of exile in other countries, and the menace of European totalitarianism have modified his views and those of other *Apristas*.  They have become less radical as to reforms, and have also lessened their anti-imperialism and now favor co-operation with the United States as a democracy.  There are indications of a legal compromise as to party existence, and peaceful reform of some of the abuses seems possible.

**Venezuela.**  When death ended the twenty-six-year tyranny of Gómez, anarchy seemed certain to follow.  But in spite of the abuses of his régime, Gómez left Venezuela with practically no governmental debt, and the nation as a whole economically sound. It enjoyed increasing employment and revenues from the oil industry.  Though many of the national leaders had been killed or exiled, others had been able privately to disagree with his tyranny and brutalities while serving Venezuela faithfully in posts such as those of cabinet ministers or head of the national bank.  One of them, Minister of War Eleázar López Contreras, took control and was later elected president.  Whether or not by plan, he allowed the populace the emotional relief of a brief orgy of revenge against the worst of Gómez's family and followers.  He then clamped down on further disorder, invited exiles to return, tried to restore confiscated property, and revived civil liberties.  He proved to be an excellent president, and preferred democratic to arbitrary rule.  A new constitution (1936) continued federal government, with liberal provisions as to suffrage and other rights.  The Church is still established, but all religions are tolerated, all education is free, and secondary as well as primary education is compulsory.  The national government has complete control of financial institutions, national resources, social security, and

public health.  Laws under the constitution have given labor a
highly favorable status.

**The New Régime.**  The government has vigorously attacked
the problems of malaria, tuberculosis and other common diseases,
of maternal and child welfare, and of public sanitation.  A three-
year plan (1938) of water supply and sewerage systems for the
towns is well advanced.  Banks must keep eighty per cent of their
deposits invested in Venezuela, and other legislation has made
foreign investment a direct benefit to the nation.  There is much
to be done in such fields as education and railroad building.
Another real problem is found in the low standard of living for
most, and the appalling cost of living for persons who aspire to
white standards.  The supply of gold from Venezuela's mines, the
revenue from oil, the heavy import duties, and a certain license on
the part of the newly important labor have combined to make
middle-class life approximately two and a half times as expensive
as in New York City.  Neglect of agriculture and ranching for the
rising oil industry probably has something to do with that fact.
Revival of those interests is beginning to concern far-sighted
thinkers.  In spite of all the difficulties, modern government has
apparently come to stay.  As the end of López Contreras's term
of office approached, a seemingly genuine movement arose to
persuade him to continue in office for the sake of the nation's welfare.  He resolutely refused.  On April 28, 1941, the Congress in
its electoral capacity chose a former cabinet member, Isaías
Medina, to succeed him.

**Mexico.**  The men who, in the National Revolutionary party,
began to rule Mexico in 1920, inherited numerous and perplexing
problems.  They must give peace to a war-ridden country, suppress
banditry, reorganize the finances, and withdraw vast quantities of
depreciated paper money from circulation.  They must satisfy the
industrial workers, who evinced a strong drift toward radical
socialism, secure the adoption of agrarian reforms enabling the
peasants to acquire land of their own, and attract the foreign
capital needed for development of Mexican resources without
allowing the foreign lenders to secure a strangle hold on Mexican
economic life.  They must overcome the opposition of the clerical
elements to an entirely secular state, provide for adequate popular
education and, in general, foster among the common people the

habits of thrift, industry, and obedience to law. Any one of these problems would tax the abilities of the best statesmen. In Mexico they had all to be faced at once and to be solved under a constitution which, drawn up without free debate in a time of revolutionary fervor, is extreme in its details even for many who agree with its aims. Finally, solution of some of the problems would almost surely interfere with the solution of others.

**General Character of Mexican History.** The Mexican leaders, consciously or not, adopted a policy of opportunism. Execution of some parts of the program was postponed, while the government worked on essentials and such "safe" things as land distribution, and social welfare projects. As time wore away the revolutionary aspects of Mexican thought, and as the government gained popular approval, it tended on the one hand to decrease in social radicalism and antiforeignness, and on the other hand to begin the execution of the highly controversial anticlerical clauses of the constitution.

**Political History since 1920.** For more than twenty years now, Mexico has enjoyed fairly stable and efficient government, under a succession of able men with advanced social views. There have been several revolts of limited extent, but they were all suppressed with increasing ease. They were even to some degree helpful in that they resulted by 1929 in eliminating from Mexican life practically all the older "generals" who had grown up in the tradition that the army was the proper road to the presidency. The government has been a dictatorship, but it has been the dictatorship of a party even though that party has in turn been dominated by "strong men" such as President Plutarco Elias Calles (1924–1928). The leaders have been sincerely interested in the needs of the people, and desirous of bringing about honest self-government as soon as possible. It is interesting to observe that for a while the presidents were each time more civilian in character. This trend was reversed in 1932, when a general of the new army, Abelardo L. Rodríguez, became provisional president following the resignation of Ortiz Rubio, and was succeeded as the elective president by General Lázaro Cárdenas (1934–1940). Only time can tell if this is of permanent significance. Foreign relations remained for many years in a most unsatisfactory state. The antiforeign provisions of the constitution were in themselves no legitimate concern of foreign governments, but in the early days of high revolutionary emotion Mexico attempted to apply them retroactively. Foreign ministries, on the other hand — especially those of the United States and Great Britain, already hostile to the revolutionary aspects of Mexican ideals — not merely protested the genuine breaches of international comity, but interfered with internationally permissible or purely domestic affairs as well. A deadlock ensued. In later years, both sides became better advised and less aggressive. When approached in a rational and conciliatory frame of mind, there proved to be no insuperable difficulties in the way of adjusting disputes by peaceful negotiation or arbitration, and for years Mexican intercourse with the world was on a normally friendly basis.

**Nonpolitical Change.** The administrations have made, on the whole, notable advances toward the solution of other problems. Before the depression, finances had been put on a sound basis, and mining, agriculture, and industrial production improved. A tremendous program of schools, libraries, public health work, and agitation for temperance is under way. In its earlier days it showed such amusing aberrations as loading the new libraries for newly literate peasants with translations of the works of Homer and Virgil. That phase soon passed, with the passing from influence of the earnest but impractical revolutionaries, and the program has for years been brilliantly conceived and well carried out by men who know that the basis of the Mexican state is, and probably always will be, the farmer of Indian race. All the work now specially aims at remaking the Indian into a self-respecting and self-helping member of a modern society, without losing sight of the fact that the inherited culture of the Indian is in many things worth preserving, and in others impossible to eradicate at once. The whole idea centers about the distribution of lands, averaging some twenty to twenty-five acres per person, to the previously landless. By June, 1931, over sixteen million acres had been so distributed. Several million more acres were given out by 1935, to the direct benefit of some 900,000 persons in all. Irrigation projects, land banks to finance the new farms, and agricultural schools to assure good use of the land round out the program.

**Problems of Labor.** Execution of two parts of the 1917 provisions, respectively concerning labor and the Church, is still far from having reached equilibrium. The constitution definitely permitted labor to organize, and favored it in many ways which gave it almost a privileged status in the nation. The "C. R. O. M." (*Confederación Regional de Obreros Mexicanos*) was organized in 1918, and soon became the major representative of the labor union viewpoint. President Obregón, and for a time President Calles (1924–1928), favored it personally, and it grew from some fifty thousand members in 1920 to about two and a quarter millions in 1928. Its leaders finally suffered such delusions of grandeur that they became ambitious to supplant the National Revolutionary party in the political power, and they nearly paralyzed the economic life of the country by a series of strikes of doubtful necessity. As a result, Calles practically destroyed the C. R. O. M. in his last year. Aided by the Labor law of 1931, the C. T. M. (*Confederación de trabajadores mexicanos*) replaced it in national affairs, led by the Marxist, Vicente Lombardo Toledano.

**Church *versus* State.** The clerical provisions of the constitution were left in abeyance until 1926. Calles, then president, was apparently indifferent to religion, if not then as hostile to it as he later showed himself, but the Church forced his hand and incurred the responsibility for the first overt act. On February 4, 1926, the Archbishop of Mexico published an announcement in a Mexican newspaper that the clergy did not recognize the validity of the anticlerical clauses of the constitution and would combat them. Calles promptly had laws passed to execute the constitutional provisions, closed the religiously controlled schools, and deported some clergy. The Church retaliated by stopping all religious offices, and for three years Mexico had no real churches. As time passed, it became apparent to the church leaders that the populace would not back their stand if that meant opposing the only beneficial government that the common man had ever had in Mexico. Also, some of the exaggerated suspicions on both sides were quieted through the friendly services of the very popular United States Ambassador, Dwight Morrow, who served as a go-between without attempting to impose his views as to proper outcome. In June, 1929, a settlement was reached. The Church agreed to abide by the laws, and to return the clergy to the churches, while the State more or less formally assured the Church that it was concerned only with the nonspiritual aspects of Church activity. Unfortunately the 1929 bargain has since been widely broken on both sides in spirit, if not always in the letter. Many states have passed laws (1931–1933) stringently limiting the number of clergy allowed to officiate within their confines, usually setting a figure of something like one priest to twenty-five thousand of the population.  Some have by circumlocution barred all Roman Catholic priests, as did Guanajuato by banning as foreigners any clerics who professed allegiance to foreign potentates — that is to say, any who professed allegiance to the Roman Pontiff.  On the other hand, the Church has clearly violated the laws about such things as political activity and education. It is impossible to establish which side was primarily to blame for renewal of the conflict, but it created a situation deplorable for the best interests of either side, and dangerous to the peace of the country.

**Cárdenas.**  Though Mexico avoided the complete upheavals of most Latin American countries during the depression, its recent history has shown a somewhat troubled character.  The University of Mexico, regarded as a center of reaction, became a political storm center, and religiously inspired unrest and conservative discontent caused apprehension and some riots and revolts.  Most notable event was the rise of Lázaro Cárdenas as the real leader of the National Revolutionary party.  Apparently Calles, grown rich and more conservative with years, had become lukewarm on the land and labor provisions of the constitution. Cárdenas, presumably the choice of Calles when elected in 1934, flatly defied his leader on matters of policy in June, 1935, and thereafter successfully maintained his position.  Calles, announcing that he had been misunderstood and that he desired only peace and constant good government in Mexico, retired to his Sinaloa ranch.  In view of his self-denying action at the time of Obregón's assassination (1928) he was quite probably sincere. At any rate, he made no further move.  Cárdenas chose a new Cabinet from men not previously prominent in politics, but recognized as industrious, able, and moderate sympathizers with the Socialist theories.

**Socialist Era.**  They energetically revived the agrarian and labor program — with a subsequent epidemic of strikes — promoted "Socialistic" education, and strengthened the attacks started by Portes Gil (1928–1930) against gambling, prostitution, and alcohol. By his speech at the opening of Congress (September, 1935) Cárdenas planned a program of government ownership of basic industries like those of paper, petroleum, mining, sugar, and alcohol. He also declared in favor of women's rights and equal suffrage. He accomplished much of his hopes. Distribution of lands jumped until the total given out between 1915 and 1939 reached 57,000,000 acres, benefiting 1,600,000 heads of families or perhaps half the population. Education and the campaign against social evils advanced, railroads were nationalized in 1937, and the oil fields expropriated in 1938. Production of sugar and cotton, and of textile, shoe, and paper goods increased. The Church crisis receded through neglect of extreme aspects of the laws. But serious troubles appeared. In spite of the increased lands for small farmers, basic foods had to be imported. The cost of living rose faster than incomes, currency depreciated, and the worker-operated railways steadily lost money and declined in efficiency. The oil industry incurred a deficit of 68,000,000 pesos by 1940. Whether this last was due to poor handling or to loss of a market is uncertain, but much of the other economic crisis was clearly a result of lack of experience and foresight on the part of the farmers and workers, and of the political tinkering of the C. T. M. Relations of the government and the C. T. M. became increasingly bitter over questions of policy as well as over the personal ambitions of the leaders.

**Recent Events.** In 1940 the official candidate, Manuel Ávila Camacho, was announced as the winner of a bitterly fought contest: The campaign and the election were marred by violence, and the result was manipulated beyond the average, but no serious revolt followed. Ávila Camacho, from the start of his campaign, denounced Communism, and made it plain that he would welcome foreign capital on fair terms, would ameliorate the condition of the Church, and would reform some of the excesses of "Socialization" of education and industry. Soon after his inauguration he introduced bills to correct some of the abuses in railway management and operation, and began issuing individual though inalienable titles to lands in the communal holdings. The C. T. M. and radical and fascist groups were brought under control. British relations, broken over oil expropriations were renewed, and a series of agreements (November, 1941–April, 1942), largely

*Courtesy American Supply Company, Mexico City*

IXTACIHUATL

*Courtesy "La Rochester"*

XOCHIMILCO

settled disputes with the United States. Loans from the United States are aiding establishment of basic industries and improved transportation systems.

**Guatemala.** The "Unionist" revolt that overthrew Estrada Cabrera in 1920 is still a subject for unofficial celebration in Guatemala, and is likely to be regarded in the future as a milestone in Guatemalan history. But it did not solve the basic problems of the nation, nor end more than temporarily the rivalries of parties and leaders. The currency had greatly depreciated under Cabrera, and the destruction of the capital by earthquakes in 1917 and 1918 had not been overcome. The Indians, who form at least seventy per cent of the population, suffered from debt peonage and lived in squalor, although mostly in possession of their ancestral lands. Even the one per cent of the population which was white was sunk in political apathy and suffering from economic depression. The first president lasted only a year and a half, but General José María Orellana (1922–1926) and his successor made real advances. The country went on the gold standard in 1924, railroads and highways were built, foreign commerce thrived, and primary education was improved in quality and quantity. A constitutional amendment (1928) forbade reëlection of a president for twelve years.

The disabling illness of President Lázaro Chacón permitted street fighting late in 1930, but his resignation (January, 1931) led to election of General Jorge Ubico. The latter is regarded as a Conservative. He has suppressed all political opposition, and has "permitted" a plebiscite (1935) and a Constituent Assembly (1941) to extend his term until 1949. But even his enemies agree that he is enlightened, honest, and energetic in promoting his country's welfare. He has largely eliminated the official graft and sinecures that bled Guatemala's revenues without benefit to the nation. The budget is balanced, good roads cover the republic, the railroads are clean and run on schedule, and order and sanitation prevail even in remote corners of the land. The tourist trade, new banana plantations, and recent trials of rubber represent efforts to overcome too great dependence on coffee. Intellectual life has been aided. The Labor Law of 1934 abolished debt peonage. It substituted an obligation to work somewhere 150 days annually, but realists agree that the system is less evil that the system that it displaced. Indian exclusivism and illiteracy are being broken down through drafting men into the army and educating them while there.

**Costa Rica.** The generally peaceful history of Costa Rica has been interrupted only by the Tinoco régime (1917–1918). This sprang directly from the plan of President Alfredo González Flores to succeed himself under a legal quibble. The president had previously stirred opposition by advocacy of land and property taxes, and a land policy in general, that offended the wealthy, and there was widespread dislike of his proposed violation of the intent of the constitution. When Federico Tinoco set himself up as dictator in January, 1917, the puzzled voters for the time preferred this to the alternative. Tinoco declared a general amnesty and caused amendment of the electoral system. The United States now had to choose between breaking its Central American policy of nonrecognition of governments that rose by force, or opposing a government acceptable to the people. Basing its decision on political principle — and it really had no other reason for blocking Tinoco — it chose nonrecognition. Its pressure and growing popular opposition to his rule forced Tinoco out in August, 1918. A literacy test for voting, and other reforms, were introduced in 1920. Since then peace and the promotion of education, sound finances, transportation, and a satisfactory status for labor have occupied the nation's attention. Electric power was nationalized in 1928, and governmental control has been extended over banking and insurance. Costa Rica has long prided itself on spending more on education than on its army. Political activity and civil rights are in a healthy state, in spite of minor abuses. A self-governing middle-class nation is approaching reality. A new law establishing secret and compulsory voting was first used in February, 1940, resulting in the election of Dr. Rafael Angel Calderón Guardia.

**Cuban Problems.** The Republic of Cuba began its independent life, only a little less than four decades ago, with nearly the same problems and handicaps as those of the other Spanish American nations a century earlier. Its history has been markedly affected by two other factors: its close political and economic relations with the United States, and its peculiar advantages for growing sugar better than any other large area in the world. The right of the United States to intervene in Cuban political life under the Platt

Amendment, as already described, was objectionable to all Cubans in theory, but it is only too evident that many of them, when in power, preferred United States intervention and protection to fighting the opposition or allowing it to take over control. Also the United States, judging Cuban political conditions by its own, tended until very recently to maintain any incumbent in office as a matter of principle, not realizing that under Latin American conditions revolution is sometimes a lesser evil than, and the only corrective for, tyranny. It goes without saying, probably, that Cuban policies were also influenced to favor United States investments. All observers agree, whatever their other divergences, that the Platt Amendment slowed up the growth of the Cubans' political self-reliance and abilities by saving them from the consequences of their errors.

**Cuban Sugar.** Sugar crops had been increasing in Cuba throughout the nineteenth century, but did so with tremendous rapidity in the early twentieth century and after the World War. Whereas in 1900 sugar accounted for only forty-two per cent of all Cuban production, in 1929 it made up over eighty-one per cent. This was partly due to the natural tendency of capitalists in the United States to invest in near-by lands, and to the preference which Cuba enjoyed in the United States market by location and under the reciprocity treaty of 1903. Much of it, however, was due to Cuban geography, and to world conditions not subject to effective control by anyone. For many years the imposing sugar crops brought great prosperity to Cuba as a whole, but they produced many undesirable effects upon individuals. As in some other Latin American countries, dependence on one export crop made Cuba exceptionally sensitive to fluctuations in the world market, and in Cuba both the one crop, sugar, and the second crop, tobacco, were commodities which were partly in the luxury class. In the second place, sugar plantations offer practically no employment from July to November, and the lack of other large crops caused serious seasonal unemployment. Finally, the nineteenth-century tendency toward ownership of small farms by the men who worked them was reversed. Modern large-scale methods concentrated more and more land under one owner, and put both laborers and surviving small farmers at the mercy of the owners of the great *Centrales*, or sugar mills. These, often worth a million

dollars each, were impossible for the little man either to get along
without, or to compete with. That they were frequently owned by
absentees, or by foreign and "soulless" corporations, was an ag-
gravation of other evils.

**The Machado Tyranny.** The Cuban situation came to a head
under the influence of the world depression. The storm had been
gathering long before, as Cuba came nearer and nearer to growing
enough sugar for the whole world, at the same time that many
former markets like the United States and Great Britain developed a national supply for themselves behind the protection
of increased tariffs or quotas. General Gerardo Machado, who
was president (1925–1933) when the storm broke upon Cuba, was
a despotic dictator of the modern type. Within the limits of his
unformed ideology he may have meant well. Certainly he had
been making an effort to solve Cuba's economic problems by encouraging diversified industries and agriculture, and by a program
of highways and other public works, and by fostering the tourist
trade. He also coöperated in domestic and international efforts
at sugar crop restrictions. But he had no idea that economic development could be bought at too high a price if it destroyed individual freedom and learning, and he indulged in graft and favored
foreign capital to an unprecedented degree. He ruled ruthlessly
and violently through intimidated courts and an enlarged and well-
paid army; he was indifferent to the status of the peasant; he
neglected the lower schools and stifled the formerly excellent university. Illiteracy, officially rated at twenty-three per cent in
1929, was estimated by nonofficial Cubans at about fifty-three
per cent. Though all opposition was forced underground, it became increasingly vigorous as the world-wide economic crisis
brought greater and greater woe to Cuba. Some of it was purely
the jealousy of politicians among the "outs," but much of it represented the anger of a new "Youth" group against unconstitutional
government, public corruption, and social wrongs. It rather
naturally, though erroneously, blamed all Cuba's troubles on
foreign influence and capital. Equally naturally its social liberalism and dislike of foreign capital became extreme because so long
repressed. For a time, as its only resource, the opposition met
Machado's terror with a terror of its own. Meantime United
States public opinion had been educated to a fair understanding

of the facts in the case, and after it became apparent that the United States government was no longer supporting Machado, a final rising forced him to flee in August, 1933.

**Upset Years.**  In less than five months after Machado's fall, Cuba had three real presidents, as well as others who lasted only a few days.  The three represented the violent fluctuations of public opinion that would be expected after so long a period of tyranny.  Carlos de Céspedes, though an able and personally respected man, was not radical enough in his social views for the newly released reform elements, and suffered in popular esteem because of the fact that he was so evidently approved of by the United States representatives.  After three weeks of turmoil he was succeeded by Ramón Grau San Martín, an able and reasonable professor of the old University of Havana, but a man politically inexperienced and too radical in his ideals for most of the older Cubans.  After a little over four months, he resigned under pressure.  He was succeeded on January 18, 1934, by Carlos de Mendieta, a man whose moderation and good intentions were agreed to even by his opponents.  But he largely represented the older ruling groups in his personal views, and remained in office lacking any constitutional mandate, supported by the army under the "strong man" of present-day Cuba, Fulgencio Batista.  The rise of the latter from a sergeant under Machado to the self-bestowed rank of colonel — truly a modest promotion considering his opportunities and Latin American precedent — is the most interesting single aspect of Cuban history since the original revolt.

**Batista Régime.**  Though fairly well educated, and intelligent, Batista had a military viewpoint on life, and ran Cuba on conservative dictatorial lines offensive to great numbers of Cubans. There were nevertheless one or two encouraging events for friends of good government in Cuba.  In 1934 the United States agreed to the abrogation of the Platt Amendment, and replaced it by a new treaty which in effect put Cuba on the same basis as any other independent nation.  On June 12, 1935 — probably under unofficial pressure by the United States so far as Batista was concerned — the constitution of 1901 was restored to vigor in its original form.  Machado had amended it to permit his continued rule. Grau San Martín had replaced it with a provisional and rather radical constitution promulgated without popular vote, and Mendieta had earlier annulled Grau San Martín's instrument and soon thereafter had in effect suspended all constitutions under martial law.  The 1901 basic law, so far as carried out, guaranteed popular liberties and self-government on a framework that had proved adapted to Cuba's needs.  Elections were as steadily postponed since June as they were before it, but every declaration of intention to restore constitutional government made it harder to refuse the deed, and in January, 1936, Dr. Miguel Mariano Gómez, son of Cuba's second president, was elected.

**Recent Events.**  Gómez's régime was aided by world-wide economic recovery, but he faced heavy opposition.  Though too conservative to please the Cuban masses, he had the courage to oppose Batista's pet idea of rural schools under army domination.  He was soon impeached and removed from office.  Under his successor, Vice-President Federico Laredo Bru, Batista regained a free hand.  He used it strongly, chiefly in an effort to control the sugar and tobacco industries, to restrict immigration, and to preserve jobs in Cuba for the Cubans.  Debate about a new constitution, and preparations for the next election, occupied Cuban attention until 1940.  Preparations for the election consisted mostly of efforts to settle on the best man to oppose Batista, whose candidacy was taken for granted.  Bargaining for lesser offices among the numerous parties had, by June, created a coalition behind Batista of the Conservatives and the Communists, which assured him a majority.  In that month a new constitution was approved.  This created a semiparliamentary régime, under an appointed prime minister who requires approval from the Chamber.  Apparently land could be confiscated, mortgages seriously impaired, and other anticapitalistic action could be taken, if the government chose so to interpret the sweeping provisions of the document.  Voting is compulsory.  In July Batista was elected, apparently without serious manipulation of the ballot.  He is now dissolving his relations with the Communists, a troublesome inheritance from his days as an army sergeant.  He has transferred control of the rural schools to the Ministry of Education, though army officers will still teach them, and plans expansion of other education, of diversified industries, and of public works.  In February, 1941, he startled foreigners by exiling two former associates, respectively heads of the army and the navy.  Cubans were less startled. Personal motivations were of course involved, but they had threatened the constitutional government and the country approved the act. Even the leader of the major opposition party, the "A.B.C.," declared that no one could disapprove if he had a "sense of responsibility toward the nation." Cuban politics and progress are still painfully dependent on world events, but there is real promise that her worst days are over.

## Words and Phrases You Should Know

| | | |
|---|---|---|
| *Apra* | homestead law | "Popular Front" |
| *Centrales* | Indian Servitude law | São Paulo |
| "Córdoba Clique" | *Integralistas* | social reforms |
| Cosach | peon | socialistic |
| C.T.M. | peonage | universal education |
| disestablishment of the Church | Petroleum Code | |

## Questions You Should Be Able to Answer

1. How has twentieth-century development in Latin America differed from nineteenth-century development? Why?
2. How were Latin American countries affected by the World War? by the depression?
3. In what four ways did the laws and revised constitutions of Latin American countries attempt to meet modern conditions?
4. What reforms were adopted in Argentina in 1911? What groups of people really forced these reforms?
5. What groups of people were supposed to benefit from the reforms in Argentina in the years 1912–1930?
6. How would you compare Argentina's political and social progress up to 1930 with that of Brazil?
7. How was coffee an important factor in the unrest of the 1930's in Brazil?
8. How did Varges's rule before 1937 differ from his rule after that date?
9. Why did political development in Chile which had been comparatively orderly in the nineteenth century become disorderly after 1920?
10. Why did Chile feel the effect of the depression so keenly?
11. What is the Argentine "Popular Front"?
12. What progress has been made in Colombia in recent years?
13. What is the Indian problem of Perú?
14. How have gold and oil worked hardship on some people in Venezuela?

15. What is meant by the statement that Mexican leaders since 1920 have followed a policy of opportunism?
16. How has the Mexican government attempted to deal with the oil problem?  the land problem?
17. Describe the problem of Church *versus* State in Mexico.
18. Has the Platt Amendment worked to the advantage or disadvantage of Cuba?
19. How has the United States been influential in Cuban economic affairs?  in Cuban political affairs?

## PROJECTS AND ACTIVITIES

1. Make a chart illustrating the problems that have confronted one or more Latin American countries in the twentieth century.  Use these headings: Country; Problems; Attempts at Settlement of Problems.
2. Which Latin American country do you think has made the most progress in the twentieth century?  List your reasons.
3. Let a committee prepare short oral reports on some of the twentieth-century leaders of Latin America.  Each member of the committee should be responsible for one leader.
4. Write a short essay on "New Social Ideals of Latin America."
5. Make two lists of Latin American rulers.  In one list include the names of rulers who governed democratically and in the other the names of rulers who were dictators.
6. Write an imaginary dialogue between a Conservative and a Radical as they discuss proposed reforms for their country.
7. List the good features and the bad features in the régime of any one outstanding Latin American ruler.
8. Prepare a brief talk on how Chile, Mexico, and Cuba were affected by the depression of 1929.

# CHAPTER X

# Economic and Social Conditions in Latin America

**Population.** There are no reliable statistics of population for many of the Latin American republics. In some of them a census has never been taken; in others it is not taken regularly or so carefully as to provide a complete enumeration of the inhabitants. Liberal estimates about 1930 gave Mexico 17,000,000; the six Central American states, 6,300,000; Cuba, Haiti, and the Dominican Republic, 8,000,000; the nine Spanish South American states, 43,000,000; and Brazil, 43,000,000. Latin America would thus contain upwards of 120,000,000 people, as compared with perhaps 20,000,000 at the close of the colonial period. States of the temperate zone rather naturally show the most marked growth in numbers; the population of some other states seems to have increased very little during the past century. But Mexico since 1810 has nearly trebled its inhabitants, and Argentina in recent decades has outstripped the once more populous Colombia and Perú. Brazil at the present time is growing more rapidly than any other Latin American country.

**Density of Population.** Latin America, though larger than Anglo-America, has fewer inhabitants. It has fewer inhabitants than the United States, which, excluding Alaska, is smaller than either Brazil or the Spanish American republics taken together. The average density of population in the United States, according to the census of 1940, was 41 per square mile. The average density in Latin America cannot exceed 9 or 10 per square mile, and in South America it probably does not reach that figure. Either Mexico, Venezuela, Colombia, or Perú could alone contain and support the entire population now scattered from the Mexican boundary on the north to Tierra del Fuego on the south. If Chile were as densely peopled as the Japanese Archipelago, it would have 90,000,000 inhabitants. If Argentina were as densely peopled as England, it would have 800,000,000 inhabitants. Were Brazil peopled in the same proportion as Belgium, all mankind might dwell there.

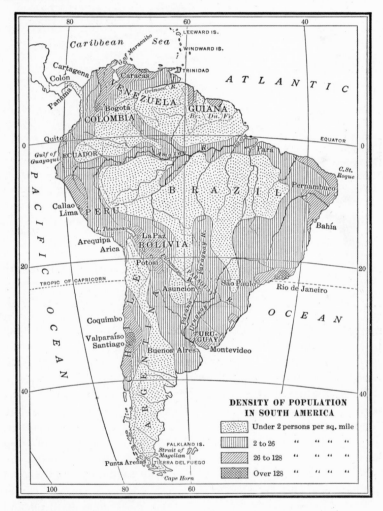

**Rural and Urban Population.** Taking the Latin American states as a whole, their population is rural rather than urban. This reflects the usual situation in new and undeveloped countries, where the extractive industries, and not manufacturing and com-

STATISTICS OF LATIN AMERICA [1]

| STATES | AREA (In square miles) | POPULATION | CAPITAL | INDEPEND- ENCE DECLARED |
|---|---|---|---|---|
| Argentina | 1,153,119 | 13,130,000 | Buenos Aires | 1816 |
| Bolivia | 514,155 | 3,430,000 | Sucre | 1825 |
| Brazil | 3,275,510 | 44,120,000 | Rio de Janeiro | 1822 |
| Chile | 289,829 | 4,640,000 | Santiago | 1818 |
| Colombia | 440,846 | 8,700,000 | Bogotá | 1813 |
| Costa Rica | 23,000 | 610,000 | San José | 1821 |
| Cuba | 44,215 | 4,230,000 | Havana | 1898 |
| Dominican Republic | 19,332 | 1,580,000 | Santo Domingo | 1844 |
| Ecuador | 116,000 | 3,200,000 | Quito | 1811 |
| Guatemala | 48,290 | 3,050,000 | Guatemala City | 1821 |
| Haiti | 10,204 | 3,000,000 | Port Au Prince | 1804 |
| Honduras | 44,275 | 1,000,000 | Tegucigalpa | 1821 |
| Mexico | 767,198 | 19,500,000 | Mexico City | 1821 |
| Nicaragua | 49,200 | 1,170,000 | Managua | 1821 |
| Panamá | 32,380 | 470,000 | Panamá | 1903 |
| Paraguay | 75,673 | 1,000 000 | Asunción | 1811 |
| Perú | 722,461 | 6,670,000 | Lima | 1821 |
| Salvador | 13,183 | 1,700,000 | San Salvador | 1821 |
| Uruguay | 72,153 | 2,100,000 | Montevideo | 1828 |
| Venezuela | 398,594 | 3,500,000 | Caracas | 1811 |

merce, naturally hold the first place. A special reason, applying to Latin America, is found in the large number of Indians, who are predominantly country folk. The whites, as during colonial times, tend to concentrate in towns and cities.

**Race Mixture.** The interbreeding of yellow man, black man, and white man, which began with the colonization of Latin America, has continued there without interruption to the present day. Never during historic times has any similar experiment in miscegenation been made elsewhere on so extensive a scale. No other part of the world can show such an extraordinary mingling of really alien stocks.

**Racial Types.** Crossings of the races result in a great variety of racial types. Mestizos, the offspring of Indians and whites;

[1] The figures for area and population are taken from the *World Almanac*, 1941. Most are approximations, though some are census figures and others are based on older censuses. Figures for areas are also estimates.

mulattoes, the offspring of Negroes and whites; and zambos, the offspring of Indians and Negroes, themselves freely intermingle. There exists, in consequence, an infinite variety in skin color, stature, head form, and other physical traits, from the pure European to the pure Indian and African.

**Proportions of the Races.** Mexico, Central America, and Spanish South America, except Argentina, Costa Rica, and Uruguay, are predominantly Indian or mestizo in blood. Haiti is a black republic, and Santo Domingo is strongly mulatto. Cuba has a considerable percentage of colored people. There remains Brazil, the most populous of all the republics. Whites, or those who pass for whites, are here in the majority, but Brazil also has many Indians and a great many Negroes, mulattoes, and zambos. While the proportions of the races have altered in some Latin American countries since the colonial era, largely as the result of foreign immigration, it still remains true that for Latin America as a whole the European element is numerically inferior to the native element (pure Indian and mestizo).

**Indians.** No definite statement can be made as to the number of Indians in Latin America. The aborigines, especially in the wilder regions, run away from the census taker or else refuse to answer his questions. Even when a complete enumeration has been made, the difficulty arises of distinguishing with exactness between Indians of pure blood and those of mixed blood. The pure Indians in Mexico probably constitute half of the population and in the Central American states much more than half. The proportion is far less — fifteen to twenty per cent — in both Venezuela and Colombia. In Ecuador the pure Indians rise to two thirds and in Perú and Bolivia to more than half of the population of each state. Their number in Chile is not large and in Argentina and Uruguay is negligible. Paraguay, on the other hand, contains so many that the Guaraní language is there the prevailing tongue. The Indians of Brazil, most of them savages living in the interior districts, may amount to between two and three millions, or under ten per cent of the total population. According to some estimates, however, the number of aboriginal Indians in Brazil does not much exceed half a million. If we omit Argentina and Uruguay as well as Brazil, a safe estimate would put the number of pure Indians in the other Latin American republics at more than double that of the whites and a little less than that of the mestizos.

**Indian Characteristics.** As in colonial times, the Indians continue to be divided between the wild, semi-independent tribes (*bravos*), and the relatively civilized aborigines (*mansos*) who live in villages, sometimes speak the European language of the country, as well as their own native tongue, profess a nominal Roman Catholicism, and have more or less contact with mestizos and whites. The former class is especially numerous in Brazil, and the latter class in Perú and Bolivia. The Indians differ considerably in mental endowment: striking contrasts exist, for instance, between the virile Araucanians of Chile and the gentle, submissive Quechuas of the Andes tablelands. Speaking generally, their virtues and their vices are those of primitive peoples in other parts of the world.

**Condition of the Indians.** The wild Indians live much the same lives as did their ancestors at the time of European discovery. Some are cultivators of the soil, others are pastoralists, and others are simple hunting and fishing folk, such as many aborigines in the Brazilian wilderness and the miserable inhabitants of Tierra del Fuego. Their condition appears stationary, where it is not retrograding. As respects the relatively civilized Indians, one may say that their condition has improved all too little since colonial times. They form the poorest and most neglected part of the population. Free in the eye of the law, they are often really serfs. They are ignorant, superstitious, brutalized by excessive indulgence in alcohol, and exploited by everybody above them. In most Latin American countries an Indian seldom casts a vote or presents himself as a candidate for office. He fights in the armies, but otherwise stands outside the political life of the nation. He has no literature, not even a newspaper or a magazine; he rarely rises into the educated class; he exercises little or no influence on the destiny of the country of which he is a nominal citizen. Many leaders and some groups in the countries from Mexico to Paraguay are now trying to aid, but are handicapped by Indian apathy and suspicions as well as by the general indifference or outright hostility of the ruling class to all such efforts toward improvement.

**The Mestizos.** The mixture of Indians and whites in Latin

NATIVES OF PISAC, PERÚ

FIESTA OF ARAUCANIAN INDIANS IN SOUTHERN CHILE

240 HISTORY OF LATIN AMERICA

America has produced the large class of mestizos. They comprised perhaps a fourth of the total population at the end of the colonial period; today the proportion is larger — perhaps a third. The pure Indians are decreasing, but the Indian half-breeds are increasing. Estimates as to their number in the various countries differ considerably, because official statistics usually count all the more educated mestizos as whites and all Indians with any infusion of white blood as mestizos. Those in Mexico may be between forty per cent and fifty per cent of the total population, in Chile sixty per cent, and in Brazil thirty per cent. Venezuela, with at least seventy per cent of mestizos, has the largest proportion of any South American country, while Argentina and Uruguay have the smallest proportion.

**Condition of the Mestizos.** The facile generalization that the union of two parent stocks, one more advanced, the other more backward, necessarily produces a hybrid stock without the virtues of either, is disproved by Latin American experience. In general the mestizo (*ladino*) shows no inferiority to the Europeans that cannot be explained by opportunity. He learns Spanish, gets an education, enters business and politics on the same terms with the white man, and, if otherwise desirable, many marry into a white family even of the highest position in society. For political and social purposes the Iberian (Spanish or Portuguese) and the mestizo stand on the same level. These statements apply most accurately to mestizos who are the issue, not of one crossing, but of several crossings with the whites. On the whole, it appears that education, industrial and commercial activity, and political responsibility are developing in the mestizos a self-contained, independent, and progressive race throughout large areas of Latin America.

**Colored Peoples.** The distribution of the colored peoples remains substantially what it was during colonial times. They constitute the great bulk of the inhabitants of the West Indies and a very appreciable percentage of the population along the Caribbean coast of Central America and South America. In Brazil, where the African slave trade continued until the middle of the nineteenth century, they may equal or outnumber the whites. The colored population of Brazil is found mainly in the central and northern coast states. Except in Haiti, Negroes are everywhere less numerous than mulattoes, quadroons, octoroons, and other crossings with the whites.   Zambos, the offspring of Negroes and Indians, do not form a large or important class.

**Results of Race Mixture.**   Latin America has practically no color problem.   Neither law nor custom interposes any barriers to the free intermingling of the races.   Such distinction as exists between them is one of inherited status rather than of color.   The admixture of Indian, African, and European blood seems destined to produce in this part of the world a new division of mankind. It will be Ibero-American in Mexico, in Central America, and in most of Spanish South America.   It will be Ibero-American-African in most of Brazil.   Argentina and Uruguay, without either Indian or African elements, and southern Brazil, where these disappear before the tide of European immigration, will probably remain the only really white countries in Latin America.

**European Immigration.**   Spain and Portugal excluded aliens from their possessions overseas.   The three centuries of the colonial era saw no movement of Old-World peoples across the Atlantic to Latin America, other than the very limited migration of Spaniards and Portuguese.   Conditions did not at once change with the advent of independence.   Latin America was less attractive than the United States to the English, Germans, and other North Europeans who formed the bulk of the earlier immigrants. They preferred to come to a country geographically and climatically like their own, and to live among peoples like themselves in race, religion, and customs.   It must be remembered, also, that for a long time after the Latin American countries became free, most of them were vexed by revolutions and civil wars, in striking contrast to the peaceful progress of the United States.   European immigration on an extensive scale is, therefore, a comparatively recent phenomenon in this part of the New World.

**Distribution of Immigrants.**   Latin American countries, needing labor and capital for their development, try to attract foreigners by offering free passage from European ports, free transportation into the interior, and often free land, livestock, seed, implements, and the like.   Such inducements have been effective in the southern republics of the temperate zone.   Argentina between 1857–1920 had over 5,000,000 immigrants, and Brazil, during the century 1820–1920, had over 3,500,000.   Chile and Uruguay, especially the latter, are also being settled by Europeans. On the other hand, they avoid the northern republics. The foreign population of Mexico, including all nationalities, reached only 116,000 in 1910, and 158,000 in 1930. Cuba is the only northern republic which at the present time shows a marked increase of immigration.

**Nationality of Immigrants.** The great mass of immigrants come from southern Europe. They are Spaniards, Portuguese, and Italians, who blend easily with peoples, like themselves, of Latin origin. Argentina, according to the last census (1914), contained 929,000 Italians and 829,000 Spaniards who had not so far merged with the general population as to be classed as Argentines. Brazil between 1908 and 1916 received 926,000 immigrants, of whom 355,000 were Portuguese, 191,000 Spaniards, and 153,000 Italians. No general census has been taken in Argentina since 1914, and no census figures for Brazil since 1920 are available. (They are being compiled from data gathered late in 1940.) Official estimates give Argentina nearly twenty per cent of foreign born, mostly Spanish or Italian. Brazil has four million persons of Italian descent and many of Spanish blood. A large proportion of these were born outside Brazil. The Brazilian state of São Paulo has a compact colony of over a million Italians. Many Italians are found in Perú. Other nationalities increasingly represented in the population of these countries include Germans, French, British, Swiss, and Slavs from Central Europe. Germans, the largest group, have settled chiefly in southern Chile and the Brazilian state of Rio Grande do Sul. Those in Brazil may number half a million. Argentina is believed to have 237,000. Unlike the Italians, the Germans tend to preserve their own language and customs and do not readily assimilate with other elements of the population.

**Oriental Immigration.** The assumed menace of the "Yellow Peril," leading to the exclusion of Chinese and Japanese from the United States, is scarcely felt in Latin America. Perú and Ecuador have recently placed restrictions upon Oriental immigration; Brazil, on the other hand, permits a limited number of Japanese agricultural laborers to enter annually. Japanese and Chinese are established along the northwest coast of South America, and at various points in Central America and Mexico. Nowhere are they sufficiently numerous to affect the character of the population. The total number of Orientals in Latin America probably does not exceed 100,000 at the present time, though some estimates triple that figure.

**The White Race in Temperate Latin America.** White peoples, multiplying rapidly during the last century, have filled nearly the whole of the United States and much of Canada. They are filling other parts of the temperate zone, such as South Africa, Australia, and New Zealand. As the growth of numbers continues and population presses more relentlessly than ever upon food supply, white peoples will turn more and more to Latin America. It is the only extensive region on the globe remaining greatly underpeopled. It contains enormous tracts capable of settlement. Its temperate area comprises not only the pastoral and arable territory of Chile, Argentina, Uruguay, southern Brazil, and southern Paraguay, but also the Mexican plateau, the alpine districts of Central America, the higher parts of the West Indies, and those parts of South America which, by reason of great elevation, reach literally out of the tropics. That temperate Latin America has not been sooner occupied by whites is due mainly to its disordered politics and to its inaccessibility (as compared with Anglo-America). Both these adverse conditions no longer apply to the southern republics, which have had most European immigration during the last century. Doubtless they will continue for many years to attract the largest number of Europeans. Viscount Bryce, a shrewd observer, thought that by 2000 A.D. the countries south of the Tropic of Capricorn might contain at least one hundred million inhabitants. But other parts of temperate Latin America may also be expected to receive an increasing white immigration, as political life becomes stabilized in them and the development of good roads, railways, and steamship lines brings them out of an agelong seclusion.

**The White Race in Tropical Latin America.** The question may be raised whether, as the free or cheap land in temperate Latin America is exhausted, the white man who wants to establish himself in this part of the world will not go more and more to the tropical regions. Here are rich soils that have never been tilled, virgin forests that await the woodsman's ax, and mineral wealth yet to be exploited. Consider, for instance, the forest-covered Amazonian plain, which includes nearly all the western half of Brazil and the eastern parts of Ecuador, Perú, and Bolivia. All this vast area supports only a few thousand white inhabitants. Here is the largest unoccupied fertile area in the world. Can it be reclaimed by white men? Europeans and North Americans have not gone to the tropics in large numbers, principally because they feared the climate and the tropical diseases. Modern science has proved that yellow fever, malaria, and other plagues may be conquered by elimination of insect carriers, proper sanitation, and medical treatment. Even so, however, much doubt exists whether white men can long thrive in the hot, moist climate of equatorial lowlands. Still more doubtful is their ability, under such physical conditions, to do hard, continuous, open-air work. The whole subject of tropical acclimatization requires careful investigation. In the light of our present experience it seems probable that while white peoples may continue to control tropical lands, they will not thickly settle them. If the natural resources of tropical Latin America are ever fully utilized, this will be by native labor, both Indian and Negro, and perhaps also by the labor of Orientals.

**Scarcity of Labor.** Latin America, in mines, forests, grazing land, and fertile, arable soil, possesses natural resources which may be equaled elsewhere on the surface of the globe but are nowhere surpassed. These resources have been little developed. One obvious reason is the scarcity of labor, especially of skilled labor. The natural increase of the population, even when supplemented by foreign immigration, does not yet supply enough workers. Nor are the people distinguished for industriousness. Their wants are modest; climatic conditions and malaria, hookworm, and malnutrition foster indolence; and a general tendency exists to put off until tomorrow (*mañana*) what *Norte Americanos* think they should do today. There has also survived from the colonial régime a disdain for manual toil on the part of the upper classes. The descendants of Spanish and Portuguese always had Indians or Negroes about them, not only on the farms but also in the households, so that to work with one's hands became associated with servitude and exemption from it, the hallmark of social superiority. The separation from Spain and Portugal and the adoption of republican institutions did not affect the old tradition in this matter, any more than in the southern states of the Union before the Civil War. It is still characteristic of many Latin American countries.

**Lack of Capital.** The Industrial Revolution of the late eighteenth and early nineteenth century, bringing in machinery and the factory system, scarcely affected Latin America. Foreign capitalists avoided countries where political conditions remained so uncertain. Latin American citizens themselves, if they owned available capital, preferred to invest it in mines and landed estates, instead of in industrial enterprises. Mining, stock raising, and agriculture, which required superintendence but not actual work, enjoyed social esteem, and, for the reasons just given, they yielded a greater immediate return than did manufacturing.

**Absence of a Mercantile Class.** Trade and commerce never flourished in colonial Latin America. These occupations attracted Spanish and Portuguese scarcely more than did manufacturing. The policy of the home governments in excluding alien foreigners from the colonies also tended to prevent the rise of bankers, wholesale merchants, shopkeepers, and other substantial businessmen, who have contributed so greatly to the building of the United States. The mercantile class in Latin America is generally small, and the towns and cities where it exists are too few and too far apart from one another for it to become as yet a very important factor in economic development.

**Economic Backwardness.** Scarcity of labor, lack of capital, and the absence of a mercantile class go far to explain the economic backwardness of Latin America. All the republics, except Chile, Argentina, and Brazil, and in a somewhat less degree several others, are poor countries, whose vast potential resources have been so imperfectly utilized as to bring in little wealth to the native population. They are also, without exception, nonindustrialized countries. Such manufacturing as exists has usually a direct association with mining, stock raising, or agriculture, for instance, nitrate plants, packing plants, flour mills, and sugar refineries. No marked development along industrial lines may be looked for in the distinctly tropical areas, at any rate not within the near future. In the temperate regions local industries, adapted to the requirements of the home market, have recently become of increasing importance and will lessen dependence on foreign lands for manufactured products. The chief manufacturing centers seem likely to be Mexico, Chile, Argentina, and southern Brazil. As a whole, however, Latin America must continue to export

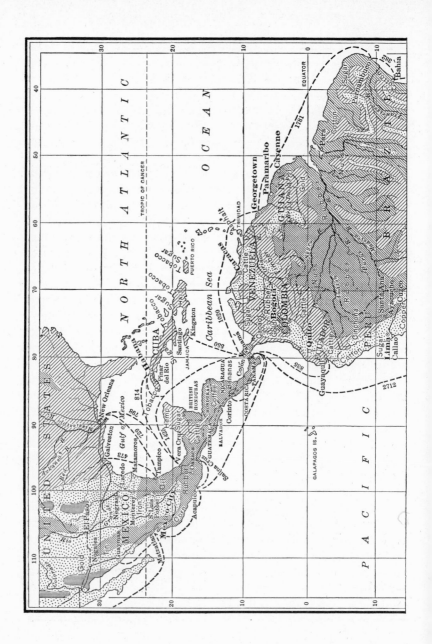

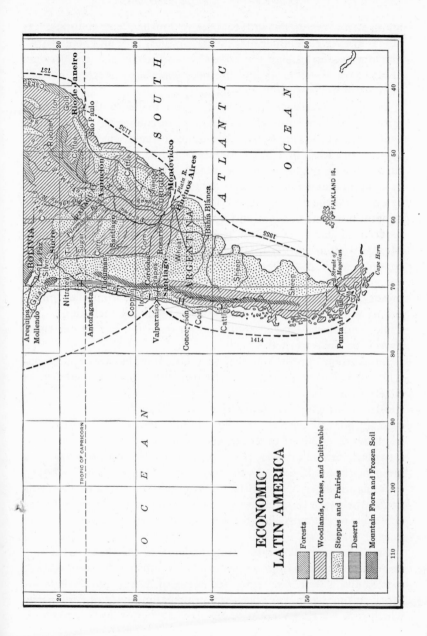

ECONOMIC
LATIN AMERICA

Forests

Woodlands, Grass, and Cultivable

Steppes and Prairies

Deserts

Mountain Flora and Frozen Soil

mainly raw materials and to import finished commodities. It offers an ever expanding market for textiles, iron and steel wares, machinery, and general merchandise, and needs also the services of an army of engineers and business experts to develop its commerce and industries.

**Mining.** Reference has already been made to the enormous mineral resources of most Latin American countries.[1] In Mexico, Colombia, Perú, and Bolivia the mines of gold, silver, platinum, copper, tin, lead, and other metals continue to be, as in colonial times,[2] the principal source of wealth. Emeralds are still mined in Colombia and Ecuador, and diamonds in Brazil. The nitrates of Chile and the oil fields from Mexico to Patagonia comprise other mineral products of great and growing value. Those essentials of modern industry, coal and iron, also exist in Latin America. Mexico, Colombia, Perú, Chile, Brazil, and some other countries contain much coal, both anthracite and bituminous, probably enough to supply in time the needs of the home market. At present, however, most of the coal is imported from the United States and Great Britain. Many of the republics, including Cuba, Chile, and Brazil, have extensive iron deposits, but as yet these have been little worked.

**Lumbering.** Latin America, save Uruguay, possesses great potential wealth in its forests. Santo Domingo, for instance, is covered with virgin timber, and the Amazonian plain is all a forest, the trees growing so thickly that no way of traveling exists except by boat along the streams. Lumbering, until recently, has been chiefly confined to dyewoods and cabinet woods, while wood for construction purposes, paper pulp, and industrial uses has been imported from abroad. As the result of the high cost and scarcity of foreign lumber, Chile, Brazil, and other countries now begin to utilize their own illimitable forests, and lumbering promises to become one of the most important of the extractive industries in this part of the world.

**Stock raising.** The extensive grasslands of the Plata River and its tributaries have afforded pasturage for immense herds of horses, cattle, and sheep ever since the days of European settlement. Stock raising has always been the principal industry of Argentina, which now leads the world in the exportation of beef, surpassing

[1] See page 12.          [2] See page 112.

*Courtesy Pan American Union*

COPPER MINE, CHILE

*Publishers' Photo Service*

A COFFEE PLANTATION

both the United States and Australia, and also holds first place in the export of wool. Uruguay, Paraguay, and southern Brazil are likewise great and growing cattle centers. Stock raising and its affiliated occupations are much less important elsewhere, though Mexico, Venezuela, Colombia, Perú, Bolivia, and southern Chile enjoy favorable climatic conditions and possess ample pasturage. These countries are well placed, geographically, for the development of a large export trade in cattle and animal products, now that the Panamá Canal has brought them so much closer to the great cities of the United States and western Europe.

**Farming.** As far as Latin America is concerned, a distinction must be drawn between domestic agriculture to meet the needs of the inhabitants and agriculture for export. Farming is and always has been the chief industry of the Latin Americas, with the exception of Bolivia and perhaps Chile. For simple lower-class foods they are self-sufficient, but their agricultural exports consist chiefly of a few staple products for which they possess special advantages. Examples are *henequén*, or sisal hemp, in Mexico, bananas in Central America, tobacco and sugar in Cuba, and coffee and cacao in Brazil. Argentina, among the Spanish republics in South America, has become by far the most important for its export of cereals. It was in 1920 the world's largest exporter of maize, and only the United States and Canada surpassed it in the export of wheat. Despite favorable conditions in many countries, little cotton is produced except in Brazil. But almost certainly the highlands of Brazil, the plains of northern Argentina, eastern Bolivia, and Paraguay, and the more limited coastal valleys of Perú and Mexico may some day vie with Egypt, India, and the United States as sources of supply for this commodity. In general, agriculture throughout Latin America is extensive rather than intensive, the natural result of underpopulation. But modern scientific methods of farming are being introduced more and more in the progressive states.

**Land Tenure.** A characteristic feature of Latin American society is the absence of that class of small landowners which forms so considerable an element in the population of the United States. There are exceptions to this statement. In Costa Rica the peasant proprietors comprise two thirds of the population. In Argentina and Mexico the number of landholders possessed of farms of some

25 acres is increasing rapidly. In southern Brazil many Italian and German immigrants have settled down as small but prosperous farmers. Land in some other republics is held by Indians on communal tenure. More than a third of the Peruvian Indians belong to agricultural communities, resembling the old German *mark* and (until recently) the Russian *mir*, in which the land is distributed afresh every year to the members. With such exceptions it may be said that Latin America is a region of great estates owned by a few thousand white families who ventured forth to the Western world in search of wealth.

**Great Estates.** This situation reaches back to colonial times. It originated in the lavish land grants made by the Spanish and Portuguese governments. After the separation from Spain and Portugal the public domain was alienated to capitalists, speculators, and persons with political influence or a military record; it was not divided and sold on favorable terms to actual settlers. The Latin American countries, in short, never adopted the homestead system of the United States. The estates which arose in this way truly deserve the adjective "great," for some reach the size of European countries. The largest was a Mexican ranch embracing eight million acres, or as much as Connecticut and New Jersey combined. There is a ranch in Argentina so extensive that a train takes the best part of a day to cross it. The owner of one of these principalities often lives on it only a few months in the year, spending the rest of the time in the city and leaving an overseer to act as his representative. On the other hand, the Chilean *hacendados* (with many exceptions) and the Brazilian *fazendeiros* are as attached to rural life as the planters of the South before the Civil War. The country gentry everywhere keep up a semifeudal state, surrounded, it may be, by thousands of laborers and dependents. They form the real aristocracy in Latin America.

**Peonage.** Unable to acquire a farm of his own, the common laborer (*peón*) must work on these estates. He must work several days a week for the proprietor, receiving as compensation a small wage and permission to cultivate a little tract of ground for himself. Ignorant, improvident, and poverty-stricken, he easily falls into debt to the proprietor for money or supplies. Such a debt is seldom paid, but he may not leave the estate until it is paid. He thus becomes virtually a serf; peonage becomes serfage. Such was the condition of the semicivilized Indians and poorer half-breeds in Mexico, and such it still is in most of Central America and tropical South America.  Agricultural labor is better off in Chile, where wages are higher, and far better off in Argentina, where, under the dictatorship of Rosas, the peons long ago got rid of their feudal fetters.  The recent revolutionary movement in Mexico has produced notable improvement of the peasants' condition there.  Ecuador and Guatemala have now abolished peonage and canceled the debts owed by peons to their masters.

**Highways.**  The immense extent of Latin America, so much of it either mountainous or swampy and densely forested, the sparse population, and the poverty and inertia of the rural class are formidable obstacles to road building.  These might be overcome more rapidly if foreign capitalists, who invest in railroads and steamships, could be sure of a satisfactory return from investments in highways.  But rich or geographically favored countries like Argentina, south Brazil, Chile, Cuba, Guatemala, Mexico, Uruguay, and Venezuela already possess extensive road systems, and all countries are building.  Paving is relatively uncommon, but most highways have an all-weather surface.  Public busses run on all of them.  The Pan-American highway from the United States to Argentina and Chile is pushing toward completion, except that the terrain between Panamá and Colombia will prevent construction for years.

**Railroads.**  Latin America has about 75,000 miles of railroads.  Argentina leads with 23,000 miles; Brazil comes next with 19,000 miles; Mexico ranks third (16,000 miles); and Chile fourth (6,000 miles).  Cuba has over 3,000 miles, the largest mileage of any country in proportion to area.  All these republics possess more or less elaborate trunk systems, but elsewhere railroads are generally short lines running between seaports and interior cities, and thus forming a series of scattered, unrelated units.  However, Argentina is now joined by rail with Chile, Bolivia, and Paraguay and, including short water links, with Perú, Uruguay, and Brazil.  Chile, through its northern stretching line, also has direct connection with Bolivia.  Main lines connect Uruguay and Brazil, and the latter country has a short interior line connecting it to Bolivia.  Several lines connect Mexico City with the United States, and another reaches Guatemala City with only a break at the border.

From Guatemala City trains run to San Salvador. The networks of Argentina and Mexico furnish indirect routes between the oceans, and other lines have that crossing as their main purpose. These include the short Panamá Railroad, opened in 1855, and the Trans-Andean Railroad. This connects Buenos Aires with Valparaíso, Chile, via Santiago, through a three-mile tunnel which pierces the Andes at a height of 12,000 feet. The first trains ran in 1910. Three other lines cross at the Isthmus of Tehuantepec or through the republics of Guatemala and Costa Rica.

**Aviation.** The great distances between settlements, and faulty land transport, have encouraged the rise of aviation to the first rank. Freight as well as passengers and mail is carried on regular schedules. Many more or less national companies exist, in addition to extensive international systems. United States interests started the Pan-American Airways, that serves both coasts of both Americas, and have recently (1941) acquired the "Taca" of Central America. Until 1939 the German *Lufthansa* controlled much of the interior of South America through the "Condor" syndicate or the "Scadta" of Colombia. Dutch, French, and Italian concerns were active in some areas. Between 1939 and 1942 European control was practically eliminated.

**Maritime Routes.** Along the coasts and on navigable rivers and large lakes, water travel and transport is well developed. Only Brazil and Chile have a merchant marine of really international character, but all countries have coastal or river steamers and motor launches in regular service. The Pacific coast rivers lack value, and some useful ones like the San Juan in Nicaragua and the Magdalena in Colombia have serious obstacles to navigation. But the Orinoco, Amazon, and Plata river systems carry a heavy share of interior trade and travel, which will be increased as roads and railways reach out to them across the Andes. At present even the great river port of Iquitos, Perú, is connected to the centers of population only by air or by arduous trails.

**The Panamá Canal.** The idea of an artificial waterway at Tehuantepec, Nicaragua, Panamá, Darién, or some other point was broached almost as soon as the Spanish conquest of Mexico and Central America. The government of Spain, anxious to preserve a monopoly of communication with its possessions in the New World, did not look with favor upon the idea. Nothing was done during colonial times to break down the narrow barrier which nature had raised between the two oceans. After the Central American republics secured independence, interest in the canal question revived. The acquisition of California by the United States, as a result of the Mexican War, and the Spanish-American War, which made the United States a Caribbean power, intensified that interest. Meanwhile, accurate surveys narrowed down the practicable routes to one through Nicaragua and another across the Isthmus of Panamá. Two attempts were made to construct a canal by private enterprise. A company organized in the United States began work on the Nicaragua route, but soon went into bankruptcy. A French company, headed by De Lesseps, famous as the promoter of the Suez Canal, started excavations

RELIEF MAP OF THE PANAMÁ CANAL

at Panamá. Extravagance and corruption marked its management from the first; it failed in 1889, and operations came to a standstill. A second French company then took up the task, but made slow progress. The government of the United States in 1902 bought its property and rights for $40,000,000. Shortly afterward, the secession of Panamá from Colombia enabled the

United States to obtain from the new republic occupation and control of a canal zone, ten miles wide, for the purposes of the canal.[1]  Digging of the "big ditch" began in 1904.  It was opened to traffic ten years later, but was not entirely completed until 1920.  United States Army engineers, under the direction of Colonel (later General) George W. Goethals, have the credit for this engineering feat, the most notable, perhaps, that the world has ever known.  In spite of unexpected "slides," or breaks, in the walls of the Culebra Cut, where the greatest difficulties were met, the canal cost less than had originally been estimated.  The cost, including interest for early years, and payments to the French Company and to the Republic of Panamá, was officially estimated at over $540,000,000 on June 30, 1938.  Tolls levied on traffic now provide for the expenses of operation and maintenance, and approximately enough more to pay the interest on the bonds issued to raise money for building the canal.

**Commercial Aspects of the Panamá Canal.**  The Hay-Pauncefote Treaty,[2] between the United States and Great Britain (1901), provides for the use of the canal on equal terms by ships of all nations.  They are using it more and more.  In 1915, total cargo passing through amounted to 4,969,792 tons.  In 1929, the last pre-depression year, the total reached 30,660,000 tons.  It fell sharply thereafter until 1933, but began to rise in 1934 and reached 27,866,627 tons in 1939.  Much of this tonnage was in transit between Latin American countries and the rest of the world.  The canal places Guayaquil, Callao, Valparaíso, and other Pacific ports of South America several thousand miles nearer than before to the Gulf and Atlantic ports of the United States.

Obviously, the distance across the Atlantic to Liverpool, Havre, and Hamburg is also diminished, though not to so great an extent.  The canal likewise gives renewed importance to the Caribbean

---

[1] See pages 145 and 185.

[2] By the Clayton-Bulwer Treaty of 1850 the United States and Great Britain had mutually renounced the right of colonizing, fortifying, or occupying any portion of Central America.  They also agreed not to construct any canal between the Atlantic and Pacific oceans, except as a joint enterprise.  The treaty tied the hands of the United States in the isthmian region for half a century.  It was superseded by the Hay-Pauncefote Treaty, which gave the United States the right, not only to construct an interoceanic canal, but also to fortify it and keep it under her exclusive control.

republics, by putting them once more on the highways of international trade. Panamá is now the gate to the Pacific.

**Commerce.** Over fifty steamship lines connect Latin America with Europe, and over twenty-five lines, with the United States. Most of this shipping is owned and operated by foreign nations, among which Great Britain ranks first and the United States second. For many years the three nations having the largest shares in Latin American commerce have been Great Britain, Germany, and the United States. The war [1] upset all the natural

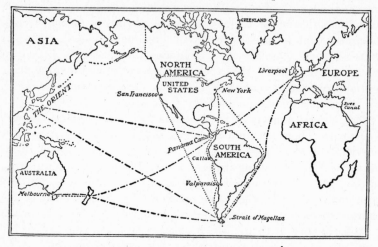

ROUTES PASSING THROUGH THE PANAMÁ CANAL

currents of international trade and made Europe economically impotent both as producer and as consumer. The result was that the commerce of the United States with Latin America rose from $790,567,811 in 1914 to $3,256,295,601 in 1920 — an increase of 311 per cent in money value. The increase in volume of exports and imports was much less, of course, because the prices of all commodities advanced so tremendously during the war period. The United States was, however, able to hold only part of the new business thus developed, and that chiefly with her neighbors, Mexico and Cuba. Many of the countries are bound to have, under normal circumstances, a greater trade with Europe than with the United States. Europe needs their raw materials, and

[1] Of 1914–1918. The same trends are evident since 1939.

they need European manufactures. The United States, on the other hand, is to a very large extent a self-contained country, producing the raw materials which it requires and consuming its own manufactured articles. Natural economic factors, rather than any special sympathy for Europe, impel the Latin American countries to seek their chief markets across the Atlantic. Their exports and imports totaled some $5,000,000,000 annually before 1929. Argentina and Brazil led in foreign trade, followed by Cuba, Chile, Mexico, and Uruguay. The other republics are much less important, commercially.

**Taxation.** Latin American countries levy few direct taxes, but often resort to government monopolies of alcoholic liquors, tobacco, salt, and other commodities. Most reliance is placed, however, on import and export duties. Import duties are primarily for revenue. As manufacturing develops, protective tariffs are now making their appearance, in order to enable home producers to compete on equal terms with foreigners. Some republics enter into treaty arrangements for mutual concessions of certain duties laid upon the interchange of goods. Cuba enjoyed reciprocity with the United States until 1934. Almost all the republics secure a part of their revenue from export duties. Chile in some years derived nine tenths of its income from the export duty on nitrate of soda (*salitre*) found in the Atacama Desert.

**Foreign Investments.** The economic development of Latin America has been accomplished so far on borrowed money. European financiers for over a century, and more recently those of the United States, have invested billions of dollars in railroads, harbor improvements, public works of every description, banks, manufacturing industries, plantations, ranches, forests, oil wells, and mines. Such investments may be expected to increase rapidly as political conditions become stabilized in one Latin American country after another.

**Finances.** Nearly all the countries are deeply in debt, often as the result of financial mismanagement and reckless borrowing. The burden of indebtedness is the greater because of the comparatively small revenue. Failing to make both ends meet, some of the less prosperous states have either repudiated their foreign obligations or defaulted in the payment of interest and principal. Honduras adjusted an immense debt (1926) after paying no

interest on it for more than half a century. The pecuniary mis-
fortunes of Nicaragua, Haiti, and the Dominican Republic led to
the setting up by the United States of fiscal protectorates over
those republics. Similar troubles in Venezuela furnished the
excuse for attempted intervention by European powers, though
the country since the Gómez régime has scrupulously settled its
debts. Thus default in or repudiation of public debts may lead
to serious international complications. Even the more progressive
states have sometimes been embarrassed by their financial obligations to Europe and the United States. Argentina in 1890 became
practically bankrupt, and Brazil in 1914 postponed for several
years the payment of interest on all foreign loans. Nearly all the
countries ceased payments about 1930. But the financial situation in general shows marked improvement throughout most of
Latin America, with the development of its industries and commerce.

**Currencies.** The gold standard has been officially adopted in
all the countries, although in most of them paper money, which
may or may not be redeemable in coin, forms the medium of
exchange. The issue of depreciated paper, upsetting domestic
prices and producing fluctuations in foreign exchange, has long
been a serious obstacle to economic progress. Argentina, Chile,
Colombia, Cuba, Mexico, Paraguay, and Uruguay have the gold
*peso.* The monetary units of the other countries are the *boliviano*
(Bolivia), *milreis* (Brazil), *colón* (Costa Rica and Salvador), *dollar*
(Dominican Republic), *sucre* (Ecuador), *quetzal* (Guatemala),
*gourde* (Haiti), *lempira* (Honduras), *córdoba* (Nicaragua), *balboa*
(Panamá), *bolívar* (Venezuela), and *libra* (Perú). United States
currency circulates freely at its nominal value in Mexico, the
Dominican Republic, and Panamá; in Cuba it is legal tender.

**Social Betterment.** Hospitals, almshouses, asylums, reform-
atories, and other institutions for the relief of suffering and mis-
fortune are maintained by the national governments and the
municipalities. The Roman Catholic Church also supports numerous benevolent societies, either of recent origin or established
during the colonial period. Hitherto, Latin Americans have not
devoted much attention to social betterment in the broader sense,
that is, to movements and activities for the well-being of the
community as a whole. But this situation tends to disappear, as

the result of increased contacts with the outside world. Physical culture and athletics, once neglected, are now encouraged by the governments and by various societies. The Boy Scout movement spreads rapidly in the different countries. Child-welfare organizations, antituberculosis leagues, Red Cross societies, and other humanitarian agencies multiply everywhere. Agitation against the abuses of intemperance has become very marked, especially in Mexico, Perú, and Bolivia, where alcoholism is so terribly destructive of the Indian population, and in Chile, where the mestizos suffer equally from its ravages. A general adoption of prohibition, as tried in the United States, seems unlikely, at least for a long time to come; the ruling white class is not given to inebriety.

**The Legal System.** Latin America inherits its jurisprudence from Rome. The legal system is based ultimately on old Roman law, with such later modifications as are found in the Spanish and Portuguese codes and the French *Code Napoléon*. Legal enactments are generally codified in exact form, thus contrasting with the "judge-made" law of Anglo-Saxon countries. The Chilean civil code, which went into force in 1857, was the first to be framed; it has been adopted, with modifications, by Ecuador, Colombia, and Nicaragua. The Brazilian civil code was promulgated as recently as 1917.

**Religion.** Roman Catholicism is the prevailing faith in all the republics. It was, in all of them, the only recognized faith when the era of independence began. A century of political freedom has also brought religious freedom. Protestants everywhere enjoy the right to worship in their own way and to proselytize without restrictions. A good many Protestant missionaries are now at work; if they make comparatively few conversions, their schools, hospitals, and other humanitarian agencies help to introduce the ideals of modern Western civilization. The movement for religious liberty has also led to the passage of laws providing for secularization of cemeteries, civil marriage, and birth registration, and abolishing the legal right of the clergy to collect tithes. Church and State are separate in most of the republics, though Argentina, Bolivia, Costa Rica, the Dominican Republic, Paraguay, and Venezuela grant annual subsidies for the support of the ecclesiastical establishment. The Church is a large property owner, especially on the west coast of South America.

SANTIAGO, CHILE

Entrance to Santa Lucia Park

THE CITY OF KINGS, LIMA, PERÚ

**Marriage and the Family.** The domestic relations prevailing among the upper class perpetuate southern European traditions. Large families prevail. Even society women do not evade the responsibilities of motherhood, while the childless wife considers herself the most unfortunate of beings. Marriages are generally arranged by the parents. Unmarried girls are kept under surveillance; if they appear in public, they must be properly chaperoned. Married women, also, continue to be more or less secluded. Their sphere is the home; their duties are those of the household. Divorce is rare,[1] and breach of promise cases are practically unknown. Latin America is not a stranger to the movement for the emancipation of woman from dependence on man. Various feminist organizations conduct an agitation to secure for women equality before the law, equal educational opportunities, and permission to engage in business or enter the professions. Woman suffrage associations have also appeared in Argentina, Paraguay, and other states. Costa Rica in 1920 gave women the vote and made them eligible for all offices. Ecuador gave them votes in 1928, Brazil and Cuba and Uruguay in 1934. Mexico did so in 1935 by presidential decree. They now vote in local elections in Chile and Perú.

**Common Schools.** The colonial governments in Latin America neglected popular education; the Church opposed it as being secular; members of the upper class saw no need for it on the part of those who must always remain hewers of wood and drawers of water. The masses themselves were indifferent to it. These conditions, plus poverty and isolation, have made the task of giving the populace the rudiments of education tremendously difficult. The early leaders tried such experiments as Lancasterian (monitorial) schools, with some temporary success. But the effective movement for popular education is of recent date. Even Argentina, the leader, did not begin to do very much in this direction until 1868, when the famous Sarmiento became president. He founded normal schools for the training of teachers, introduced teachers from the United States, and molded the educational system along democratic lines. Sarmiento's influence was also strongly felt in Chile. About the same time President

[1] Only Uruguay had a divorce law before 1934. In that year Perú passed one, causing the president to resign in protest.

Díaz initiated a remarkable development of common schools in
Mexico, which has been greatly amplified by the present régime.
Years ago, Uruguay, Cuba, and Costa Rica, together with the
southern states of Brazil, began devoting more attention to their
schools, and other nations have since joined the educational
procession.

**Illiteracy.** The constitutions of all the republics make primary
education free and all but Brazil and Colombia make it compulsory. Enforcement has been incomplete, and illiteracy remains
common. Costa Rica, with only 23.6 per cent in 1927, has the
best record. Argentina, with 35 per cent (1922), Chile, with
25 per cent (1936), and Uruguay, with 40 per cent (1923) are
perhaps the only other countries even today with less than a
majority of illiterates. Several are over 80 per cent illiterate.
As might be expected, the tropical nations and the country
districts where laws requiring school attendance cannot be well
enforced show a much greater extent of illiteracy than do other
regions.

**Higher Education.** The *colegio* or *liceo*, as the secondary school
is called in Latin America, provides a six-year liberal course pre-
paratory to the specialized work of the university. It thus covers
much the same ground as the high school and "junior college" in
the United States. *Colegios* and *liceos* are not very numerous as
yet, and the enrollment in them is only a fractional part of that
in the primary schools. All the republics have at least one national
university, supported by the government. Some of the institutions
of higher learning go back to colonial times, but many others are
of recent foundation, such as the Universities of Rio de Janeiro
and of Panamá. They follow European models in being combi-
nations of professional "faculties" for instruction in law, medicine,
engineering, and other advanced subjects. The teachers themselves are usually professional men, who devote only a part of
their time to instruction. Agencies for higher education of a more
practical type than that furnished by the universities include
normal schools, of which Argentina alone has more than seventy,
and agricultural, trade, and commercial schools in growing
number. The rapid economic development of Latin America
creates a demand for instruction which will produce skilled workers
and technical experts for its industries. All the countries provide

scholarships enabling talented young men to complete their training by travel and study abroad, and thus to bring home the latest scientific discoveries and the most approved educational methods. There are probably 2,000 such students in institutions in the United States. Most of them are studying engineering or medicine, with considerable numbers also in education, business administration, and dentistry. It may be noted, finally, that co-education seems to be becoming popular, partly from the example set by the United States. Primary and normal schools are sometimes co-educational, and the universities in the southern republics now open their doors to women.

**Science and Scholarship.** Practically all the countries, in their universities and institutes, have long supported a class of learned men. The "intelligentsia" of Mexico City, Bogotá, Lima, Santiago, Buenos Aires, Rio de Janeiro, Havana, and other metropolitan centers make contributions to knowledge in such fields as medicine and surgery, jurisprudence, geography, biology, anthropology, archæology, sociology, and history. Oswaldo Cruz, the Brazilian expert in municipal sanitation; Gastão de Cunha, also a Brazilian, chosen to preside over the Council of the League of Nations; Luis Drago, of Argentina, an authority on international law; Ernesto Quesada, the Argentine sociologist; the Chilean legalist, Alejandro Alvarez; and Carlos Finlay, of Cuba, the discoverer of the cause of yellow fever, have a high reputation, not only in Latin America, but abroad as well. These are only a few out of many brilliant scientists and scholars. They no longer work in isolation. Since the close of the nineteenth century coöperation among them has resulted in a series of congresses, held at frequent intervals. The United States was represented at the meeting in Santiago de Chile (1908), and, to mark the entrance of that country into intellectual fellowship with its southern neighbors, the name of the assemblage was changed to Pan-American Scientific Congress. Several later meetings have been held.

**Arts and Literature.** Love of music, drama, dancing, painting, and belles-lettres has always characterized the Latin American. Governmental maintenance or subsidization of art schools, conservatories of music, museums, opera houses, and theaters is as widespread and as old a custom as support for scholarly bodies. But until recently literary and artistic products were unimportant, since Latin American workers in those fields tried to be Europeans instead of accepting inspiration from their surroundings. The illiterate masses, and lack of even an inter-American clientele, prevented hope of living by unorthodox or creative effort. Most painters and musicians studied abroad, and became imitators. Popular taste at home supported only the sentimentalities of European romanticism. Sculpture, dancing, and architecture, in spite of recent stirrings, are still in the imitative stage. Other fields of effort are only recently better off. During the first century of independence, there were many facile musicians and painters, but their abilities were stifled by their environment. Before the twentieth century no painter achieved other than local fame, and among composers only the Brazilian Carlos Gomes had a European audience. Writers, perhaps because they needed less formal training, were less inhibited by awe of Old World masters. Most of them were no better than the painters. But among other good poets, José Joaquín Olmedo (Ecuador), Andrés Bello (Venezuela and Chile), José Martí and José María Heredia (Cuba), Doña Salomé Ureña de Henríquez (Dominican Republic) and Goncalves Dias (Brazil) stood out. The charm of the "best-selling" but sentimental novel *María* (1867) by the Colombian Jorge Isaacs is today difficult to understand, but it includes vivid sketches of life in the isolated Cauca Valley. Other novelists reflected or examined the American scene in more penetrating tales that remain valuable today. Among the most important were José Joaquín Fernández de Lizardi (Mexico), Antonio José de Irisarri (Guatemala and Chile), Manuel Jesús Galván (Dominican Republic), José Mármol, José Hernández, and Domingo Faustino Sarmiento (Argentina), Alberto Blest Gana (Chile), Doña Clorinda Matto de Turner and Ricardo Palma (Perú), and José de Alencar and Escragnole Taunay of Brazil. Essayists and critics were of high quality nearly everywhere.

**Modern Literature.** Much is now changed. Belles-lettres still suffer under serious handicaps. Readers are few, as compared with the situation in the United States and western Europe, and public libraries are rare. Authors consequently find it necessary, in most cases, to publish books at their own expense and in limited editions. Often they do not publish in book form at all, but confine their efforts to magazines and newspapers.

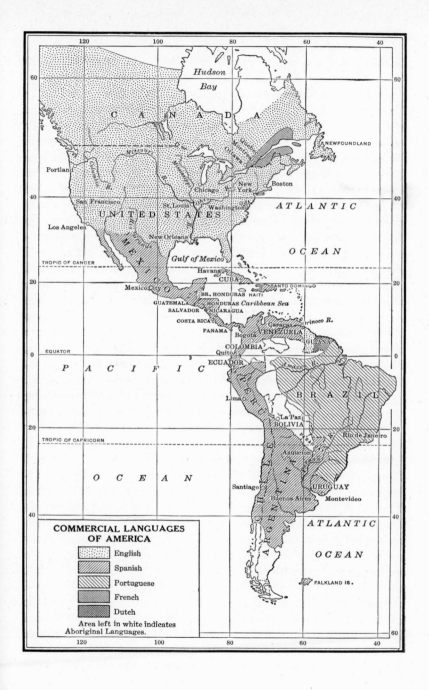

COMMERCIAL LANGUAGES
OF AMERICA

English
Spanish
Portuguese
French
Dutch

Area left in white indicates
Aboriginal Languages.

Such periodicals are numerous and compare favorably with those of Europe and the United States. A new spirit has appeared in the literature. Part of this came from the foreign "modernist" movement and generally is dated from publication of the Nicaraguan Rubén Darío's *Azul* (1888). Fundamentally more important is the emphasis upon local and native themes. This was powerfully advocated by the Uruguayan José Enrique Rodó in such works as the *Ariel* and *Motivos de Proteo*, as an offset to *modernismo*. Since 1918 it has become the major trend of Latin American literature, with a notable focus upon social problems, especially those of the Indian or Negro lower class. So far as one can select among the many, critics regard the outstanding poets as Salvador Díaz Mirón, Manuel Gutiérrez Nájera, and Amado Nervo of Mexico, José Santos Chocano of Perú, and Ricardo Jaimes Freyre of Bolivia. Top rank novelists include the Mexicans Mariano Azuela and Martín Luís Guzmán, the Argentine Ricardo Güiraldes, the Colombian José Eustacio Rivera, and the Venezuelan Rómulo Gallegos. Brazilian literature shows the same trends, beginning with Olava Bilac's *Poesías* (1888), Euclydes da Cunha's *Os sertões*, and Graça Aranha's *Chanaan*, both of 1902. The novels of José Lins do Rego are now outstanding.

**Modern Arts.** Students and artists, returning from Paris during the War of 1914–1918, were inspired to apply their modern techniques to the little developed American scene and tradition. They were affected also by the social problems then so newly evident. The Mexican Diego Rivera, and his contemporaries Orozco and Siqueiros, not only started the school of socially conscious painting centering about the Indian, but revived the art of the fresco. The Argentine Cesáreo Bernaldo de Quirós, the Brazilian Candido Portinari, and the Peruvian José Sabogal, drawing inspiration respectively from the gaucho, the Negro, and the Indian, are only a few of the men doing significant work elsewhere. Musicians are no longer content with pallid imitations of Chopin and Verdi, but are combining the resources even of atonality with the novel rhythms, melodies, harmonies, and instrumentation of the music of the colored races. The Mexican Carlos Chávez, the Brazilian Heitor Vila-Lobos, and the Uruguayan Eduardo Fabini lead this group. All of them also write in other idioms. The Argentine Juan Carlos Paz and the Chilean Domingo Santa Cruz, less given

RIO DE JANEIRO, FROM MOUNT CORCOVADO

A view showing the crescent-shaped Botafogo Bay and the granite rock of Sugar Loaf, which, from a height of 1,383 feet, overlooks the entrance to the harbor.

BUENOS AIRES

to obvious use of American themes, are other original composers. They and many others are deliberately elevating public taste as leaders of symphony orchestras or heads of schools of music. Their work is aided by the internationally written and published *Boletín latino-americano de música*, edited annually since 1935 by the Uruguayan Francisco Curt Lange. Alongside this development of intellectual music, men in various countries have recently become concerned to record or revive folk music and dances.

**Municipal Progress.** The urban drift has become very marked within recent years, especially in Mexico, Chile, Argentina, and Brazil. South America now has twenty-four cities with a population over 100,000. There are seven in Middle America and three in Cuba. Those between three and five hundred thousand include Pará (311,000), Porto Alegre (322,000), Bahía (364,000), and Pernambuco (473,000) in Brazil, Bogotá (330,000), Caracas (300,000), and Lima (370,000). Next in size are Rosario, Argentina (511,000), Havana (569,000), Montevideo (683,000), Santiago, Chile (829,000), and São Paulo, Brazil (1,151,000). Mexico City (1,754,000) passed Rio de Janeiro (1,711,000) in the last decade. Buenos Aires (2,364,000) is the eleventh city of the world. It is second only to Paris in Latin countries, and surpassed only by New York and Chicago in the Western Hemisphere. Guatemala City (200,000) is the largest of Central America. The cities' characters vary with their sites. Mexico City and Guatemala City, Bogotá, Caracas, São Paulo, and Lima are high above sea level, though the last three are close to the sea. The others are busy seaports. They mostly date from the sixteenth century, but Guatemala City and Montevideo are of the eighteenth century and Rosario and Porto Alegre are more recent still. They usually preserve a picturesque if crowded "old quarter," but around that has grown a city modern in every respect. The buildings and appearance of the modern parts tend to imitate those of nineteenth-century Paris. All possess an adequate and pure water supply, sewage system, paving, lighting, and transportation. Their fine public buildings, boulevards, and parks, together with many handsome private residences, make a most pleasing impression upon the traveler.

**Latin American Civilization.** The twenty republics between the Rio Grande and the Strait of Magellan differ among themselves in many respects; and yet, as a whole, they possess a distinctive civilization, unlike that of Anglo-America. Culturally, the republics are nearer to Spain, Portugal, Italy, and France — the so-called "Latin" countries — than they are to the United States and Canada. Their white population (exclusive of Germans) comes chiefly from those countries, speaks Romance tongues, accepts Roman Catholicism, and finds in the literature, art, and intellectual life of southern Europe (including France) both models and inspiration. Even the customs, the general ideas, the psychology are essentially South-European.

## WORDS AND PHRASES YOU SHOULD KNOW

| | | |
|---|---|---|
| *bravos* | Hay-Pauncefote Treaty | Pan-American Airways |
| *Code Napoléon* | *ladino* | Pan-American highway |
| Culebra Cut | land tenure | *peso* |
| density of population | *liceo* | public domain |
| extractive industries | *Lufthansa* | serf |
| fiscal protectorate | *mansos* | "Yellow Peril" |
| foreign capital | mercantile class | |

## QUESTIONS YOU SHOULD BE ABLE TO ANSWER

1. From the statistics given in this chapter would you say that Latin America could or could not support any more people than already live there?
2. Which countries in Latin America contain more Indians than people of other races? more Negroes than others?
3. Have the Indians of Latin America benefited from the white man's civilization?
4. Have the mestizos been able to rise in society to be the equals of the white man?
5. How do you account for the fact that Latin America has no color problem?
6. From what European countries have people emigrated to Latin America in recent years?
7. Why will it prove difficult for the white race to settle in tropical Latin America?
8. Why is the attitude of the upper classes toward work a handicap to the development of Latin America?
9. Why has there been comparatively little industrial development in Latin America?
10. What are some of the chief exports of Latin American countries?

11. Why have there been so few small farms in Latin American countries?
12. How has the system of peonage handicapped many farmers?
13. Why has aviation become so important in Latin America?
14. Why did the French company fail in its attempt to construct the Panamá Canal? How long did it take the United States to complete the canal?
15. Can the ships of any country use the canal?
16. What was the effect of the World War upon trade between the United States and Latin America?
17. Why are many Latin American countries bound to have more trade with Europe than with the United States?
18. How have Latin American countries often obtained money to carry on government and develop industries?
19. Do women in Latin America have as many opportunities to participate in activities outside the home as they do in the United States?
20. How do you account for the fact that so large a number of people in Latin American countries cannot read or write?

## Projects and Activities

1. Using the statistics in this chapter, indicate the following: the country with the largest population; the country with the smallest population; the countries which have fewer people than New York City; the countries which have more people than your own state.
2. Work out a comparison of the effect of immigration upon the population of Latin America and the United States.
3. By means of a chart show the percentage of Indians and mestizos in the population of several Latin American countries.
4. Make a list of Latin American countries that contain large numbers of European immigrants and indicate the approximate proportion of the total population that each group represents.
5. Make an economic map of Latin America showing the chief economic activities in each country.
6. Make a transportation map of Latin America showing some of the important highways, railroad lines, aviation lines and shipping routes.
7. Make a chart in which you compare education in Latin America and in the United States.
8. On a map of Latin America place on or near the proper countries the names of outstanding men in science, literature, and art.

# CHAPTER XI

# International Relations of Latin America

**Basic Status.** The international relations of the countries of Latin America have, since their independence, shown the influence of three basic elements, which have changed only in detail. They are: (1) the ambitions and rivalries of the Great Powers, (2) the weakness, compared to those Powers, of even the strongest Latin American nations, and (3) the fact of location in a "New World." The ambitions of the Powers and the weakness of Latin America were formerly such that the story often related to the struggles over Latin America among the Powers, rather than to the foreign relations among the Latin Americans or their ideas as to the outside world. That situation became less true as time passed. Location in a "New World" has become increasingly important. The ocean that separates Latin America from the "Old World," though no insurmountable barrier to a naval power, has at least discouraged large-scale interference. The New World location also isolated the Americas from the inherited and dynastic quarrels of crowded Europe, and furnished a basis for the rise of common principles and ideals within the Western Hemisphere.

Until about the close of the nineteenth century, the nations most involved in Latin American affairs were Great Britain, the United States, and France. Germany and Italy had no national existence until late in the century. Spain gained some importance, in spite of its weakness, through its status as a mother country, but Portugal has not tried to play even that part. The Powers were, for the whole nineteenth century, in an era of imperial expansion throughout the world. Their greeds as to Latin America involved lands, trade and investments, and canal sites or strategic bases. Fortunately for Latin America, their interests conflicted, and one Power was itself an American nation. Whatever the faults of the United States within the Americas, from the start it worked on the principle of eliminating European interference and encroachments. As a result of the rivalries, and what resistance

the Latin American nations could offer to aggression, Latin
America survived practically intact while the "partitioning" of
Africa, Asia, and Oceania into European zones of influence proceeded to the end.  But it did not survive without struggle, and
it had international problems within its own limits.  Most of the
latter were disputes, such as those over trade, tariffs, and treatment
of nationals, that are common to all peoples.  Boundary disputes,
however, were numerous and had distinctively American aspects.
During the colonial period political limits had been uncertain.
Settlements rarely spread far enough from their centers to run into
each other, and so long as Spain controlled eighteen of the present
states, there was no point in surveying lines through uninhabited
forests, jungles, and deserts.  The legally stated limits of the
provinces and viceroyalties were vague and conflicting, owing to
ignorance of the interior and to a succession of carelessly worded
grants.  The Portuguese-Spanish treaty of 1777 furnished a
reasonable basis for the bounds of Brazil, but even that had not
been fully carried into effect, and shifts of population and of *de
facto* control had occurred after 1777.

**The Early Years.**  The Latin American nations were themselves
responsible for many of their earlier troubles.  This was partly due
to interference by ambitious dictators with their neighbors' affairs.  Domestic turmoil also weakened them against foreign aggressions, and furnished the Powers with excuses or causes for
demanding redress of grievances.  Warfare (1825–1828) between
Brazil and Argentina for possession of Uruguay, and the internecine troubles of Central America, have been mentioned.  Wars
(1828–1829) in connection with the breakup of Bolívar's Colombia
had an international character, and Chile (1837–1839) forcibly
destroyed the confederation of Perú and Bolivia.  Under Rosas,
Argentina interfered with Uruguayan politics almost constantly,
and Rosas's forces besieged Montevideo for nine straight years
(1843–1852).  Boundary disputes also began early.  Colombia,
Bolivia, Perú, Brazil, and Central America had raised the issue
over one or more of their possible frontiers by 1826, and most of the
others had joined the discussion by 1845.  In 1832 part of the line
between Ecuador and Colombia, involving ownership of the
southern part of the Cauca Valley, was delimited in favor of Colombia.  But most of these questions concerned areas that were

not yet of value, and discussions were not pushed with vigor. Generally speaking, negotiations were peaceful and broke down without result or led to an inconclusive treaty.

**Early Congresses.** In spite of the exceptions that must be expected in all human affairs, relations between the new nations proved to be animated by a more general desire for peace than was common in the Old World. They reflected also a desire for some form of federation. Such a movement appealed to the leaders' emotions in terms of size and power, and offered the answer to weakness before the Powers. The tradition of a great empire, and the unity of language, religion, laws, institutions, and customs that prevailed throughout Spanish America and partly included Brazil, encouraged the idea and promised to facilitate its execution. As has been seen, several efforts at governmental amalgamation broke down from internal pressures, but international associations seemed less difficult to achieve because less extensive in their purpose. Bolívar admitted that the Chilean José Gregorio Argomedo first suggested such an experiment. But Bolívar's prestige enabled him to put his ideas into execution, and he is regarded as the father of the idea of a League of American Nations. As early as 1814 he expressed the hope that some day there might meet on the Isthmus of Panamá "an august Congress of the representatives of the republics, kingdoms, and empires, to treat of and to discuss the high concerns of peace and war with the nations of the other parts of the world." Such a congress was convoked in 1826 by the Liberator, who wished to convince European statesmen that the new republics should be recognized as independent states. Somewhat against his own wishes, Bolívar invited the United States to participate, and both President Adams and his Secretary of State Henry Clay favored acceptance. After long debate Congress appropriated money to send delegates, but they arrived after adjournment of the congress. Great Britain and the Netherlands had observers present, and the British observer took an active though informal part. Only the four countries nearest the isthmus — Mexico, Central America, Colombia, and Perú — were officially represented. Their delegates framed conventions establishing a "perpetual union, league, and confederation," and providing for mutual assistance in time of war. The acts of the congress were never ratified by the separate states.

**Relations with the Powers.** Foreign nations promoted their interests with energy during the years of general weakness in Latin America. Spain retained hope of reconquest, and refused even to discuss recognition until after the death of Ferdinand in 1833. In 1829 a Spanish expedition landed in Mexico aiming at reconquest, but was decisively beaten. By 1834 Spanish statesmen realized that they had estranged Latin America and lost its trade without achieving anything of value, and announced a willingness to negotiate. Venezuelan parleys, begun in 1833, broke down, but a treaty recognizing Mexican independence was signed in 1836. Ecuador, Chile, Venezuela, and Bolivia signed similar treaties between 1840 and 1847. Other states established partial trade relations. In spite of this evidence of a technically friendly international status, Queen Mother María Cristina, seeking realms for her sons by an earlier marriage, continued to think of the former colonies as fair game. There is a disputed story that in 1846 she planned to enthrone one son in Mexico. In that and the following year she actually appointed a general and ordered an army prepared to assist the exiled General Flores against Ecuador. Domestic politics forced abandonment of the project.

The major powers were Great Britain, France, and the United States, in that order of strength. All were concerned over the control or possession of Mexico, Cuba, and the Middle American canal zones, and to a less degree about the Plata and the Amazon river regions. Cuba was left to the control of weakened Spain, in spite of complicated maneuvering, because no one of the three would see it held by any strong power except itself. France, which had originally backed Spanish plans of reconquest, expecting to pick up a reward in the process, branched out for herself as Spanish hopes receded. Her absorption in Europe, Africa, and Asia prevented the use of her full strength in America, and she took no positive action in questions concerning Cuba and Texas that might have brought conflict with the United States. But she refused to recognize any of the new nations until the overthrow of the Bourbons in 1830. Her recognition of her own lost colony of Haiti (1825) was an example of her aggressive attitude and of her disregard of the eighteen-month-old Monroe Doctrine. Threats from a sizable French fleet forced Haiti to accept a

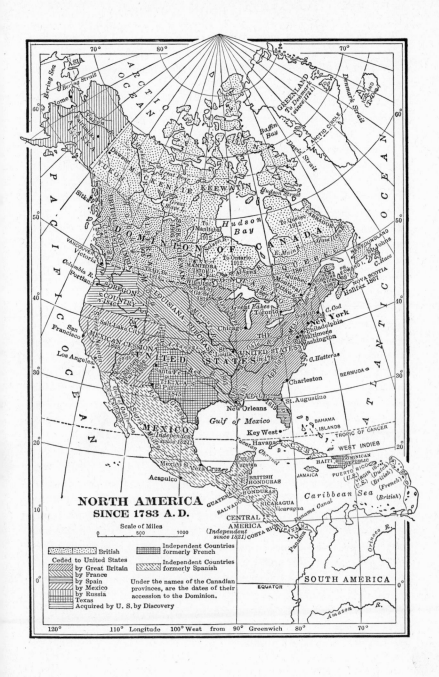

# NORTH AMERICA
## SINCE 1783 A. D.

Scale of Miles

0          500          1000

British

Ceded to United States
by Great Britain
by France
by Spain
by Mexico
by Russia
Texas

Acquired by U. S. by Discovery

Independent Countries
formerly French

Independent Countries
formerly Spanish

Under the names of the Canadian
provinces, are the dates of their
accession to the Dominion.

"grant" of independence, and to agree to pay an indemnity of 150,000,000 francs in five years. In 1838 France bombarded Vera Cruz in the "Pastry Cook's War," so called because it started over the trivial claims of a French baker against the Mexican government. In 1839 she blockaded Buenos Aires and landed troops to aid Uruguay against Rosas. From 1845 to 1849 she joined England in again blockading the Plata.

**Great Britain** *versus* **the United States.** Much of the history of the period centered about the struggle in the Caribbean between Britain and the United States. Fear that the latter might achieve hegemony and then strangle British trade caused Great Britain to oppose her absorption of Texas and her expansion across the northern frontiers of Mexico. Much the same fear, plus a partly unselfish wish to keep European aggression from the Americas regardless of direct danger to the United States, actuated the policy of the growing North American power. The latter looked with a doubtful eye on British activities anywhere in the Western Hemisphere, though she remained quiescent when her rival seized the Falklands against Argentine protests in 1833. She bitterly opposed Britain in Central America. The manner in which Great Britain used her vague protectorate over the Mosquito Indians to expand her control of the Central American coast has been told as part of the history of Nicaragua and Honduras. England used an equally vague foothold in British Honduras to claim still more. Her loggers and smugglers had been in the region since the seventeenth century. A succession of treaties with Spain, 1763 to 1814, permitted them to remain there within stated bounds, but specifically reserved the sovereignty to Spain. Those terms were repeated in the British-Mexican treaty of 1826, after settlers had begun moving south of their legal limit at the Sibun River. By the 1840's the British Crown was claiming sovereignty, and bounds enormously enlarged to the Sarstoon River. The United States was too busy with domestic problems and with her quarrels with Mexico to do more than protest, and her protests achieved little. Her sole victory came in a treaty with Colombia in 1846. This guaranteed United States citizens transit of the Isthmus of Panamá on the terms enjoyed by Colombians, and barred special concessions to Great Britain by granting the status of "most favored nation" to the United States.

**The Monroe Doctrine.** Long before much of the above, the United States had crystallized and published to the world its intention of safeguarding Latin American freedom from European interference. Washington, in his neutrality proclamation of 1793 and his Farewell Address (1796), had laid down the principle that the "primary interests" of Europe had "only a remote relation" to the interests of America, and that political isolation should be the policy of his nation. Jefferson at the time of the Spanish cession of Louisiana to France (1800) and Madison a few years later in connection with West Florida had declared that the United States "could not see, without serious inquietude, any part of a neighboring territory in which they have so deep and so just a concern pass from the hands of Spain into those of another power." The successful struggles of the Hispanic colonies for independence brought out a new aspect of the problem. The overthrow of Napoleon had been followed by restoration of the "legitimate" dynasties in Europe and the revival of the "old régime" of absolutism, privilege, and divine right. The sovereigns of Austria, Prussia, Russia, and France had formed an alliance, agreeing to aid one another in suppressing democratic or nationalist movements that might threaten the security of their thrones. In 1823 France, acting under a commission from the three other powers, crossed the Pyrenees, put down a liberal revolution in Spain, and placed Ferdinand VII once more on his throne. Ferdinand besought the alliance to complete their work by subduing the rebellious American colonies. Modern research shows that France had no real intention of complying, but contemporary opinion, on the basis of speeches by French statesmen, credited it with definite plans for an intervention.

Great Britain and the United States were alarmed. The latter had recognized the independence of four of the republics, and Great Britain was about to take the same step. Both countries had built up a large trade with the revolted colonies after the end of Spanish control. The new market would be lost if Spain were to recover her possessions and revive her monopolistic trade laws. Another cause for anxiety was found in the situation on the northwest coast of North America, where Russia, long established in Alaska, had begun to claim also the Oregon country. This claim was incompatible with the pretensions of Great Britain and the

United States to the same territory. George Canning, as foreign
minister of Great Britain, began in 1822 to declare that Great
Britain could not tolerate Spanish cession of American colonies to
any other power. Late in August, 1823, Canning approached the
United States envoy at London, proposing a joint declaration by
the two governments against the measures which the autocratic
European sovereigns seemed likely to employ. Discussion within
President Monroe's cabinet showed a realization that British interests would lead Canning to support a unilateral declaration by
the United States, and American sentiment was strong against

JAMES MONROE

any sort of entanglement with Great
Britain. The United States decided on
an independent course. What has become famous as the Monroe Doctrine
appeared without drama or emphasis,
in scattered and unconnected passages
of President Monroe's message to Congress, on December 2, 1823.

**The Doctrine Stated.** The language
used by the president can be arranged
and abbreviated as follows:

"At the proposal of the Russian Imperial Government, made through the
minister of the Emperor residing here, a
full power and instructions have been transmitted to the minister of
the United States at St. Petersburg, to arrange, by amicable negotiation, the respective rights and interests of the two nations on the
northwest coast of this continent. . . . In the discussions . . .
the occasion has been judged proper for asserting as a principle in
which the rights and interests of the United States are involved,
that the American continents, by the free and independent condition which they have assumed and maintain, are henceforth not
to be considered as subjects for future colonization by any European powers. . . . In the wars of the European powers in matters
relating to themselves we have never taken any part, nor does it
comport with our policy so to do. It is only when our rights are
invaded or seriously menaced that we resent injuries or make
preparations for our defense. With the movements in this hemisphere we are, of necessity, more immediately connected. . . .

We owe it therefore to candor, and to the amicable relations existing between the United States and those powers, to declare that we should consider any attempt on their part to extend their system to any part of this hemisphere as dangerous to our peace and safety. With the existing colonies or dependencies of any European power we have not interfered and shall not interfere. But with the governments who have declared their independence, and maintained it, and whose independence we have, on great consideration and on just principles, acknowledged, we could not view any interposition for the purpose of oppressing them, or controlling in any other manner their destiny, by any European power, in any other light than as the manifestation of an unfriendly disposition toward the United States. . . . Our policy in regard to Europe, which was adopted at an early stage of the wars which have so long agitated that quarter of the globe, . . . remains the same, which is, not to interfere in the internal concerns of any of its powers, . . . [and] to cultivate friendly relations with it. . . . But in regard to these continents, circumstances are eminently and conspicuously different. It is impossible that the allied powers should extend their political system to any portion of either continent without endangering our peace and happiness; nor can anyone believe that our Southern brethren, if left to themselves, would adopt it of their own accord. It is equally impossible, therefore, that we should behold such interposition, in any form, with indifference."

**Growth of the Doctrine.** The restatement of the United States principle of isolation, though not strictly part of the Monroe Doctrine, was closely related to it in the minds of American statesmen. The true Doctrine, it will be seen, included two parts: a warning directed immediately against Russia, that the Western Hemisphere was closed to further Old World colonization, and a declaration addressed to the allies of Europe against extension of the absolutist political "system" to the New World. It said nothing about United States relations with Latin America, and nothing about possible transfers of American territory from one European power to another. But the Doctrine as an executive policy, not an act of Congress or a treaty, has always been open to modification. Spain's rumored intention of transferring Cuba or Puerto Rico to France soon afforded the opportunity for restating Jefferson's and Madison's objections to such acts. In 1825 President John Quincy Adams notified the French government that the United States could not consent to the occupation of Cuba or Puerto Rico "by any other European government than Spain under any contingency whatever." In 1848, Yucatán offered sovereignty over itself to Great Britain, France, or the United States, if one of them would aid against the frightful Indian rebellion then devastating the country. President Polk thereupon disclaimed any desire for the annexation to the United States, and stated that the United States could not consent even to voluntary transfer of territory by American nations to European powers. This so-called "Polk Corollary" was clearly the basis of later policy, as appeared in connection with events of the 1860's and 1870's, but is often forgotten entirely. No further developments in the Doctrine took place until the late nineteenth century.

**Effect of the Doctrine.** In spite of Canning's anger over the single-handed action of the United States, Great Britain's interests compelled her to continue to follow the same policy against allied interference that the United States had proclaimed. Into the bargain, the United States failed to follow up its chance for American leadership, being absorbed in domestic affairs. For those reasons the Doctrine was less discussed, and had less immediate weight, than is now commonly assumed. It was welcomed by most Latin Americans and by many Englishmen. It was railed against or ridiculed by the European nations against whom it was aimed. But Great Britain was so much more important than the United States in 1823 that many parts of Latin America received their early news of the Doctrine from British sources, and all showed themselves more interested in the British reaction than in the United States declaration. Even twenty years later the day of the Doctrine had hardly dawned. The Doctrine's early history is important chiefly to show the paper's origin and its true character, since careless speech distorted both in later days. The Monroe Doctrine was not a part of international law. It did not represent a pact or agreement among the American nations. It was not a self-denying ordinance, and was never so claimed. The United States proclaimed it on her own authority, as a measure of self-protection. The Doctrine did not forbid and it did not permit any action by the United States within the hemisphere. Whether such action conformed to or violated international law, it had nothing to do with the Monroe Doctrine.

**Rise of the United States.** The growth of the United States in size and strength finally ushered in a new era in the relations of Latin America with the outside world. Between 1845 and 1849, the incorporation of Texas, the Oregon country, and northern Mexico into the Union, and the discovery of gold in California, fostered a rapid rise of United States population on the Pacific coast. That the process of incorporating Mexican territory began the alienation of Latin America is significant of other changes brought about by the appearance of an American Great Power. Purchase of the Louisiana territory (1804) and acquisition of the Floridas had given the United States an interest in Cuba as the key to the Gulf of Mexico, through which an increasing trade must pass. From 1845 the nation owned more than half the Gulf coast and all of its good harbors except Havana. From 1849, possession of Pacific as well as Atlantic seaboards changed the question of assuring transit through Middle America from a policy for the benefit of trade to an imperative necessity of national life. As will be seen, this resulted in eliminating British and later Spanish and French influence from the Caribbean. In the long run it encouraged establishment of near hegemony there. It caused less change in other parts of Latin America. The countries without Caribbean shores — Salvador excepted — are in South America, and lie wholly or partly south of the equator. They had their best market in Europe, and their east coasts were closer to Europe than to the United States. For practical purposes the same was true of the western coasts until the opening of the Panamá Canal. The large states of Argentina, Brazil, and Chile soon established domestic quiet and national strength, and had less than did the Caribbean lands to attract aggression.

The relations of these southern nations continued to be closer with Europe than with the United States, but usually involved no threat to their independence. The Monroe Doctrine therefore had no concern with their affairs. The United States made it clear throughout the period that she did not intend to shut Europe out of Latin America as to normal diplomatic or trade relations. For a time she probably realized her inability to do as much as she would have liked, and joined Britain and France in various moves, partly to prevent them from acting alone.  In 1850, for instance, she was associated with them in the so-called mediation to force Haiti to recognize the independence of the Dominican Republic, and started a peaceful international movement to persuade Brazil to open the Amazon to all nations.  The first move achieved nothing.  The second finally led Brazil to open the river to navigation in 1866, but only after straining the normally friendly relations of the two governments.  The United States also associated herself with France and Britain in "bestowing the moral weight and influence of diplomatic relations" upon Urquiza's government in Argentina, when the state of Buenos Aires withdrew from the new Confederation in protest against treaties that opened the Uruguay and Paraná rivers to the world on liberal terms.

**Great Britain *versus* the United States.**  The changing status of the United States first became visible in the rivalry with Great Britain over the West Indies and Central America.  Britain had no real wish for new territory in the West Indies, but wanted to keep the islands from the United States.  Many citizens of the latter country favored the acquisition of part or all of Cuba or Hispaniola.  The United States tolerated their filibustering expeditions against Cuba, and harbored the Cuban revolutionary juntas.  It several times tried to buy the island from Spain, but would probably not have used force regardless of the British attitude.  Certainly it turned down or neglected bona fide offers of annexation from the men in power in the Dominican Republic, as it had in 1848 from Nicaragua and Yucatán.  But the slaveholders and others in the United States who favored such expansions were more vocal than those who opposed them, and both Great Britain and the United States suspected the other's intentions.  Diplomatic interchanges and intrigues were lively, but led to no change in the situation.

The Central American question was more serious, because of canal possibilities.  Part of that story has been told while discussing the domestic history of Central America.  Great Britain foresaw the result of the war between the United States and Mexico.  In January, 1848, she seized control of Greytown at the mouth of the San Juan River in Nicaragua, theoretically acting for her ward, the ridiculous "Mosquito King."  The United

States countered vigorously. In 1849 her diplomatic agents secured treaties with Nicaragua and Honduras. The first granted the United States transit privileges and the right to charter an exclusive transportation company. The second ceded Tigre Island in Fonseca Bay as a Pacific naval base. British naval forces temporarily occupied both Tigre Island and Trujillo Town on the east coast. This was supposedly to collect a claim for damages to British subjects, and both forces soon withdrew, but Britain clung firmly to Greytown. The United States did not ratify the 1849 treaties, but for a time the two nations hovered on the verge of war. Better judgment led to negotiation and ratification of the Clayton-Bulwer Treaty (1850). By this the two governments agreed to neutralize any canal, and not to occupy or exercise any control over the Mosquito Coast or other parts of Central America. The United States had expected this to force Great Britain out of the Bay Islands and the Mosquito Coast. The British, claiming that the terms were not retroactive, refused to withdraw and in 1852 formally created the "Colony of the Bay Islands." The conflict flared anew.

While Washington and the Court of St. James quarreled, nationals and agents of the two countries struggled in Central America. Here the United States had the advantage. It was less of a menace to sovereignty than was Great Britain, and the flow of its citizens to California benefited the economic life of Central America. A concession from Nicaragua in 1849 had permitted formation of a transportation corporation, and the American Transit Company put a combined river, lake, and stage coach route into active operation from 1854. In 1850 Colombia granted a concession to the American-owned Panamá Railroad Company, and in 1855 trains began to make the complete crossing. A Mexican treaty (1853) granting unrestricted transit use of the Tehuantepec Isthmus, and a Honduran charter (1854) for an Interoceanic Railroad, led to no immediate accomplishment, but completed United States control of all the practicable crossings except that through Nicaragua. There Britain used possession of Greytown to obstruct the migration of United States citizens, and local altercations and riots were frequent. Finally (July 13, 1854) an American man-of-war bombarded Greytown and burned it to the ground. Great Britain, engaged in the Crimean War, could only protest. The two nations next came into conflict over Walker in Nicaragua. Great Britain opposed his filibustering by every measure in her power. In the spring of 1856 the United States recognized Walker's government and broke off relations with Great Britain. The latter was now free from the Crimean struggle, and the two powers moved close to war.

**Great Britain Withdraws.** Open conflict between the English-speaking peoples probably was averted only because Britain receded from its thirty-year policy. Her statesmen, desirous of concentrating on the shifting European balance of power, had at last realized the strength and determination of the United States in Caribbean waters. They had also decided that United States dominance would not menace their true interests. Britain desired only trade and use of any canal. The latter was assured by treaty, and the United States was most unlikely to interfere with trade if friendly to Great Britain. Many Englishmen even believed that the United States, by encouraging or enforcing order in Central America, would foster prosperity and increase the value of British trade as well as of its own. The Dallas-Clarendon Treaty (1856) nearly settled all questions between the two, but ratification broke down over the status of the Bay Islands. Most of the provisions were incorporated in separate treaties that Great Britain made with Honduras (1859) and Nicaragua (1860). By these she recognized Central American sovereignty over the Bay Islands and the Mosquito Coast, though she included safeguards for land grants and for the rights of the Mosquito Indians in Nicaragua. By another treaty of 1859 Guatemala recognized British sovereignty over British Honduras, with the southern limit set at the Sarstoon River. For practical purposes, these treaties ended the Anglo-American conflict over Central America.

**France and Spain.** Like Great Britain, France and Spain were increasingly aggressive after 1848. To some degree this was the result of the struggle between Great Britain and the United States, which diverted the attention of both and somewhat encouraged Great Britain to coöperate with, or tolerate, European policies in America to which she was normally opposed. To some degree also it was due to the growing value of Latin American trade, and to conditions in Europe. French trade in Latin America, for instance, had been worth only three million dollars in 1825. It totaled thirty million in 1848, eighty in 1855, and over one hundred and twenty million in 1860. It was, obviously, worth a struggle and some risks. A major factor in the struggle was the personal and dynastic ambition of Napoleon III of France, who was interested in American expansion before he acceded to the throne in 1848. But until 1861 activities remained within bounds. Those of Spain consisted of little more than propaganda against United States imperialism, and an effort to associate herself with the acts of France and Great Britain in the West Indies. She also pressed strongly for settlement of claims against Mexico from 1856, and against Venezuela just before 1861. Before 1865 she consented to add only Nicaragua, Argentina, the Dominican Republic, Costa Rica, and Guatemala to the states that she recognized. France used diplomatic pressure and naval demonstrations freely, to advance her interests and oppose those of the others in Cuba, Haiti, the Dominican Republic, and Central America. She acted frequently in association with Great Britain. Her participation in joint moves as to the Plata and the Amazon rivers has been mentioned. She also interfered at times in other parts of South America. The weakening of American foreign policy by the War between the States (1861–1865) gave the signal for open attacks on Latin American sovereignty. The French intervention in Mexico (1861–1867) and incorporation of the Dominican Republic with Spain (1861–1865) have been mentioned earlier. Both had some excuse in the wishes of an important element in those countries' national life, but there was no such circumstance behind Spanish seizure of the Chincha Islands, which developed into war against Perú, Ecuador, Bolivia, and Chile, 1864–1866. The United States protested, but could do nothing more for a time. Its emergence from its internecine war as the strongest military nation of the world was not the only reason for the withdrawal of France and Spain from their ventures, but it had something to do with the withdrawals and with the fact that no further invasions were tried.

**Three Peaceful Decades.** For more than a generation after 1865, the relations of Latin America with the outside world were about the same as those of any other peoples. Disputes and the making of treaties over such things as commerce, extradition, and claims of foreigners occupied the attention of the authorities.

Ships of the Powers occasionally bombarded some port to enforce claims. Great Britain's interpretation of her relations to the Mosquito Indians under the treaty of 1860, and British and French interest in a canal, caused a few acrid interchanges with the United States. Only in 1894 did Spain complete her admission that a war of independence had been fought, by recognizing Honduras. But truly serious aggressions were lacking. United States policy, though hardly more objectionable in itself, suffered from the quality of its envoys. These were all too often low-grade politicians, who gave offense by their manner even when their aims were legitimate. They caused trouble, for instance, while encouraging union among the Central American republics in 1871, and while attempting to mediate disputes and wars in Latin America. Many of the rising capitalists of the United States, moreover, were anxious to acquire territory or almost sovereign concessions in Cuba, Haiti, the Dominican Republic, or Central America, and sometimes the American government reflected their views. It further safeguarded the canal routes by treaties with Honduras (1864) and Nicaragua (1867). It several times seriously embarked upon the annexation of all or part of the Dominican Republic and Haiti. It quarreled with Mexico over the river boundary and over Mexico's failure to prevent depredations along that frontier. Its relations with Chile were inflamed over relatively senseless incidents during most of the period. At one time or another it was at odds with Paraguay and Perú. But the canal treaties and the projected annexations were desired at least by the factions in power in the countries involved, and yet the annexations were defeated by opposition in the United States Senate. And of course not all the faults in the other disputes lay with one side. Citizens of the United States can hardly be proud of their relations with Latin America during the period, but the relations were by no means so bad as they were sometimes painted by more recent writers in an era of greater respect for the rights of small countries. Had nothing worse followed, their evil features would long ago have been buried beneath gratitude for protection against a far more imperialistic Europe.

**Latin American Aggrandizement.** The relations between the Latin American states concerned the same issues as earlier.

Ordinary economic questions played a large part, as did embroilments over aid given to insurgents or over the harboring of political exiles. The successful efforts of the Powers to open the Amazon, already mentioned, brought about bitter and complicated quarrels, alliances, and breaches of peace or of relations among the nations surrounding the Amazon Valley. The boundary disputes became major issues. Expansion of the population into new areas and the changing demands of the world market brought the peoples into more real contact, and made the resources of many of the frontier zones of greater value. As gold and silver had been a main motive for settlement under Spain, few mines of those metals were found in the now disputed regions, and it was Latin America's good fortune that the richest oil fields have been discovered in areas already clearly delimited. But coal mines in South Chile and oil prospects on the Amazon slopes of the Andes have played a part in boundary quarrels, as have the nitrates and guano of Chile, Bolivia, and Perú, the rubber of the Amazon, the banana lands of the Caribbean, and valuable harbors and rivers wherever found. Old handicaps to friendly relations decreased with more stable home government, but as Latin American nations became strong they all too often showed the aggressive traits of the Powers. Though their freedom from international wars surpasses that of most of the world, minor clashes along frontiers were frequent, and petty "wars" were almost endemic in Central America. Three major Latin American wars have occurred since the end of the Rosas attack on Uruguay in 1852. They are the Paraguayan War (1865–1870), the War of the Pacific (1879–1884), and the Chaco conflict (1932–1938). All involved boundaries and all had clear elements of national aggrandizement.

**Boundary Settlements.** At least thirty-four bilateral frontiers existed within Latin America as it was in the mid-nineteenth century. Each of them presented some question. The contestants claimed to be trying to apply the principle of *uti possidetis* — that is, to decide the limits as they were at the start of independence. Though the claim was usually sincere, legal documents of the colonial era contradicted each other or called for divisions impossible to reconcile with geography, and history showed that colonial practice had often conflicted with colonial law.   Nevertheless, the principle afforded a basis for settlements. In spite of many acrimonious exchanges, direct negotiations decided many cases.   Others were handled through mediation, often by a technical commission with a neutral member, or by arbitration.   The last has been common.   Between 1870 and 1930, for instance, special treaties sanctioned twenty-four bilateral arbitrations.   Three of these were left unfinished.   Of the twenty-one awards, only three were rejected, though the results were frequently calamitous from the viewpoint of one or the other party.   However the boundaries were finally settled, almost all were still uncertain as late as 1875.   By 1900 those of Argentina, Brazil, Uruguay, Chile, and Mexico were well advanced toward permanent status, as were some of those between smaller states. Delimitations occurred steadily thereafter.

**International Peace.**   Reliance upon arbitration is no new thing in Latin America.   From the days of early independence, the republics made a practice of entering into treaties providing for arbitration of specific questions.   In 1902 Argentina and Chile ratified a treaty providing for the arbitration of *all* differences between them.   At the same time they agreed to a restriction of land and naval armaments — the first recorded instance of insuring against war by diminishing the means of making war. Many later cases have occurred.   The idea of congresses, begun at Panamá in 1826, was also developed further.   A congress representing Colombia, Ecuador, Perú, Bolivia, and Chile met at Lima in 1847–1848, mainly to consider joint opposition to the plans of General Flores and the Queen Mother of Spain.   In 1856 delegates from Perú and six Caribbean nations met at Washington, and those of Perú, Chile, and Ecuador conferred at Santiago. Both these meetings were primarily concerned with danger from the United States.   Another group convened at Lima in 1864–1865, and at least twenty-eight more met in various cities between 1877 and 1920.   Many were for scientific or commercial purposes, and a series were concerned with Central American problems.   But the general keynote was a search for peace and security, joint resistance to foreign aggression, and development of international law to forbid practices objectionable to the weaker nations.   The conferences achieved little political result, since treaties were rarely ratified, but they provided a medium for an

THE CHRIST OF THE ANDES

Erected in 1904 to commemorate the peaceful settlement of a boundary dispute between Argentina and Chile. The monument stands about three thousand feet above the tunnel on the Trans-Andean Railroad. The figure of the Christ, twenty-six feet high, was cast from bronze cannon. The following inscription, though universally quoted, does not exist. "Sooner shall these mountains crumble into dust than the people of Argentina and Chile break the peace which they have sworn to maintain at the feet of Christ the Redeemer."

interchange of views and helped to keep alive the spirit of inter-
nationalism.

**Federation.** Except in Central America, the idea of federation
retained little vitality. The three great states of South America,
Argentina, Brazil, and Chile — popularly called the "A–B–C
Powers" — have long maintained close relations. The ties between Argentina and Chile went back to the days of independence
and were strengthened by adjustment of their boundary quarrels
(1899 and 1902), and by completion of the Trans-Andean Railway.
Brazil, as the largest of all American states, was a natural third
member. No formal alliance was made, but some publicists looked
forward to a time when the three nations as a group might serve
as a counterpoise to the United States and thus set up a New
World balance of power. In the nineteenth century it was also
urged that Cuba, Haiti, and the Dominican Republic should form
a confederation of the Antilles. Some have favored renewal of the
ties between Colombia, Venezuela, and Ecuador, and others have
suggested a Confederation of the Plata — Argentina, Uruguay,
and Paraguay — or a Confederation of the Pacific — Perú, Bolivia, and Chile. Including Mexico, a Central American Federation, and Brazil, Latin America would thus have seven or eight
great states united by geographic common interests, instead of the
twenty present states. But in view of the growth of the spirit of
nationalism since independence, it has become steadily less likely
that any existing people will consent to merge their identity with
that of any other.

**Imperialism.** The last decade of the nineteenth century inaugurated an era of renewed aggressions by the Powers. This
seems to have been an offshoot of the process by which European
nations divided Asia and Africa into colonies or spheres of influence. As they neared the end of the areas to partition in those
continents, their struggle for land became more vigorous and they
transferred some of their energies to the New World. Among
them now was Germany, which had become a unified nation too
late to seize a satisfactory share of the spoils. The United States
tended to regard Germany as the principal menace to America.
This was partly due to German tactlessness, and to chauvinistic
German speeches intended largely for home consumption. There
was also hostility over a real conflict of interests in the Pacific

islands, and a private Pan-German League undoubtedly wished to extend some German control over American areas with a large German-descended population. But the governmental policy was independent of such considerations. The world situation made Germany as eager as was Great Britain to avoid offending the United States, and the government never planned to disregard the Monroe Doctrine. The Netherlands, Belgium, and Italy began to participate, and the United States became openly imperialistic. That is, its people as a whole became generally desirous, for the first time, of owning or controlling lands outside its "natural" or continental limits, without regard to special strategic or canal values. This is supposed to have been associated with the disappearance of the frontier as a zone of opportunity on the mainland. It was also part of the economic development of the United States, which had reached a stage where the home market for goods and investment failed to satisfy the more venturesome manufacturers and bankers. The European balance of power and United States policy prevented European threats to sovereignty, as in the preceding half century, but other acts by both Europe and the United States became more energetic and more directly injurious to Latin America. All the nations employed naval demonstrations and landed troops, or bombarded ports, in the Caribbean. The Dominican Republic, Haiti, Venezuela, and to some degree Central America, as lands of incessant disorder and injury to foreign citizens and investments, were special targets.

**The Venezuelan Episodes.** The most famous incidents concerned Venezuela. The first was the Guiana boundary controversy between Great Britain and Venezuela, 1895–1899. In 1895 Britain was less a new aggressor against Venezuela than a victim of a new temper in the United States, but for a half century she had expanded her claims to Guiana territory. The expansions had markedly coincided with the discovery of new mines, or had reached out toward the mouth of the Orinoco River. Great Britain had refused to arbitrate unless Venezuela would first concede the Schomburgk line, surveyed by a British engineer in 1841. Though Venezuela also made unreasonable claims, it had mostly been willing to arbitrate everything. The United States had only slowly taken an interest, but by the 1890's the American public was, for other reasons, hostile to Great Britain.

Grover Cleveland, who became president in 1893, believed firmly in arbitration and in the Monroe Doctrine. His mind gradually hardened to the conviction that Great Britain was adding to her American possessions under a new guise. As he began in 1895 to press for a solution, death of his secretary of state caused appointment of an able but inexperienced aid, Richard Olney, to that position. The resulting despatch of July 20, 1895, which the secretary himself later called "bumptious," startled Great Britain and the world. It and later papers virtually served Britain with an ultimatum to arbitrate. As Britain played for time, Congress set up an investigating commission, whose report the United States proposed to enforce. Facing an African crisis with Germany, Great Britain at last agreed to arbitrate. Venezuela had agreed that fifty years' possession should be accepted as evidence of title, and the arbitral award gave Britain most of the disputed territory. Venezuela saved the mouth of the Orinoco, and some less important areas. The episode forcefully reminded European nations of the position of the United States, and probably guarded Venezuela against larger losses. The documents addressed to Great Britain are regarded as having extended the Monroe Doctrine to cover a new type of encroachment.

Two other incidents occurred during the misrule of Cipriano Castro (1899–1908). Frequent insurrections against Castro injured foreign property, and Castro treated foreigners harshly. By 1902 a dozen nations, including Mexico and the United States, had outstanding claims against Venezuela. Many of these antedated the revolutionary damages. Castro dodged all efforts to negotiate. Late in 1902 a joint fleet of British, German, and Italian warships seized and sank the Venezuelan navy, blockaded the chief ports, and bombarded Puerto Cabello. The United States had been assured that no acquisition of territory was contemplated, and had given the consent of silence to the operation. As the scope of action broadened, the United States became restive, and Germany and Great Britain began to differ. Early in 1903 the tripartite powers accepted arbitration of their cases along with all others, on equitable terms. The arbiters awarded about one sixth of the sums claimed. As Castro still evaded payment of a part, handled foreign investments arbitrarily, and treated foreign envoys discourteously, his troubles continued. He was seriously at odds with the United States from 1904, and France broke off relations in 1906. In 1908 the Netherlands again destroyed the Venezuelan navy and blockaded harbors. None of these troubles were cleared up until the start of the Gómez régime.

**Caribbean Policy of the United States.** To the United States, the Caribbean had become an area of prime importance. The Spanish-American War and the building of the Canal were part of an era of United States imperialism and "dollar diplomacy." As has been related elsewhere, between 1898 and 1917 the United States successively freed Cuba from Spain, annexed Puerto Rico, aided Panamá's independence, established protectorates over Cuba and Panamá, brought the Dominican Republic and Nicaragua and Haiti under its tutelage, intervened in Mexico, and bought the Danish islands. Far too much of this was instigated by private economic interests or by governmental officials sympathetic with such interests, though it sometimes had good intentions as well. Regardless of its motive, it reflected a basic necessity of United States life: security for Caribbean trade routes and for the Canal. Obviously it was dangerous to allow European nations to intervene as in Venezuela, even though they disclaimed territorial ambitions, but it was impracticable to refuse them all redress for grievances. To President Theodore Roosevelt, who took power politics and the rights of the strong for granted, the answer seemed simple. The United States would prevent abuses arising against foreigners, and thereby eliminate excuses for foreign action. In his fourth message to Congress (1904) he asserted: "Chronic wrongdoing, or an impotence which results in a general loosening of the ties of civilized society, may [anywhere] . . . require intervention by some civilized nation, and in the western hemisphere . . . may force the United States . . . to the exercise of an international police power. . . . We would interfere . . . only if . . . [their failure] to do justice . . . had violated the rights of the United States or had invited foreign aggression." Though this so-called Roosevelt Corollary was apparently regarded by its author and others as part of the Monroe Doctrine, it really was a different policy, based on the relation of the Caribbean to United States safety. It added nothing to world doctrines, being merely a statement of the "right" of intervention for national self-preservation that has always existed on the fringes

of international law.  The true Monroe Doctrine was extended by
the Lodge Resolution, passed by the Senate in 1912.  This resulted from rumors that a Japanese corporation might buy out an
American concession in Magdalena Bay.  That bay is strategically
important for control of the sea lanes between the Pacific coast of
the United States and the Canal.  The resolution stated that
"the United States could not see, without grave concern, the possession of such harbor or other place, by any corporation or association which has such a relation to another government, not
American, as to give that government practical power of control
for naval or military purposes."

The "Pan" Movements.  As part of the rivalry of the Powers,
a number of movements arose to enlist Latin American sympathies
for a sponsoring Power, and more or less against other Powers.
Spain early began an effort to capitalize on her status as a mother
country.  She established newspapers in Mexico, hostile to the
United States, in 1852, and offered leadership against the United
States in 1856.  Her losses in 1898 stripped her of all illusions as
to her place in the world, and intensified her efforts to regain importance.  By the early twentieth century a full-fledged "Pan-
Hispanic" (or "Pan-Iberian") movement had emerged, with
governmental subsidies or encouragement for congresses, for institutions, publications, and individuals carrying on Pan-Hispanic
propaganda in Latin America, and for Americans studying or
traveling in Spain.  Portugal, theoretically included in the movement, has taken little active part.  France has headed a "Pan-
Latin" movement.  She became conspicuously hostile to the
United States position in Latin America after 1867, from envy or
from fear of losing her trade and perhaps her West Indian islands.
Private French organizations have, since the early twentieth
century, conducted the same sort of campaign as have the Spanish.
These groups obviously have governmental approval, and ability
to gain French decorations for prominent Latin Americans, though
they are not known to have the use of public funds.  The French
and Spanish movements oppose each other, but their major attack is against the United States.

Pan-Americanism.  In 1882 James G. Blaine, secretary of state
under President Garfield, sincerely desired to secure and preserve
peace throughout the hemisphere, and he felt a natural interest in

THE PAN AMERICAN UNION BUILDING, WASHINGTON, D.C.

This white marble structure, erected through the munificence of Andrew Carnegie and the contributions of the American republics, houses the international organization known as the Pan American Union. In architectural design and in its decoration, the building is throughout suggestive of Latin America.

President Roosevelt speaking at the opening of the Inter-American Conference for the Maintenance of Peace, Buenos Aires, December 1, 1936.

promoting United States trade.   In his mind the first objective
was a necessary step toward the second, and he projected a peace
congress of all the independent American nations.   Garfield's assassination ended the project, but Blaine revived it when he again
became secretary of state, under Harrison.   In 1889 he presided
at Washington over the first "International Conference of American States," popularly called the Pan-American Conference.   The
delegates discussed a variety of subjects: reciprocity treaties;
uniform weights, measures, and coinage; extradition; patents and
copyrights; and arbitration of international disputes.   The major
result was the foundation of the Pan American Union, an international organization of the twenty-one American republics, with
headquarters in Washington.   The Union is supported by quotas,
which each republic contributes on the basis of population, and is
controlled by a governing board normally composed of the secretary of state of the United States and the Latin American envoys
to Washington.   The Union has for its aim the "development of
commerce, friendly intercourse, good understanding, and the
preservation of peace" among all the American peoples.   Its activities are based on the principle that all the republics, however
unlike in some respects, are one in their independence of Europe
and detachment from European concerns, in their governmental
principles, and in their political ideals.   They form a distinct
family of nations, able to coöperate for furtherance of their
common interests.   Through its monthly bulletins and other publications, the Union serves as a clearing house of information.
Subsequent conferences have met at Mexico City (1901–1902),
Rio de Janeiro (1906), Buenos Aires (1910), Santiago de Chile
(1923), Havana (1928), Montevideo (1933), and Lima (1938).
The gatherings are deliberative in character.   The delegates have
no power to bind their governments, and conventions framed by
them are often not ratified.   Moreover, the sovereign status of
each nation makes it impossible to adopt any resolution without
unanimous consent.   So long as Latin America and the United
States were at odds in their policies, this prevented the solution of
most political questions.   Thus at Santiago the so-called Brum
Doctrine, sponsored by Uruguay and calling for creation of an
American League of Nations to replace the Monroe Doctrine, was
not even discussed, as obnoxious to the United States.

**Other Pan-American Gatherings.**  The intellectual leaders of America associate, as well as the political leaders.  Pan-American Scientific Congresses, beginning with the one at Santiago in 1908, conferences dealing with fiscal and commercial interrelations, beginning at Washington in 1901, and conferences on sanitation have been frequent.  Many others have been devoted to child welfare, highways, postal affairs, aviation, eugenics, customs, status of women, education, or other nonpolitical subjects.  An important outcome of these gatherings was the creation of the Inter-American High Commission, a permanent body composed of the financial officers of the various nations.  The American Institute of International Law, organized in 1912, has held sessions in several countries.  The Pan-American Institute of Geography and History, inaugurated in 1929, has sponsored conferences and valuable publications.

**The "Yankee Peril."**  The Latin American nations exhibited mixed reactions toward these movements.  Their sympathies never really needed to be enlisted for France, which was the second homeland of all cultured Latin Americans.  They were hostile to Spain, remembering her colonial régime through the words of men who fought against Spain for independence, and having reason to dislike Spain's later acts.  They deeply feared the United States.  Their leaders realized that the latter had virtues as well as vices, and had protected them against Europe, but as they became stronger themselves that fact seemed less important, and the Caribbean expansion of the United States, and "dollar diplomacy," aroused tremendous apprehension.  The United States was commonly represented as a giant destined to gobble up during the next century whatever of Mexico, Central America, and the Antilles she had not already taken.  Misunderstandings also occurred due to the different cultural ideals of the "Anglo-Saxon" and the "Latin," and to tactless actions of the United States.  So long as the latter's policy justified the accusations of French and Spanish propagandists and sympathizers, Pan-Americanism could have little immediate meaning.  The Pan-Hispanists slowly improved their position, as the last men born under Spanish rule passed from national life.  The four-hundredth anniversary of the discovery of America furnished the occasion of a Congress at Madrid, in which the Latin American republics participated. Other reasons were found for expositions or congresses in 1900, 1914, 1921, and 1929–1930. These received increasingly cordial coöperation from the American nations. Both the French and Spanish movements, therefore, seemed to have more influence on Latin American minds than did Pan-Americanism. But neither, unfortunately for their sponsors, could offer a concrete plan of action as a solution for international problems.

**The War of 1914.** The World War that began in 1914 stirred Latin America deeply. All the nations were basically sympathetic to France. The presence of large German colonies in Argentina, Brazil, and Chile complicated governmental policy, but that influence was probably more or less counteracted by the Italian colonies of Argentina and Brazil and the strong British ties of Argentina and Chile. Public opinion, though pretty clearly pro-Ally, frequently turned against Great Britain because of that nation's use of sea power against neutral shipping, until the United States declared war on Germany in 1917. In that year Brazil, Cuba, and Panamá ranged themselves with the United States. During 1918 Costa Rica, Guatemala, Haiti, Honduras, and Nicaragua did likewise. The Dominican Republic, Ecuador, Perú, Bolivia, and Uruguay broke off diplomatic relations with the Central Powers, and Salvador declared a "benevolent neutrality" as to the United States. The remaining nations — Mexico, Venezuela, Colombia, Chile, Argentina, and Paraguay — continued strictly neutral. This was currently ascribed to pro-Germanism on the part of the governments. That belief was perhaps justified, especially in the first year, as to one or two of the nations. But Colombia and Mexico were strongly motivated by enmity for the United States, and all were trying to guard their own interests rather than to help those of Germany. Brazil hoped to gain South American leadership when she became the only large Latin American nation to enter the war, but she was also playing the part called for by a traditional friendship for the United States and liking for Pan-Americanism. She announced a desire to give her foreign policy, at a critical moment in world history, a practical form of "continental solidarity." Only Brazil got men and ships to Europe before the armistice. All the nations were awakened to a greater interest in world affairs, and were aided in various ways to appreciate their own resources.

**Latin America in the League.** Except Costa Rica and the Dominican Republic, the countries that had entered the war or had severed relations with Germany took part in the Peace Conference and signed the Treaty of Versailles. They thus became original members of the League of Nations, since its Covenant was part of the treaty. Argentina, Chile, Colombia, Paraguay, Salvador, and Venezuela soon accepted an invitation to accede to the Covenant. Costa Rica was admitted in 1920, the Dominican Republic in 1924, and Mexico in 1931. Ecuador failed to ratify the action of her delegates at the Peace Conference until 1934, when she became a member of the League. Latin American fervor for peaceful methods of international intercourse made membership seem natural in the earlier days. The countries hoped also to find a counterpoise to United States hegemony under the Covenant, which provided for settling controversies among members through the agency of the Council. This hope proved vain, as the United States never entered the League and the latter rigidly avoided actions objectionable to the great American Power. Article twenty-one of the Covenant stipulated that nothing in the document should be deemed to affect the validity of "regional understandings like the Monroe Doctrine." Since the Doctrine never had been more than a unilateral declaration of the United States, the other American nations risked giving it validity in International Law by signing the Covenant, but several efforts to persuade the Council to define the phrase failed of result. The League took no American action of any kind until 1933, when it collaborated with the United States and Brazil — already a nonmember — to settle the Leticia boundary clash between Perú and Colombia. Latin American delegations took able parts in all deliberations and committee work, but were unable to gain permanent seats on the Council. The cost of membership was high for the poorer nations. Disappointed in the benefits hoped for and disinterested in the Old World orientation of the League, one country after another dropped out. Argentina and Mexico withdrew soon after joining, but returned later. By 1941, Brazil, Chile, Costa Rica, Guatemala, Honduras, Nicaragua, Paraguay, Perú, Salvador, and Venezuela had permanently ended their membership.

**The Modern Era.** The war of 1914–1918 inaugurated an era of greater Latin American importance in world affairs. Several of the nations had risen to the rank of minor Powers, and all could better resist aggressions. Their trade and their market for loans, and their support in the League and other international bodies were increasingly valuable to the rival industrial and imperial Powers. The latter now included Italy and Japan. Italy had little capital to invest, but her trade, which was worth annually thirty million dollars in 1896 and forty-six millions in 1905, had reached one hundred and fifty-five millions in 1923. The presence in Argentina and Brazil of millions of first or second generation Italians gave the Italian government — Fascist from 1922 — hope of extending its influence in America and Europe through their help. Japan showed its first official interest in Latin America in a Mexican treaty of 1888, and a small migration occurred from 1897. But Japanese trade was worth only about a million dollars in 1907, and migration was small. Trade increased enormously during the war, but stabilized near twelve millions annually about 1922. There probably were fewer than fifty thousand Japanese in Latin America in that year, and neither trade nor migration increased as rapidly thereafter as Japan had expected. But hopes for improvement induced the government and the businessmen to carry on an active promotion campaign. As with all the other powers, part of the Italian and Japanese activities consisted of efforts to undermine their rivals' positions.

**Power Politics in Latin America.** Except as to the United States, specific events in the international relations of Latin America were comparatively unimportant for years after the close of the war (1919). Relations among themselves remained fairly peaceful. They held a few conferences under their own leadership, and settled nearly all their boundary quarrels by the 1930's. But it is interesting to note that as some of them became stronger and somewhat industrialized, their foreign policies showed the same quarrels over trade and tariffs, and the same struggle for leadership, that had earlier appeared between the Powers of Europe and the United States. During the 1920's, Mexico several times tried to assume leadership of Central American disputes with the United States. In the 1930's a tariff war between Argentina and Chile forced suspension of traffic over the Trans-Andean Railroad. Partly because of this, flood damage was so great in 1934 that the road was unusable in 1940. It was rumored, apparently with some basis, that Argentina and Brazil guardedly backed opposite sides during the Chaco conflict between Bolivia and Paraguay. The decades from 1919 to 1939 saw an unending struggle for position among the Great Powers. The Pan-Latin and the Pan-Hispanic drives took on new vehemence. To them were added the propaganda and the commercial campaigns of the newer contestants for Latin American favor. From about 1933 Germany and Italy gave these a special character. Both carried on ordinary activities. But their propaganda also sought to encourage totalitarian tendencies among the Latin American peoples. Trade proceeded largely in a regimented manner. "Dumping," exchange control, use of "black lists," pressure on agents, and all the other mechanisms of private "trusts" were applied by the totalitarian governments to the promotion of their trade and the stifling of that of others. Trade became virtually international barter, dealing a serious blow to the free international exchange of goods upon which modern prosperity had been built. Germany's prestige and trade rose — the latter apparently at the cost of Great Britain. The Faculty of Economics of the University of São Paulo was staffed and supported by Italy. The Dominican Republic had a German-dominated School of Tropical Research whose functions were broader than its title implied. Old newspapers were subsidized, or new ones were established, with totalitarian funds. The ideas spread by such papers and by Nazi or Fascist radio programs began to acquire something of the wide circulation formerly possessed only by the ideas of France. Nazi or Fascist organizations appeared in such countries as Argentina, Brazil, Chile, Perú, and Mexico, and the dictators of a few countries at least played with the corporative or totalitarian idea. The situation undeniably became serious for the "democratic" Powers, though alarmists somewhat exaggerated the successes of their rivals. Regimented trade began to break down under its own clumsiness and weight before Europe went to war in 1939, and individualism and idealism made Latin Americans unlikely to adopt the worst aspects of the totalitarian assault on personal liberty.

**Toward Hemisphere Friendship.** "Dollar diplomacy" had always been attacked by part of the North American public. An enormous increase in United States trade with Latin America from 1914 to 1919, and some decline thereafter, awakened the people as well as the government to the desirability of friendly relations with their southern neighbors. President Woodrow Wilson had promised a new policy in 1913, but the exigencies of domestic and world events prevented him from putting the promise into execution. The return of peace in 1919 was accompanied by a popular revulsion against Big Business anywhere, and imperialism and force in foreign relations. Liberal magazines and speakers drew attention to the expansion that had taken place while the nation's attention was on Europe. A Big Business president took over the White House in 1921, but the election had nothing to do with national feeling about Latin America, and led to a vigorous debate over foreign policy. Governmental actions long remained unchanged. But the debate (1921) over ratification of a treaty between the United States and Colombia concerning Panamá showed a general desire in the Senate for restoring harmony in order to improve economic relations, and began to educate the public as to how the interests of private investors had been allowed to direct United States policy. In 1922 the State Department announced that it wished to see the terms of loans to foreign nations before they were closed. This was an honest effort to forestall future claims for aid in collecting loans that never should have been made, but was perverted by some bankers into a guarantee that the United States would assist in collecting loans upon which the Department had passed. From 1924 to 1927, a series of Congressional hearings informed a startled public of the connection between oil imperialism and ratification of the Colombian treaty, of the evils of State Department loan supervision, and of the flimsy titles behind many of the North American claims as to Mexican land and oil.

The first indication of a new Latin American policy concerned the Isle of Pines, off the Cuban coast. No intelligent statesman had ever believed that the United States owned this island, but the Senate had refused for twenty years to ratify a treaty surrendering the United States claim, in order to safeguard the interests of North American residents. In 1925 the Senate ratified the treaty without serious debate. The withdrawal of marines from Central America, even though temporary, was another step.

Partly under the influence of Herbert Hoover as secretary of commerce, the last years of the Coolidge régime showed a generally conciliatory tendency. This appeared in Mexican relations by 1927. The next year saw the amicable compromise of a dispute with Colombia over the San Andrés Islands in the Caribbean, and clarification of the Monroe Doctrine through the so-called "Clark Memorandum." This paper, drawn up for and adopted by the State Department, stripped the Monroe Doctrine of all but its original meaning of banning foreign encroachments against Latin America. At the Havana Conference in 1928, Secretary of State Hughes followed this up in a brilliant speech. He appealed to the legalistic minds even of hostile statesmen by the precision of his distinction between the Monroe Doctrine and the United States Caribbean policy, and by his frankness in dealing with the latter. Under President Hoover, who had made a tour of Latin America as president-elect, the government continued to reverse the trend of its policy. Though Hoover was handicapped by the political difficulty of changing an old party practice, he largely dropped the idea of preventing revolution, quietly forgot the Roosevelt Corollary, and withdrew the marines from the Dominican Republic and Nicaragua and prepared to take them from Haiti.

**The Good Neighbor.** In 1933 Franklin D. Roosevelt became president of the United States. He had long cherished convictions as to need of discontinuing aggressions in Latin America, and cultivating close relations. He has never been reluctant to reverse an old policy, and as that policy was unpopular with the electorate and associated with the "old régime" of the opposition party, his acts were entirely unhampered. He announced the "Good Neighbor" policy in his inaugural address and later. What will probably go down in history as his doctrine, however much it was foreshadowed by other men, was stated most clearly on December 28, 1933, at a dinner of the Woodrow Wilson Foundation. Recalling Wilson's earlier renunciation in the name of the United States of the right of acquiring territory by conquest, Roosevelt added, "The definite policy of the United States from now on is one opposed to armed intervention." The speech, timed to be heard at the Pan-American Conference then meeting at Montevideo, made a favorable impression, and that impression deepened as the United States acted in accordance with its words. Much of the story has been told as part of the history of the separate countries.  Except for interference in Cuba, the essence of which took place before the Montevideo Conference, the record has been excellent.

**Improved Relations.**  The United States delegation to Montevideo, carefully chosen for ability and prestige, followed a conciliatory course.  It avoided too much leadership, and it made no effort to block discussion of Latin American grievances over interventions or trade and tariffs.  Its acquiescence in several resolutions of a vague but friendly character, when coupled to announcements of the Good Neighbor policy, assured Latin America of security from its powerful northern neighbor.  Between 1933 and 1939 United States protectorates and financial controls were practically all abolished.  United States nationals and their investments have been given little protection by their government in recent years.  Even oil expropriations in Bolivia (1937) and in Mexico called forth no more than the internationally conventional protests, though Mexico's economy could have been wrecked by discontinuance — as a "domestic matter affecting only the United States" — of silver purchases at an inflated price. An effort to improve relations by visits of distinguished men had begun in 1928, when President Coolidge traveled to the Havana Conference.  This type of propaganda was continued in later years, and supplemented by "good will" visits of warships, and navy or army planes.  Improved steamship, air, and press services and radio broadcasts, by private companies but with government approval, have increasingly broken through the barriers of ignorance between the north and the south.

The improvement in inter-American relations has been striking. Pan-Americanism does have a basis in common conditions, and Latin America has long admired the practical accomplishments of its northern neighbor.  In spite of some faults on the part of Latin America, the major handicaps to friendship had been found in the acts of the United States.  Once fear of these was removed, the helpful factors became effective.  By the time that a special conference met at Buenos Aires in 1936, the Latin Americans were mostly convinced of North American good faith.  Conventions signed there are usually interpreted as having outlawed intervention among the signatories, and having started to change the Monroe Doctrine from a unilateral declaration to a collective security pact. Another convention, for Inter-American Cultural Relations, provided for mutual exchange between all countries of students and teachers, at government expense. The general conference at Lima in 1938 revealed the same cordial relations. The Declaration of Lima, though very vague in its wording, increased the multilateral character of the Monroe Doctrine. Meantime Latin America was, as a whole, welcoming North American leadership in abolishing trade barriers through the so-called "Hull treaties," and through loans and treaties which overcame the restrictions of the regimented trade systems.

**Hemisphere Solidarity.** Inter-American cordiality became almost general in time to meet the problems of renewed European war which began in September, 1939. The preponderant sympathies would probably have been with France and Great Britain, just as a generation earlier, and German attacks on unoffending small nations stirred Latin America profoundly. But there was enough Nazi and Fascist strength and sentiment in strategic areas to menace domestic and inter-American peace, had hemisphere solidarity not enabled Latin American nations to support each other and fearlessly to accept leadership and aid from the formerly dreaded "Colossus of the North." Step after step of common policy went into the record. At the outbreak of the war, Panamá invoked the Declaration of Lima. From the resulting conference came the Declaration of Panamá (December, 1939), which affirmed a joint interest in keeping the Americas out of the war, and created a neutral zone about the continents, with a "patrol either individually or collectively." This was an unenforceable proposition, but had its place in the growth of American joint action. The collapse of France affected Latin America as it did the United States. Within a week, the American Minister to Uruguay announced, with general applause from Latin America, "The avowed policy of my government [is] to coöperate fully [for defense] wherever such coöperation is desired." Another special conference produced the Act of Havana (July, 1940) to meet the possible danger of Germany's taking control of the French and Dutch West Indies. "The status of regions in this hemisphere belonging to Europe," announced the American republics in the Act, "is a subject of deep concern to all the governments of the American Republics." This being so, they stated, no transfer could be permitted during the war. The Act provided for multipartite emergency committees to establish a provisional American control if need arose. But it agreed that if the situation could not wait, one or more American nations might act alone. In view of existing conditions, this amounted to a license for the United States to seize the islands if it judged best. That fact was well recognized, but two thirds of the countries had ratified by October, 1940, making the Act part of the international policy of the hemisphere, and completing the adoption of the idea of the Monroe Doctrine as a multilateral principle.

**Defense against the Old World.** The international existence of Latin America had begun in an era when the nations faced the possibility of an intervention by absolutist Powers. In the 1820's their only real defense had lain in European rivalries and in the Monroe Doctrine. The danger from absolutism had vanished, and with it much of the value of the Monroe Doctrine. Now in 1940 they faced a danger to their cherished liberties from totalitarian Powers, more ruthless and powerful by far than the absolutist governments of the previous century. But they had now reached a stage where they could do much to protect themselves, aside from adopting the principle of the Monroe Doctrine as a basis for joint action.

Between September, 1939, and December, 1941, various countries moved to wipe out Nazi and Fascist organizations, to nationalize their airlines, to stop their subsidized publications, and to bring foreign schools under national control. United States naval, military, and air missions replaced those of Central Europe. At the same time Latin Americans exhibited approval instead of alarm as the United States acquired naval and air bases from Great Britain that pushed her outposts a thousand miles to the south, and for the first time put them on the South American continent. By September, 1940, a joint Chilean-United States corporation received approval from the Chilean government for its plan to build a 45,000-ton dry dock at Valparaiso, a project that makes economic or strategic sense only if the dock is to be used by United States capital ships in time of war. In October, 1940, friendly discussions were publicly admitted over naval and air bases for Hemisphere use (that is, primarily for United States use), in Argentina, Brazil, Paraguay and Uruguay, and earlier, Ecuador had become willing to discuss similar use of her Galapagos Islands. The mere rumor of such a thing a decade earlier would have ended the proponents' political careers. Costa Rica, long dubious about United States policy, offered land for naval or air bases.

In the spring of 1941 Mexico buried in oblivion her memory of former territorial losses and allowed the United States Navy to use Magdalena Bay and North American flyers to use Mexican airports on the way to the Canal Zone. That summer Panamá granted the United States sites for airfields, beacons, and other installations outside the Zone. In September Uruguay announced the creation of a naval base, to be open to United States ships, financed with a gift and a loan from the United States. Brazil had approved the project. The base was so located as to command the Plata River mouth, regardless of any aid from Argentina. In November, Brazil agreed to United States occupation of Dutch Surinam, technically through an agreement with the Netherlands. It was several times rumored that Brazil and the United States had agreed that in case of necessity Brazil would o cupy the Portuguese islands in the Atlantic, as a means of handling a difficult situation with the least injury to Portuguese sentiment.

**Economic Unity.** The financial and economic program provided for at Havana (July, 1940) as a Hemisphere activity, and intended to include a contribution from the country immediately benefited as well as from the United States, was steadily advanced. Loans from the Export-Import Bank and other aid in developing communications, strategic crops like rubber, and local industries to absorb surplus agricultural labor, have been offered, and welcomed in the spirit in which they were offered. Apportionment schemes for coffee, cacao, and cotton, to overcome the loss of the European market, have been amicably worked out. On October 14, 1941, Argentina became the twelfth American nation to sign a reciprocal trade treaty with the United States, greatly aiding the trade of the whole Hemisphere. Obviously much of this is economically beneficial. But no one who knows the Latin Americans believes that they were selling their prized independence. They had simply become convinced that the United States has their interests and their safety at heart as well as its own, and that its expanding participation in their affairs no longer carries the future danger that once they would have feared.

**War Comes to the Americas.** The Japanese attack on Pearl Harbor (December 7, 1941) and the subsequent recognition or declaration of war between the United States and the Axis Powers intensified the program of Hemisphere defense and gave new evidences of Hemisphere solidarity. Within a week all the West Indian and Central American nations, including Panamá, also declared war. Mexico, Colombia, and Venezuela broke off diplomatic relations. All the states not at war declared that they would not regard as "belligerents" an American people at war with non-Americans. This legal quibble, based chiefly on the Act of Havana (July, 1940), had the enormous advantage of allowing United States naval or air forces to use ports, bases, and flying fields anywhere, without being subject to the limitations imposed by neutrals on warring nations. The Latin Americans also continued their campaign against foreign schools, airlines, and military or other missions, while those not at war attempted to stop the illegal activities of the swollen diplomatic and consular staffs of the Axis nations. The extra-territorial status of the last two groups handicapped actions against even flagrant overstepping of their proper zones of activity, but most of the other Axis bodies had been brought under control, or ejected, within a month. Brazil's seizure of the Condor (German) airlines system on January 6, 1942, practically completed elimination of foreign aviation from the Hemisphere.

**Special Conference at Rio.** A conference of American Secretaries of Foreign Affairs met at Rio de Janeiro on January 15–29, 1942. Available information indicates that a considerable part of the inspiration for its convening and for its activities came from Mexico, Colombia, and Venezuela, which desired to increase the anti-Axis effort of the American republics. The conference dealt not only with the obvious economic and political questions, but with the problems created by the Axis diplomats and consuls still accredited to most of the South American nations. Such persons, behind the cloak of diplomatic immunity, acted as dangerous spies on ship and troop movements, as directors of drives against morale, as operators of illegal radio stations, and as saboteurs. The conference successfully laid a basis for economic welfare, by a group of agreements looking toward lowered tariffs, an international currency, and pooled mercantile and naval resources.

The desire of the vast majority for a unanimous breach of relations with the Axis was blocked by the position of Chile and Argentina. Both of these had early declared the United States a non-belligerent, and neither could properly be considered an Axis sympathizer. The considerable number of residents of German or Italian ancestry did give them a greater problem than exists in most countries. Chile considered the exposed condition of its lengthy coasts to be a reason for hesitation, but was also influenced by the close division expected in the Presidential election of February first. Both candidates were reluctant to risk shifts among the blocs of extremist voters. In Argentina, the Conservative party's insecure tenure of office was a factor, since much support for the Conservatives comes from groups which include most of the Axis sympathizers.

But the trouble had more fundamental causes. Argentine produce has been barred from the United States by unreasonable sanitary embargoes, as well as by tariff walls. It has always found its natural market in Europe, where it competes sharply with produce from the United States. Naturally, Argentine policy has always had strong European and hardly less strong anti-United States slants. Finally, the sincere nationalist or "isolationist" belief that long existed in the United States, that the New World's only concern with an Old World war is to remain aloof, was strong in Argentina.

In spite, therefore, of severe pressure by other Latin American nations, and of diplomatic exchanges so acrimonious that they ruffled the surface calm usually maintained in such meetings, neither Argentina nor Chile would agree to a Hemisphere breach of relations. They did, however, line up with the others in recommending as a joint policy that all the individual nations take such action. When on January 28 Brazil, and on January 29 Ecuador, severed relations with Germany, Italy, and Japan, only Argentina and Chile still maintained them. Chile was believed likely to join the movement soon.

**Recent Events.** News of raids on Axis sympathizers, internment of Axis agents, and isolation of former Axis diplomats and consuls while awaiting repatriation, has filled the newspapers since January. Preparations for emergency uses of Latin American troops, ships, and bases have been widespread. Evidences of a more friendly spirit toward the United States have multiplied. On January 31 Bolivia, which expropriated foreign oil fields in 1937, agreed to pay the main American claimant for them. On February 11 United States troops occupied Dutch Curaçao and Aruba. Venezuela had approved the act in advance, through agreement with the Netherlands that Venezuela would "coöperate in this defense measure." In March the President of Ecuador announced that the United States was establishing a naval station at Salinas, at the mouth of Guayaquil Bay, and newspapermen were allowed to visit the airfield in Guatemala from which United States planes patrolled both coasts.

In Mexico, various friendly diplomatic exchanges, including steps toward settlement of the oil controversy, were climaxed on June 1 by a declaration of war as of May 22. This step grew immediately from mounting anger over submarine attacks on Mexican ships. The same anger is increasingly affecting the other non-belligerents which have a merchant marine. Brazil has begun using planes against submarines, and seems likely before long to join the avowedly warring nations. Argentina and Chile have taken part in preparations for defense, and in other Hemispheric activities, but have not (August 1, 1942) broken off relations. Chile seems certain to do so at some opportune time. In Argentina, the question is increasingly one of a large popular majority struggling to align itself with the democratic nations, but blocked by the Conservative oligarchy which holds political control.

**A Hopeful Future.** The millenium has not come. Minor rifts exist among the Latin American nations, and as to relations with the United States. Argentine, Brazilian, and Chilean policy will still be influenced by the presence of strong blocs of totalitarian sympathizers, and Argentina has not forgotten her trade grievances and her suspicions and jealousies of the United States. The natural markets of southern South America are still in Europe, and if the end of the war removes the pressure of fear, the new bonds will loosen. Moreover, a relatively few years of considerate treatment by the United States have not wiped out recollection of the preceding era, and many Latin Americans are of course "anti-totalitarian and pro-democratic," rather than "pro-United

States." Even sincere friends of the *Norteamericanos* have felt irritation over the sudden high-pressured goodwill campaign, and even more over the flood of books on Latin America by authors whose acquaintance was gained during a few weeks of airplane travel between capital cities, while conversing only with persons who spoke English. The inability of the United States to prevent stringencies that have resulted from the loss of European markets has also furnished ammunition for hostile groups. But all the evidence shows that the Latin Americans have, on the whole, accepted their powerful northern neighbor as a friend, whose sponsoring of Pan-Americanism has something more than immediate self-interest behind it. The United States can have confidence in a satisfactory continuance of the present status, so long as it continues to treat Latin Americans as peoples whose viewpoints and interests deserve consideration for their own sake. If it will cultivate the common interests of mind and spirit as diligently as it has those of material profit and physical security, it need not fear for the permanence of Hemisphere solidarity.

### Words and Phrases You Should Know

| | | |
|---|---|---|
| "A-B-C Powers" | hegemony | Pan-Hispanic |
| American Transit Company | hemisphere solidarity | Panamá Railroad Company |
| arbitration | imperialism | |
| balance of power | Monroe Doctrine | "Polk Corollary" |
| Clayton-Bulwer Treaty | "old régime" | Roosevelt Corollary |
| Declaration of Panamá | Pan-Americanism | spheres of influence |
| "Good Neighbor" policy | Pan American Union | "Yankee Peril" |

### Questions You Should Be Able to Answer

1. How do you account for the fact that the Great Powers which obtained control of large areas in Asia and Africa did not obtain similar control in Latin America?
2. Why is Bolívar called the father of the idea of a League of American Nations? Do you think his idea should be carried out?
3. What events in Europe after 1815 caused Great Britain and the United States to become alarmed concerning Latin America? Why?
4. What interest had Russia in North America?

5. What were the two positive parts of the Monroe Doctrine? To what two possibilities did the Monroe Doctrine not make any reference?

6. What was the reaction to the Doctrine in Europe and in Latin America?

7. Why did the United States become more concerned about Central America after 1849?

8. What was the basis of British and United States rivalry in Central America? Why did the rivalry not end in war?

9. Why did the French and Spanish cease their attempts to extend their influence into Latin America after 1865?

10. Why were there many boundary disputes in Latin America? How have many of these been settled?

11. Why did the Great Powers show increased interest in Latin America in the 1890's?

12. How did Theodore Roosevelt extend the Monroe Doctrine?

13. Do you think Pan-American conferences worth while? Give your reasons.

14. How have Italy, Japan, and Germany sought to increase their influence in Latin America since the World War?

15. Do you think the "Good Neighbor" policy will offset the fear of a "Yankee Peril"?

16. Why is there increased concern today, both in the United States and in Latin America, for hemisphere solidarity?

17. How would you compare the European threat to Latin America one hundred years ago and today?

18. What do you think will be the most important factor in building stronger friendship between Latin America and the United States in the future?

## Projects and Activities

1. Rewrite in your own words the parts of President Monroe's message of 1823 which are quoted in this chapter.

2. In two columns put items which show: What the Monroe Doctrine Was — What the Monroe Doctrine Was Not; What the Monroe Doctrine Said — What the Monroe Doctrine Did Not Say.

3. Write a brief essay on the policy of any one European nation toward Latin America.

4. On a time line indicate several events illustrating the interest of Great Britain, Spain, France, and Germany in Latin America.

5. Prepare imaginary newspaper headlines for five events in Latin America in which the United States and European Powers were involved.

6. Make a chart showing the development of the Monroe Doctrine from 1823 to the present. Use these headings: Date; President or Statesman Involved; Event; How the Doctrine Was Involved; Result.

7. Write to the Pan American Union, Washington, D.C. for a list of free publications. Several members of the class might then obtain one or more of the publications and use them as a basis for class reports.

8. Make a list of the subjects that have been discussed at Pan-American conferences. Be sure you understand each item on your list.

9. List the ways in which the United States has tried to show its good will toward Latin America since the World War.

10. Select several incidents from the chapter which illustrate the building up of good will between Latin America and the United States and use them as a basis for a short play or pageant.

11. Draw cartoons illustrating the "Yankee Peril," the "Colossus of the North," and the "Good Neighbor."

12. Write an imaginary dialogue between a Latin American citizen and a citizen of the United States as they discuss ways and means of building hemisphere solidarity.

# BIBLIOGRAPHICAL NOTES

The brief bibliography that follows is restricted to general works in the English language, usually of recent publication. Many additional references will be found in H. E. Bard, *South America: Study Suggestions* (New York, 1916, D. C. Heath and Co.); H. L. Hoskins, *Guide to Latin-American History* (New York, 1922, D. C. Heath and Co.); W. W. Pierson, *Hispanic American History: A Syllabus* (Chapel Hill, N. C., 1926); and in the textbooks listed below. Those of Robertson and Williams are exceptionally good for scholarly studies in all languages, and that of Rippy for works in English. That of Wilgus is notable for historical maps, and for its footnote guide to periodical articles in scholarly and general reviews.

Textbooks include C. I. Chapman, *Hispanic America* (2 vols., New York, 1937); T. B. Jones, *Introduction to Hispanic American History* (New York, 1939); F. A. Kirkpatrick, *Latin America, a Brief History* (New York, 1939); D. R. Moore, *History of Latin America* (New York, 1938); J. F. Rippy, *Historical Evolution of Hispanic America* (New York, 1940); W. S. Robertson, *History of the Latin-American Nations* (New York, 1932); W. W. Sweet, *History of Latin America* (New York, 1929); A. C. Wilgus, *History of Hispanic America* (Washington, 1931), and *The Development of Hispanic America* (New York, 1941); and M. W. Williams, *People and Politics of Latin America* (Boston, 1938). N. A. N. Cleven, *Readings in Hispanic American History* (Boston, 1927), makes a number of documents and other contemporary accounts available for students who lack access to the originals. *Modern Hispanic America* (Washington, 1933), *The Caribbean Area* (Washington, 1934), *Argentine, Brazil and Chile* (Washington, 1935) (STUDIES IN HISPANIC AMERICAN AFFAIRS, edited by A. C. Wilgus) are indispensable. Valuable translations of histories by Latin American writers are now appearing in the INTER-AMERICAN HISTORICAL SERIES. So far they include J. P. Calogeras, *History of Brazil*, translated by P. A. Martin (Chapel Hill, 1939); J. M. Henao and Gerardo Arrubla, *History of Colombia*, translated by J. F. Rippy (Chapel Hill, 1938); Ricardo Levene, *History of Argentina*, translated by W. S. Robertson (Chapel Hill, 1937); and Luis Galdames, *History of Chile*, translated by Isaac Cox (Chapel Hill, 1941). H. G. James and P. A. Martin, *Republics of Latin America* (New York, 1923), is valuable for political systems and economic conditions of its date, but is weak on history. A. H. Keane, *Central and South America* (2 vols., London, 1909–1911),

E. W. Shanahan, *South America, and Economic and Regional Geography* (New York, 1927), and R. H. Whitbeck, *Economic Geography of South America* (New York, 1931), are valuable on the natural conditions.

ABORIGINAL AMERICA. John Fiske, *Discovery of America* (2 vols., Boston, 1892), is still a most satisfactory book for the general reader. *The History of the New World Called America*, by E. J. Payne (2 vols., Oxford, 1892–1899), deals at length with the discovery of America and with the Indians. Three volumes by T. A. Joyce, *South American Archæology* (London, 1912), *Mexican Archæology* (1914), and *West Indian Archæology* (1916), present an excellent account of the antiquities of Latin America. Clark Wissler, *American Indian* (New York, 1922), gives the best condensed treatment of both the archæology and the ethnology of the New World. Indispensable recent works are: H. J. Spinden, *Ancient Civilizations of Mexico and Central America* (New York, 1928); and P. A. Means, *Ancient Civilizations of the Andes* (New York, 1930). H. B. Alexander, *Latin-American Mythology* (Boston, 1920), and R. Karsten, *Civilization of the South American Indians, with Special Reference to Magic and Religion* (New York, 1926), are authoritative.

THE EUROPEAN BACKGROUND. R. B. Merriman, *Rise of the Spanish Empire in the Old World and the New* (4 vols., New York, 1918–1934), covers through the end of the sixteenth century better than any other single work, though not very full on cultural developments. C. E. Chapman, *History of Spain* (New York, 1918), M. A. S. Hume, *Spain, Its Greatness and Decay, 1479–1788* (Cambridge, 1899), H. M. Stephens, *Story of Portugal* (New York, 1901), and George Young, *Portugal, Old and Young* (Oxford, 1917), are useful English treatments.

DISCOVERY AND EXPLORATION. Fiske, *Discovery of America*, Payne, *History of the New World Called America*, Sir A. Helps, *Spanish Conquest in America* (4 vols., London, 1900–1904), are readable narratives. W. H. Prescott, *History of the Conquest of Mexico* (1843 and later) and *History of the Conquest of Peru* (1847 and later), are two famous, picturesque, and interesting works, worth reading though not reflecting at all points modern knowledge of the subject. I. B. Richman, *Spanish Conquerors* (New Haven, 1919), and H. E. Bolton, *Spanish Borderlands* (New Haven, 1921) in the "Chronicles of America" series, furnish good short accounts for the general reader.

THE COLONIAL ERA. R. G. Watson, *Spanish and Portuguese South America* (2 vols., London, 1884), is still worth consulting. E. G. Bourne, *Spain in America* (New York, 1904), was long the best account in one volume, and still has much value. Bernard Moses, *Spanish Dependencies in South America* (2 vols., New York, 1914), covering from 1550 to 1730, and the same author's *Spain's Declining Power in America* (Berkeley,

Calif., 1919), for the period from 1730 to 1808, and C. E. Chapman, *Colonial Hispanic America: A History* (New York, 1933), should be widely consulted. F. W. Blackmar, *Spanish Institutions of the Southwest* (Baltimore, 1891), is good for California, Arizona, New Mexico, and Texas. C. F. Lummis, *Spanish Pioneers* (Chicago, 1893), gives a readable account of Spanish activities in the sixteenth century. Scholarly studies especially valuable for institutions and cultures are: C. H. Haring, *Trade and Navigation between Spain and the Indies* (Cambridge, 1918); J. T. Lanning, *Academic Culture in the Spanish Colonies* (New York, 1940); H. C. Lea, *Inquisition in the Spanish Dependencies* (New York, 1908); I. A. Leonard, *Carlos de Siguenza y Góngora, a Mexican Savant of the Seventeenth Century* (Berkeley, Calif., 1929); P. A. Means, *Fall of the Inca Empire* (New York, 1932); H. I. Priestley, *Coming of the White Man* (New York, 1929); L. B. Simpson, *Encomienda in New Spain, 1492–1550* (Berkeley, 1929); and I. A. Wright, *Early History of Cuba* (New York, 1916).

THE ERA OF INDEPENDENCE. A few of the pertinent English language works on the gaining of independence are: W. S. Robertson, *Rise of the Spanish-American Republics, as Told in the Lives of Their Liberators* (New York, 1918); F. L. Paxson, *Independence of the South American Republics* (Philadelphia, 1903); Bartolomé Mitre, *Emancipation of South America* (translation by W. Pilling, much abridged: London, 1893); W. S. Robertson, *Life of Miranda* (2 vols., Chapel Hill, N. C., 1929); F. L. Petrie, *Simón Bolívar* (London, 1910); A. H. Noll and A. P. McMahon, *Life and Times of Miguel Hidalgo y Costilla* (Chicago, 1910); and A. Hasbrouck, *Foreign Legionaries in the Liberation of South America* (New York, 1928). There are many others, especially biographies of Simón Bolívar, which are usually more eulogistic than trustworthy.

RECENT AND CONTEMPORARY HISTORY. A number of works are especially valuable for history since independence, though some of them also discuss the colonial era. F. García Calderón, *Latin America, Its Rise and Progress* (translated by B. Miall: New York, 1913), sets forth the viewpoint of one of the most brilliant of Peruvian scholars. M. de Oliveira Lima, *Evolution of Brazil Compared with that of Spanish and Anglo-Saxon America* (Stanford Univ., Calif., 1914), is a thoughtful book, but assumes rather too much knowledge on the part of readers. Other books that have some value are: W. R. Shepherd, *Hispanic Nations of the New World* (New Haven, 1919); W. H. Koebel, *South America* (New York, 1913); C. R. Enock, *Spanish America* (2 vols., New York, 1920); W. H. Koebel, *Central America* (London, 1917); A. K. Fiske, *The West Indies* (New York, 1899); Stephen Bonsal, *American Mediterranean* (New York, 1912). More definitely historical treatises include: C. E. Akers, *History of South America, 1854–1912* (London, 1912); T. C. Dawson, *South American Republics* (2 vols., New York, 1903–1904); F. A. Kirkpatrick, *History of the Argentine Republic* (Cambridge, England, 1931); H. G. James, *Brazil after a Century of Independence* (New York, 1925); R. Nash, *Conquest of Brazil* (New York, 1926); H. I. Priestley, *Mexican Nation, A History* (New York, 1923); E. Gruening, *Mexico and Its Heritage* (New York, 1928); D. G. Munro, *Five Republics of Central America* (Oxford, 1918); C. L. Jones, *Caribbean Backgrounds and Prospects* (New York, 1931) and *The Caribbean since 1900* (New York, 1936); C. E. Chapman, *History of the Cuban Republic* (New York, 1927); S. Welles, *Naboth's Vineyard: the Dominican Republic, 1844–1924* (2 vols., New York, 1928); H. P. Davis, *Black Democracy, the Story of Haiti* (New York, 1936). Books that offer information of more interest to many students than is political history are: A. Coester, *Literary History of Spanish America* (New York, 1916); I. Goldberg, *Studies in Spanish-American Literature* (New York, 1920); same author, *Brazilian Literature* (New York, 1922); A. S. Blackwell, *Some Spanish-American Poets* (New York, 1929); and E. Hague, *Latin American Music, Past and Present* (Santa Ana, Calif., 1934). J. L. Mecham, *Church and State in Latin America* (Chapel Hill, 1932), is the standard work in its important field. *The Civilization of the Americas: Lectures . . . Delivered in the Spring of 1938* (Berkeley, 1938) offers valuable comments by six specialists on various aspects of the growth of Latin American culture in the broader sense.

INTERNATIONAL RELATIONS. Books having value for the general reader, though many of them are already partially obsolete for specialists in the most-worked-upon field of Latin American history, so far as the English language is concerned, are: G. H. Blakeslee (editor), *Latin America* (New York, 1914); J. H. Latané, *United States and Latin America* (New York, 1920); W. S. Robertson, *Hispanic-American Relations with the United States* (New York, 1923); G. H. Stuart, *Latin America and the United States* (New York, 1922); J. B. Scott, *International Conferences of the American States, 1889–1928* (New York, 1931); J. F. Rippy, *Latin America in World Politics* (New York, 1931); C. L. Jones, *Caribbean Interests of the United States* (New York, 1916); A. B. Hart, *Monroe Doctrine* (Boston, 1915); D. Y. Thomas, *One Hundred Years of the Monroe Doctrine* (New York, 1923); and J. B. Lockey, *Pan-Americanism, Its Beginnings* (New York, 1920). Dexter Perkins, *The Monroe Doctrine* (3 vols., Cambridge or Baltimore, 1927–1937) is the authority on the history from 1823 to 1907.

WORKS OF TRAVEL AND DESCRIPTION. James (Viscount) Bryce, *South America: Observations and Impressions* (New York, 1914), is the

production of a veteran traveler and accomplished student of politics.
E. A. Ross, *South of Panama* (New York, 1915), embodies a sociologist's
observations and impressions of South America, which have not lost their
value.  Other comprehensive and fair-minded presentations of contemporary movements in Middle and South America include: C. S. Cooper,
*Understanding South America* (New York, 1918);  C. C. Griffin, ed., *Concerning Latin American Culture* (New York, 1940);  C. H. Haring, *South
America Looks at the United States* (New York, 1928);  S. G. Inman, *Problems in Pan Americanism* (New York, 1921).   Manuel Ugarte, *The Destiny
of a Continent,* translated by J. F. Rippy (New York, 1925), is the work of
a brilliant Argentine, hostile to the United States but aware of virtues in
the United States and of vices in Latin America.  Waldo Frank, *America
Hispana* (New York, 1937) is a brilliant interpretation of Latin American
life, though occasionally rather abstract.

Much practical information is accessible in the *Commercial Traveler's
Guide to Latin America,* or other publications of the Department of Commerce of the United States;  *South American Handbook* (New York, annually);  and *The World Almanac* (New York, various years).  All these
volumes are kept up to date, and as the files of past issues lengthen they
offer an increasingly valuable source of historical data.  The *Encyclopedia
of Latin America,* edited by Marrion Wilcox and C. E. Rines (New York,
1917), is still a useful work.

The HISPANIC AMERICAN HISTORICAL REVIEW (Durham, North Carolina,
1918–      ) is published by the Duke University Press.  The Pan American
Union issues a monthly *Bulletin* in three editions — English, Spanish, and
Portuguese — as well as numerous special reports and pamphlets on subjects of interest to the American Republics.

# INDEX

NOTE. — Where the pronunciation of Spanish and Portuguese words has been indicated, approximately, by means of a phonetic respelling, the diacritical marks employed are those found in Webster's *New International Dictionary*. The Castilian pronunciation of Spanish words is regularly given, though Spanish American countries have certain dialect peculiarities: e.g. *c* (also *z*) before *e* or *i* is pronounced like English *s*; *ll* like English *y*; and initial *y* often like English *j*. It should be noted, further, that many geographical and historical names have now become Anglicized, and for these the English pronunciation is allowable and indeed preferable.

Labor problems, 208, 214, 219, 221, 244
*Ladinos*, the, 176, 179, 240
Ladrone (lä-drō'nä) Islands, the, 65
Lancasterian schools, 261
Land tenure, 219, 221, 250
Lange, Francisco Curt, 268
Languages, American Indian, 17
La Paz, 149, note 1
La Plata, 79, 89, 104, 131, 133, 134, 135, 150, 153
La Salle, Robert de, 84, 85
Las Casas (läs kä'säs), Bartholomew de, 96
Las Charcas. *See* Upper Peru
Latin America, geography of, 5–14; native peoples of, 14–33; discovery and conquest of, 55–91; Spanish Portuguese colonies in, 94–122; becomes independent, 125–138; political development of, in the nineteenth and twentieth centuries, 140–162, 272, 273, 287; economic and social conditions since the World War, 203–269; international relations of, 271–307
Laws of the Indies, 102, 103, 105
League of Nations, the, 204, 207, 273, 299
Leavenworth, Fort, 168
Legation Guard, 183
Leguía, Augusto B., 149, 216, 217
León (lā-ōn'), 39, 41, 182
León, Ponce de, 66, 82, 83
Lesser Antilles, the, 10, 63, 188, 200
Leticia boundary, the, 299
Lima (lē'mä), 77, 108, 114, 116, 133, 148, 288, 296, 305
Lisbon, 57, 60, 136
Literature, colonial, 117; modern, 263–266
Lopez (lō'pĕth), Carlos, 150; Francisco, 150; Alfonso, 216
Louis XIV, king of France, 85
Louisiana, claimed by France, 84; under Spain, 85; acquired by the United States, 85, 281
Loyola (lō-yō'lä), St. Ignatius, 46
Lumbering, 248
Luque (loo'kä), Fernando de, 75
*Lusiads*, the, 57
Lusitania, 37, 38

Machado, Gen. Gerardo, 229, 230
Machu Picchu (mä'choo pēk'choo), 29, note 1
McKinley, William, 193, 194
Madeira Islands, the, 56
Madero (mä-thā'rō), Francisco L., 174
Madison, James, 277, 280
Madrid (mä-thrēth'), 103, 129, 297
Magdalena (mäg-dä-lā'nä) River, the, 8, 28, 78, 253; Bay, 294, 306
Magellan, Ferdinand, 64, 65

Magellan, Strait of, 64, 79, 153, 268
*Maine*, the, destruction of, 193
Maipú (mī-pōō'), battle of, 132
Managua (mä-nä'gwä), Lake, 8, 181
Manco Capac, 29
Manufacturing, 111, 113, 121, 172, 245
Manzanillo (män-thä-nē'lyō), 9
Maracaibo (mä-rä-kī'bō), Gulf of, 8, 78
Marajó (mä-rä-hō') Island, 9
Marcos, Friar, 85
Maria I, Queen of Portugal, 136; María Cristina, Queen Mother of Spain, 274, 288
Marranos, the, 46
Marriage and the family, 261
Martí (mär-tē'), José, 192
Martínez (mär-tē'nĕth), Maximiliano H., 180; Tomás, 182
Martinique, 10, 190, 199
Matamoros (mä-tä-mō'rōs), 8, 9
Matto Grosso (mät'tōō grō'sōō), 90
Maule (mou'lä) River, the, 29
Maximilian, emperor of Mexico, 171
Mayapan, 19
Mayas, the, 18–24, 32
Mazatlán (mä-thä-tlän'), 9
Medina, Isaias, 219
Meléndez (mĕ-lĕn'thäth), Francisco, 180
Melgarejo (mĕl-gä-rā'hō), Mariano, 149; Malgarejos, the, 149
Mendieta, Carlos de, 230
Mendoza (mĕn-dō'thä), 80, 132; Pedro de, 79, 80
Mercantilism, 107, 113, 245
Mercator, 63
Mercedarians, 98
Merchant Marine, 253
Mexican War, the, 168, 169, 254, 282
Mexico, geography of, 5–9; climate, 12; mineral resources of, 12; Aztec culture in, 24–28; conquered by Cortes, 69–73; becomes independent, 133, 134; first Mexican Empire, 134; the United Mexican States, 134, 135, 165; under Santa Anna, 166, 273; loses Texas, 166; at war with the United States, 167, 254, 282; under Juarez, 170; second Mexican Empire, 171; under Díaz, 171, 172; under Madero, Huerta, Carranza, and Obregón, 174, 175; since 1920, 205, 219–226, 298
Mexico City, 72, 114, 116, 117, 168, 268, 296
Meztizos, the, 99, 160, 217, 236, 238, 240
Militarism, 141
Minas Geraes (mē'näsh zhä-rīish'), 90, 209
Mining, 112, 248
Miranda (mē-rän'dä), Francisco de, 128, 129
Missions, 87, 88, 90, 98, 99
Mitre, Bartolomé, 154
Moluccas, the, 64, 65